A M E R I C A N ◆ C L

THUNDERBIRD
1955–66

Alan Tast

Foreword by Frank Hershey

Motorbooks International
Publishers & Wholesalers

◆

Dedication

To my loving (and evolving old-car enthusiast) wife, Marci.
If it weren't for you, my darling, the wheels wouldn't have been
put in motion to undertake this project. Your patience,
tolerance, and encouragement helped, but most of all, it was
your love for me and acceptance of my "obsession."
With all my thanks and love.

—*Alan H. Tast,* January 1996

First published in 1996 by Motorbooks International
Publishers & Wholesalers, 729 Prospect Avenue, PO Box 1,
Osceola, WI 54020-0001

Motorbooks International is a certified trademark, registered
with the United States Patent Office

The information in this book is true and complete to the best
of our knowledge. All recommendations are made without
any guarantee on the part of the author or Publisher, who also
disclaim any liability incurred in connection with the use of
this data or specific details

We recognize that some words, model names and
designations, for example, mentioned herein are the property
of the trademark holder. We use them for identification
purposes only. This is not an official publication

Motorbooks International books are also available at discounts
in bulk quantity for industrial or sales-promotional use. For
details write to Special Sales Manager at the Publisher's address

Library of Congress Cataloging-in-Publication Data Available

ISBN 0-7603-0098-4

Printed and bound in the United States of America

CONTENTS

Foreword

THE THUNDERBIRD AND THE WORLD OF MYTH

Back when we were searching for a name for the car that would become the Thunderbird, we wanted a very special name, because we knew that this automobile was destined to be something truly unique. When I saw the name "Thunderbird," proposed by the young designer, Alden "Gib" Giberson, I knew at once that there could be no other name for this wonderful car.

I had grown up in California and the Southwest, often going on long treks across the deserts in old cars with my friends when I was just a teenager. This was in this century's teens when you could still see what had made the Old West a golden place and time. I knew well the legends of the Thunderbird told by the Native Americans of the Southwest. In a way, these stories all spoke of beauty, immense power, and a particular light found only in that part of the country. This was the perfect name for this new car—a car that would make you feel free and adventurous just looking at its fresh, daring lines.

The true stories of how the Thunderbird (especially for the first three years) was designed, the real names of the men who did the truly significant work on the car, and the actual process of development have all fallen prey to quick hindsight, commercialism, popularization, and the forgetfulness that comes with time.

As head of design at Ford at the time, I had some of the best people working on my team that anyone could have asked for: Damon Woods, L. David Ash, John Najjar, and Rhys Miller. Together we worked out the concept of the little Thunderbird and developed the design, incorporating for the first time in one car a freshness, sportiness, and level of comfort unknown anywhere before that time. The little Thunderbird set the stage for Ford's larger four-passenger personal luxury cars and provided a solid tradition on which to build a series of interesting T-birds. True, I would have preferred that Ford had stayed with the smaller car concept, but that was not to be.

Too many earlier books have mistakenly named the wrong people as having been major players on the first Thunderbird design team. I was head of that team. I know who was there, how I thought through the design process, and who I relied on for assistance. Here, Alan Tast has presented a balanced report of how the first decade of Thunderbirds were developed and built—and something of what the owners did with them once they got them. The reader will find this book interesting and accurate.

—*Franklin Q. Hershey as told to James W. Howell,* fall 1995

Preface

As an architect, I find the parallels between automotive and architectural design are striking. Both involve the input of talented (and sometimes egotistical) artisans, budget-conscious administrators, impatient clients, and skilled craftsmen. The process, from conceptualization, preliminary design, and design development, through the less-glamorous aspects of engineering of systems, preparation of drawings for fabrication, and eventually assembly and "turning the keys" over to the owner, can be methodical, long and tedious. Every little detail can be worked out to ensure the best possible product, or work may be quick and haphazard with poor quality resulting. In the end, the primary difference is that while buildings are immobile objects intended to have a useful lifespan of decades, automobiles are dynamic machines which are more likely to be spent and discarded before the first major remodeling of a building completed in the same year.

This book offers a holistic view of how a specific automotive nameplate evolved. Many different disciplines and personalities are involved in the development, production, marketing, and servicing of just one car. No single person can lay claim to the Thunderbird's design. For some the Thunderbird was a mission, for others it was simply a job to put bread on the table.

If one comment during the compilation of material for this book sticks in my mind, it would have to be from a conversation I had with retired designer William P. "Bill" Boyer. When asked about the cult status that has developed over the years around the first four generations of T-birds, he replied, "I'm dismayed that people place such a religious significance on the cars which we designed for transportation, putting mere objects ahead of God and their fellow man." We must be wary of idolizing our automobiles, for lavishing affection on metal, glass, rubber, and plastic cannot and should not take the place of our need to love and be loved by our fellow man.

I have learned a lot more about the first twelve years of Thunderbirds than I thought was possible. One person once told me that "everything's been said that ever needs to be" about the marque. There were numerous topics that I would have loved to have expanded on, but there's only so much information you can cram on a page—what you see here are the most-important items. Perhaps in the future there will be follow-ups, but for now I hope you learn something new and exciting about the machines that have captivated the imagination of the automotive world since their debut in 1954.

Alan H. Tast, winter 1996

ACKNOWLEDGMENTS

Putting together a volume such as this is certainly not a one-man job. Ever since grade school, I've been thankful to God for granting me the talent to paint pictures with words. In fact, many people need to be thanked for their cooperation and involvement with this book. First and foremost, I need to thank my loving wife, Marci, for putting up with my work. If it were not for her encouragement and resolve (along with some gentle scolding once in a while) this would not have come to pass.

There are several individuals I consider key players in the telling of this story. The first is Paul Nichols, former editor of the Vintage Thunderbird Club of America's *Thunderbird Newsletter* and assistant editor for the Vintage Thunderbird Club International's *Thunderbird Scoop* magazine from the mid-1980s through the early 1990s. Without Paul's willingness to line up contacts for me in Dearborn and take the time to review the hundreds of photos that I requested from Ford, the period visual images contained herein would have been inaccessible. I am indebted to him for his help.

The other major individual to play a part in pulling many loose ends together was fellow Motorbooks International author James W. "Bill" Howell. Bill's relationship with the "father" of the Thunderbird, Frank Hershey, and other Ford designers made available many otherwise unknown contacts which helped to confirm and rewrite portions of the original manuscript. Without Bill's and the others' comments and help, some "myths"

would have been further perpetuated. For their assistance, I am most grateful.

The following provided additional support for this book:

Editorial: Zack Miller-Editor, Motorbooks International. Special thanks to fellow author Jim Benjaminson *(American Classics-Plymouth 1946–1959)*, John Lee (photographs), and Bob McKee.

Fellow long-time alumni of Vintage Thunderbirding are also due additional credit, including Bill Van Ess, former 1958-60 Technical Editor for the Vintage Thunderbird Club of America, for providing information on 1958-60 pricing which was used in the appendices, and on his special interest in 1958 convertibles; William Wonder, 1961-63 Technical Editor for VTCA/VTCI and a long-time "Thunderfriend," gave assistance on 61-63 items, especially with regard to the "M"-series; and, Larry J. Seyfarth, past president/editor and staunch supporter of the Vintage Thunderbird Club of America during the 1970s through the early 1980s, also deserves thanks: without Larry, VTCA would not have survived and expanded into the 1961-66 eras. Larry took time out to review the manuscript and provide contacts and additional information about the Squarebird era.

Ford Motor Company: Mike Moran and Mike Stoller, Public Relations-Detroit; Dan Erickson, Photomedia; Darleen Flaherty, Ford Industrial Archives.

Archives: Robert Casey, Henry Ford Museum-Greenfield Village; Marion Hirsch, Hartman Center for Sales, Marketing and Advertising History, Duke University; and Jane Barrett, Petersen Photographic Archives. Aviation photos courtesy of Jeffrey Ethell.

Libraries: National Automotive Historical Collection-Detroit Public Library; Engineering Library-University of Nebraska-Lincoln; University of Nebraska-Omaha; and W. Dale Clark Public Library-Omaha.

Additional Public Relations and Historical Services: Buick, Oldsmobile, Pontiac, Chevrolet/GEO, and General Motors' Photographic Services.

Individuals: William P. "Bill" Boyer (interview); Franklin Q. Hershey (review/comments); Rhys Miller (review/comments); John Najjar (review/comments); Bradley King, son of the late designer Maurice "Mauri" King (interview/photos); Keith Harmon and Bill McCoy, Allegheny-Ludlum Steel Co., Inc. (interviews); Doug McKenzie, Hayes Manufacturing (interview); Dale Swanson, Sr. (interview); Harry Bentley Bradley (photos/interview); Mike Alexander (interview); Ralph Nunez (review/comments); and Don Chambers (review/comments). My apologies to any others I may have neglected to mention.

Classic Thunderbird Club International (CTCI): Executive Secretary Marjory Price, Authenticity Chairman Gil Baumgartner (review/comments), and 1995 President/former *Early Bird* Editor "Red" Carney (review/comment). Special thanks to Dave Evans for his review of information on 1956 and 1957 performance versions.

Vintage Thunderbird Club International (VTCI): All officers and members of the Board of Directors, especially President Bob and Dorothy Gadra, Public Relations Director Don Donahue and wife, Linda, and Concours Director Ken Harkema, Jr.

Local chapters hosting events that I attended during my research included: The American Road Thunderbird Club/Dearborn (1994 CTCI International Convention), Vintage Thunderbirds of Florida (1994 VTCI International Convention), Rocky Mountain Thunderbird Club (1994 VTCI Southwest Regional Convention), Vintage Thunderbirds of Tennessee (1995 VTCI Southeast Regional Convention), Wunderbirds of San Diego (1995 VTCI International Convention), plus numerous VTCI International and Regional Conventions since 1985.

Members and long-time friends from the Nebraskaland Thunderbirds/CTCI, Classic Thunderbird Club of Omaha/VTCI, Nifty Fifties Ford Club of Nebraska, and many other groups involved with the Eastern Nebraska-Western Iowa Car Council were also most helpful, especially: Donald J. Chase, Rich and Pat LaMalfa, Dave and Sandy Freeberg, Clark and Sandy Savage, Tom and Gena Prazan, Martin and Mary Lou Bierman, plus Chad and Gina White, along with Ron Miller, and the staff of Auto Krafters, Broadway, Virginia.

As you read this book, remember that there are still some unanswered questions regarding the history of the Thunderbird program, and perhaps some "myths" have been repeated. If you spot any of these, please forward comments to the publisher so that future corrections can be made.

Chapter 1

DEVELOPMENT OF THE FIRST THUNDERBIRD

Product Planning

During the summer of 1951, it was apparent that the success of Ford's '49 and '50 model years had suffered an unpleasant about-face: From the division's first year of over one million sales (1,185,823 in calendar year 1950), sales plummeted by 34.6 percent to 775,307 units by the end of 1951. Market share of Ford in comparison to other manufacturers was down to 16.9 percent, in comparison to Chevrolet's 21.1 and Plymouth's 11.4. The combination of a now three-year-old basic design, plus the setback of the Korean "Police Action" enveloping the manufacturing might of the United States following the beginning of hostilities on June 25, 1950, left no doubt that planners had to look beyond the inconvenience of materials restrictions and short-term defense contracts for what became the new trend in product offerings. The 1952–54 cycle had already been put into motion, continuing along the tried-and-proven process that was pioneered with the 1949–51 programs. The trick now was to bring sales back up to similar levels of Chevrolet for the low-end line, and improve the image of midrange Mercurys and upper-end Lincolns. Among the ideas being kicked around by the product planning staff was the creation of an "image-builder" or "loss leader" that would lure potential buyers into their local Ford agencies to oogle and dream. Once in the dealership, it was reasoned, salesmen could work their magic and expose them to the less-expensive lines and gain sales. The "magnet" car would not necessarily have to be profitable, as long as a sufficient sales volume resulting from the draw of the flashy vehicle could float its expense.

Talk of producing such a drawing card for Ford had begun among the planners and others looking at ways to revive sales following 1951's miserable sales year. Lewis Crusoe, general manager of Ford Division, and others were keenly aware of the magic of the sports cars that were coming into the country, but no domestic manufacturer was actively trying to compete against them.

Among the cars that were considered as benchmarks for the Ford Sports Car program was the Jaguar XK-120. Though more expensive than the proposed two-seater, it had many traits desired by sports car enthusiasts. *Alan Tast collection*

While nothing official was being done with a Ford sports car during 1951, the allure of a sporty Ford had to be in the minds of more than one person in the design studio. The chance to design something more exciting

Introduction of Corvette at Waldorf-Astoria Hotel, January 1953. *Copyright General Motors Corp., used with permission*

1953 Chevrolet Corvette. *Courtesy of Chevrolet/GEO Photographic*

than a mundane sedan or truck would be a definite change of pace, and a way to bring fantasies of open touring with a darling companion and wind blowing through the hair to life. Behind the scenes, on the drafting boards and scratch pads of engineers and designers, dreaming was put onto paper in sketches and calculations.

The Hershey Story

While much of the credit for the spawning of the Thunderbird has been linked to a story told by George Walker about a trip with Crusoe to the Paris Auto Show during September 1951, designers involved with the program state that no movement was made toward development of a sports car until after the hiring of Franklin Q. Hershey as head of Ford division's styling section. With his past experience in the classic era of automotive design, his resume was impressive. From coachbuilder Murphy of California, then on to Hudson for a brief period following Murphy's closing in 1931, Hershey would become

9

Photographed just two days after the official beginning of studio design for the Ford Sports Car on February 11, 1953, are three of the full-size "paper car" studies. Cutout in center was chosen for development. *Henry Ford Museum & Greenfield Village*

chief stylist for the Pontiac Division of General Motors (GM) during the mid-1930s. His legacy of the "Silver Streak" motif and the beginning of the "Era of the Tailfin" with the postwar Cadillac of 1949 made him a true trendsetter in the industry, but being under the direction of the genius of the Art and Colour section, Harley Earl, would prove to be too much, so Hershey left GM in August 1947 for Taos, New Mexico, to be his own boss and make items such as ash trays and trivets with a Southwest theme from a brass-aluminum alloy. The backlash of the Korean War and its restrictions on the availability of the two metals ended this venture, so he returned to work for Packard, until an invitation from Charlie Waterhouse, Ford's chief body engineer in charge of the design section, brought him into the Ford sphere of influence, just in time for a major new project.

Hershey's drive to run with a Ford sports car was shared by Gene Bordinat, an assistant manager for styling under Waterhouse, and a few other people, but getting the project going was at best a struggle. During the spring of 1952, Ford's sales were still on the decline, with purse strings tightening on future projects—especially those not previously authorized. Development on the line to replace the 1952–54-series cars was well underway, meaning that little was left for allocation to design and build a sports car that at best was a "dream" project.

Among the young designers to help staff Hershey's studios was William P. "Bill" Boyer. Boyer, an alumnus of the Pratt Institute of Design in New York, had signed on with GM's styling department after graduation in 1950, working under Harley Earl and assisting with such projects as the LeSabre show car in the experimental studio, then moving to the body studio to refine designs for production. By early 1952, working in the pressurized culture of the GM styling section had Boyer looking for an opportunity to make a career move. The break came in March 1952 from a member of the same church he and his family attended

in Detroit—none other than the new head of Ford Division's styling department, Hershey. Boyer had spoken with Hershey about the atmosphere of working at GM and his dissatisfaction at the working conditions. Seeing a potential, talented addition for Ford's design staff, Hershey decided to offer the young man a job. In his book *Thunderbird: An Odyssey in Automotive Design,* Boyer, who was on the verge of leaving GM, recounted the call from Hershey to the GM studio where he was working at the time: "Frank definitely was not bashful . . . I was told that he was now the chief stylist for Ford division vehicles. He wanted to know if I would be interested in working in the body studio he was organizing. He said he was trying to launch a two-passenger sports car project." Ironically, the person answering the phone, Boyer later reminisced, was the burly Earl, for whom Hershey worked less than five years prior.

The 1953 Ford Sunliner is representative of a Ford "sporty" offering before the Thunderbird. Pictured is the 1953 Indianapolis 500 pace car on display at the Henry Ford Museum in Dearborn. *Alan Tast photo*

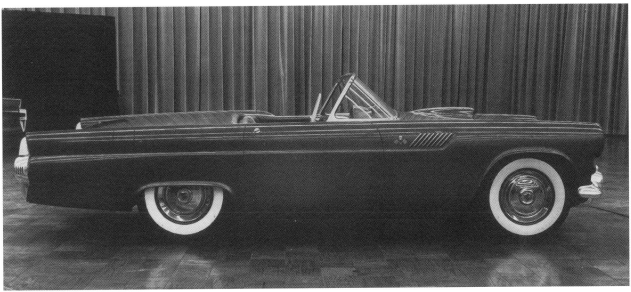

By the April 27, 1953, Product Planning show, the clay model still has midheight bumpers and Continental Mk. II-influenced "kick-up" on the driver's side. *Henry Ford Museum & Greenfield Village*

Clandestine work at first was conducted by several people, including Boyer (under direction of Body Development Studio supervisor Damon Woods), engineer William Burnett, and Hershey, while they were attempting to also develop the 1955 Ford program. Boyer's recollection was that at the time he was hired, Hershey and Woods were already working with Burnett "under the table" with their ideas on a suitable package for the car. When the pressure began to mount to get the '55 going by midspring '52, the two-seat program was put on hold, to be brought back to life in the fall of that year by rumors of a pending production two-seater from Chevrolet: the Corvette.

From Covert to Top Priority: Catching Up to Corvette

Still not an official project, the threat of Ford's number one competitor seriously considering development of the Corvette for production created a stir among product planners who knew of the "secret" project under Hershey's domain. Earlier in the spring of 1952, related Hershey, photographs of the fiberglass Stovebolt-six–powered car were obtained under mysterious circumstances from a friend who worked in the GM studios and presented to him. The result was an attempt to play "catch-up" with Chevrolet.

Not one to wait for things to happen, Hershey decided to begin work on Ford's answer to the challenge, but without the approval he would need for funds, manpower, and materials. With help from product planners Thomas B. Case, Chase Morsey, and William "Bill" Burnett acting as their engineering consultant, the effort again picked up steam. But, the veil of secrecy was soon pulled back by Earle S. MacPherson, Ford's chief engineer (the designer of the '52 Lincoln's ball-joint suspension and

namesake of the cartridge/strut suspension system), when he found Burnett laboring on the design of the chassis. Since it was an "unauthorized project," MacPherson threatened to expose Hershey and gang to upper management and possible retribution, only to have events turn in Hershey's favor in the form of consideration of a sports-car project. According to Hershey in an interview with writer Dennis Adler for the September 1985 issue of *Car Collector*, by the time his superiors learned of the surreptitious work, exterior lines and proportions were well in hand.

The Suits Get Involved

Once word got around about the Corvette in the fall of 1952, the Product Planning Committee (consisting of Henry Ford II and hand-picked vice presidents from the various divisions and operating departments) began laying the official groundwork for development of a little Ford challenger by first having the market-research department conduct studies and surveys to determine who would be potential buyers, and what they would want.

The marketing survey focused on owners of what were the most popular models, which were believed to be the two cars at the ends of the price spectrum for Ford's entry—the MG-TD Roadster and Jaguar's XK-120. The prewar styling of the "sit-up-and-beg" MG, at the low end of pricing near $2,500, and the larger, more luxurious and contemporary XK-120, in the $4,000 range, served as two extremes for comparison. With over 12,000 registered owners in the United States during 1952, there were plenty of people to sample.

From the survey, it became clear that MG and Jaguar owners enjoyed the high-profile status their cars generated.

RESTRICTED

While they loved the sporty feel they provided (snappy acceleration, fast cornering, balanced handling), they also noted that, for the most part, competition-style driving was not high on the priority list (even though many professed to be members of or associated with members of sports-car clubs that thrive on such events). They also acknowledged that even though they liked their cars, trading in their present set of wheels for a new one was a certainty if it offered more conveniences but retained the "feel" that they found so enjoyable. And, to make things more interesting for a market tie-in, most also relied on full-size cars for more mundane usage (getting groceries, travel with family, and so on).

It was also deduced that "although sports car sales had doubled every year since 1949, the total volume for 1952 amounted to only 12,000 units. Entry of Ford or Chevrolet into the field would probably propel the industry to 25,000 and even 50,000 units annually, but might tend to 'dry up' the demand in a relatively short time should this particular market prove unstable . . ."— perhaps an overly optimistic forecast in hindsight, but telling of the confidence by decision-makers that the program could be feasible.

While executives and managers were analyzing the reports drawn up to assist in developing an outline for the new car during December 1952 and January 1953, two

a hopped-up Blue-Flame Six with three one-barrel carburetors to improve performance. While at first it was not clear whether or not the sporty Chevrolet would actually become a production car, it was apparent that GM would spring it on the market sometime during 1953, one-upping Ford, Chrysler, and the independents. The opportunity to create a better sports car was now a necessity.

The results of the survey of sports car owners were folded into the product-planning letter issued on February 9, 1953, which outlined the requirements for the new model. The key to making a sales winner, though, would be in offering what others didn't: a weather-tight cockpit, which the Corvette, MG, and Jaguar XK-120, and other two-seaters from the era didn't. Performance, a growing American concern, could be improved with the new generation of overhead-valve V-8s being developed by Ford for the 1954 model year: The new motor produced more horsepower than MG's little four or the Chevrolet six and gave the sophisticated Jag mill a half-hearted challenge. Power-assisted accessories, such as steering and brakes, were unheard of on even the higher-end Jaguar, but their availability would increase the Ford sports car's appeal to people who preferred to enjoy the drive rather than build up their upper body strength and leg muscles. Power assists would also add to the profit margin.

Of course, the bottom line was a selling price that would lure owners from each end of the spectrum. Placing the Ford between the Jag and the MG in the $3,000 to $3,500 range, according to the sales analysis, ". . . would entice a segment of the market where little competition existed, and might also attract buyers of both the low- and high-priced sports cars." In fact, MG owners indicated that they would be willing to move up to a larger, more comfortable car like the Jaguar. An intermediate offering from Ford could, theoretically, capture many of those sales. Jaguar owners might move down for the amenities of the Ford car, provided that it embodied the same "flash" and styling panache as the Jag.

Based on the survey and sales and marketing's analysis, a specification was developed for the sports car:

Package size: Two-passenger open model with canvas top; have reasonable driver and passenger comfort.

Weight: Package designed for minimum weight in order to obtain high performance; curb weight objective with Ford Interceptor engine to be 2,525lb; weight distribution balanced for good roadability.

key events would help increase the urgency for a Ford sports car. First, final sales figures for the 1952 model year would reveal a disaster for Dearborn: The all-new 1952 models, even with Ford's first overhead-valve six-cylinder motor, were sold in even fewer numbers than the disappointing 1951 version.

The second spark of urgency was the official unveiling of the Corvette at the GM Motorama in New York City during January. As more became known about the car, it appeared to people at Ford that the 'Vette was a serious move to follow in the footsteps of its European cousins—a folding canvas top, detachable side curtains (no roll-up windows on this chariot), a short wheelbase (102in), and

A view toward the clay car's dash photographed during the Product Planning review of May 18, 1953. Barely visible are the tops of the bucket seats. 1953 Nash-Healey and Frank Hershey's Jaguar XK-120 Roadster are in the background. *Henry Ford Museum & Greenfield Village*

Performance: Top speed to exceed 100mph; acceleration to be superior to competition; must have good high-speed handling characteristics and roadability.

Interchangeability: Maximum use of standard production components mandatory.

With this rough outline in hand, Ford's styling and engineering teams were given a deadline of May 1, 1953, to have both a clay mock-up of the body and a preliminary chassis design. Having a head start on the design problem, work hit a frenzied pace to make the most of the eighty-odd days before deadline. Robert Maguire, taking orders from Hershey, would head the design teams that focused on exterior and interior issues.

To give an idea of how the design process evolved, a scant two days were spent between presentation of the plan and a showing of full-size airbrush renderings of five proposals. Mounted on plywood and placed next to similar renderings of an MG-TD, Jaguar XK-120, and a Nash-Healey, this first round of options (carrying the names Sportliner and Sportsman) was evaluated and whittled down by the end of the third week of February to a straight-lined car with upper rear fenders similar to the '55 Ford, which was near completion at that time. By late February, Boyer was slinging clay on a wood armature in Woods' studio for the three-dimensional embodiment of the paper cutout, changing things as the design evolved. Because of the limited amount of time to develop the final clay, the interior—which traditionally was modeled separately in its own "buck"—was initially formed inside the body clay (a separate interior mock-up would be ready by

May). This would prove to be a major plus in the final integration of the car's interior and exterior form, though the proportions of the "tub" were slightly askew due to the substructure required to hold the clay in place.

Before much more time passed, a new location for the design staff was ready for occupancy before the end of February on the west side of Oakwood Boulevard in the new Ford Styling Center complex. The new digs came with their own showroom, nicknamed the "Styling Rotunda" (so named for its round floor plan and similarity to Ford's popular tourist showcase located elsewhere in Dearborn). When they had been in the Electrical and Engine Engineering (EEE) Building, stylists and support staff were sharing space with the engineering department, to whom they were subservient. In the new complex, ample space was provided to accommodate twelve studios for full-size work, plus additional spaces for trim, instrument panels, and the like. The studio for the two-seater was located in the basement, almost as an afterthought. Though still under control of engineering, styling's growing importance in Ford's hierarchy was being acknowledged.

Throughout March, the clay was worked and re-worked to visualize different ideas. To illustrate different concepts, one side of the clay was modeled differently than the other. Appearing similar to the then-developing Mark II Continental in the Lincoln-Mercury studios (Hershey stated that there was no knowledge of the Mark II's design by him, Damon Woods, or his staff at that point in time), a kick-up was formed in front of the rear door jamb on the driver's side of the clay to give added mass above the rear

14

A 1955 Ford Victoria two-door hardtop owned by Clark & Sandy Savage (left), and a Crown Victoria owned by Dave & Sandy Freeberg (right) illustrate the styling cues shared with the T-bird. *Alan Tast photo*

A view of the 1955 Ford dash showing the "Astra-Dial" speedometer/instrument cluster adapted for the T-bird. The round heater control panel would be used for the 1958–60 T-bird. *Alan Tast photo*

wheel cutout. A feature line was sculpted into the body side that wrapped over the front wheel arch and tapered off by the kick-up. On the passenger side, what would eventually become the final form with the familiar crease that began from the top of the front fender between the wheel opening and the door jamb and running back to the Hershey-inspired "jet-tube" taillight-fin juncture. Boyer would credit Joe Oros with the front-fender crease, while Hershey would dispute the claim.

On both sides of the car, another feature that would be little modified in final form made its debut—imitation louvers, placed behind the front wheel on the driver's side and behind the valley created by the upper-body crease on the passenger side. Another bit of ornamentation that was placed aft of the rear-canted strips was a small, crown-bedecked Ford crest above a pair of crossed checkered flags. The crest, adapted from the tri-color shield originally designed by David L. Ash for the 1950 Ford and adopted as the division's identifying element through the '50s and into the '60s in abstracted forms, was being used on the full-size car's roof pillar for the Victoria, and the crest-and-flags combination was an identifying feature for Ford's Golden Anniversary Sunliner, which had been tagged for use as the pace car for the Indianapolis 500 race.

Gracing the center of the hood was a creative solution to the problem of how to lower the car's overall height and yet allow ample clearance for the motor. The proposed Y-block was slated to use a high-profile carburetor. With an oil-bath air cleaner, the assembled pairing would project above the intake manifold almost a foot. As stylists and engineers went back and forth on what package heights and clearances would be, according to writer Jonathan Katz in his book, *Soaring Spirit*, Ash came upon a novel solution: Put a dome in the hood above the carburetor and air cleaner and open the front to create a functional fresh-air intake. The scoop would remain virtually unchanged through the remainder of the design process.

But, unlike other Ford products from the period, a set of midheight bumpers was being studied. This idea

was nixed by engineering because of its "chin," which they felt would become damaged by drivers running into curb stops and other road hazards. Dictum at Ford was that bumpers were to be mounted low to avoid such problems, so the idea was shelved (the high bumper would finally come into production almost a decade later with the '65 Mustang and, to bring the idea full-circle, on the '66 Thunderbird). Another reason for ditching the high bumper was the mandate that the new car would share components with the '55 Ford. By late March, the full-size car's "jet-tube" cylinders and subtle fins (also credited to Ash, who was the source of many of the shared traits of the full-size and two-seaters' details) would be grafted onto the rear of the Thunderbird.

The Race Heats Up

March 1953 was a pivotal point in the development of the Thunderbird. The Corvette, which most people thought was another "dream" car to tease the public, was tagged to become a full-blown production car with 300 to be built at GM's St. Louis plant starting in June and continuing on into 1954. The first Corvettes were to be built with fiberglass bodies, which could be produced rapidly and would skirt the production limitations on steel still in effect because of the Korean police action, but rumors were that the car would have a steel body by the beginning of '54 production. Reports were that 7,000 orders for the Chevy sports car were in hand, and similar models were being planned by Oldsmobile and Buick. The competition was for real, but it would be at least a year and a half before Ford was able to meet it.

A stop-gap measure was reported to be in the works in early 1953 by the importing of Ford's English-built Comete with an American engine in place of the anemic four-banger used in the Dagenham-built car. But, ac-

The engine bay of Savage's 1955 Victoria illustrates what engineers had to consider when the T-bird cowl and hood heights were under development; typical carburetors and air cleaners were tall assemblies. Designers Woods, Boyer, and Ash relied on a lower-profile oil-bath air cleaner to help cheat on clearance problems. *Alan Tast photo*

cording to a report in the May 1953 *Motor Trend*, this was canceled after it was deduced that installing a larger powerplant would affect weight distribution.

Then, the Kaiser-Fraser Co. announced that it, too, was going into production during July with a two-seat tourer, designed by Howard "Dutch" Darrin, with a fiberglass body. Called the KFD-161, it would have a 161ci F-head inline six-cylinder engine, a wheelbase of 100in, a unique fan-shaped grille, and sliding doors. It appeared that even before it could hit the showroom, the new Ford would have more than a handful of domestics to do battle with.

Close to Perfect

As the design work continued into late April, the kick-up was shaved off, with Boyer adding a touch of the new XL-500 show car to the area above the rear wheel. The XL-500, which was revealed to the automotive press in March 1953, forecasted many 1955–56 (and some later) Lincoln, Mercury, and Ford design themes: the Mercury's oblong taillight assembly, the Lincoln's hooded headlights, the Crown Victoria's tiara, and the '58 Ford's faux hood intake scoop. Among its body design features was a bulge over the rear wheelhouse to accommodate rebounding of the rear wheels, allowing for additional vertical travel of the differential. The looks of the hump appealed to designer Boyer, but again, dictates of family lines—the straight body profile—would force its removal, but not before the clay was presented for the May inspection.

To compensate for the removal of the Mark II-style kick-up, a deeper fender skirt was plastered onto the side, covering most of the upper half of the rear wheel. This would create a slab-sided effect that carried the middle body through to the rear, and be a major improvement to the car's overall form.

Also appearing by this time were the characteristic "bombs" above the bumpers. The pods, mounted on pylons that tied the assemblies to the now-reconfigured bumper bars, did fill in the front end's grille cavity and provide a place for mounting road lamps, while the rears served as a place to route the exhaust pipes. By the end of April, the car's lines were firmly in place, and final detailing to the clay could commence.

Chassis Development

As dictated by the February 9 communiqué, chassis development also was to take place during the three-month period. With Burnett taking the lead, engineers wanted to find out how the desired low-engine/short-wheelbase configuration would perform in relation to braking, spring ratios, and other basic areas of interest. To quickly model the final package, Burnett instructed a team to take a production '53 Fordor sedan and, with judicious (almost haphazard) application of hacksaw and cutting torch, shortened the car's wheelbase to 102in, moved the engine down and back (most probably an early prototype of the new Y-block due for the '54), and removed the body between the center door pillar and rear jamb, filling in with an approximately 10in swath of sheet metal. While it looked ugly, the slide-rule jockeys had a "mule" to flog in evaluations.

Additional problems were worked out with the desire to lower the car's height, but limited time to get things done meant that a certain "factor of safety" was built in to design. For instance, the frame was built around an X-style cross-member, stiff enough to limit body flex at the narrow juncture between the door and rear wheelhouse.

The 1956 Continental Mark II. Early styling clays of the T-bird were heavily influenced by William Clay Ford's luxo-cruiser roofline and would be retained for the hardtop. The "kick-up" behind the door and the body side relief line would be abandoned. *Ford Motor Company*

This fiberglass and wood "Fairlane" mockup for the Detroit Auto Show of February 1954 was photographed in the Styling Studio showroom on February 15. Though the "Thunderbird" name was registered almost a month previously, no hint of the moniker could be found on the car. Crossed flags were supposedly swiped off the model by an unknown reporter. *Ford Motor Company*

Apparently the "custom" bodywork of the now-nick-named "Burnetti" was a source of humor among those involved with the project. With a prototype body shell and frame still months away from availability, one of the engineers was dispatched to the West Coast to find a suitable fiberglass body to place on the modified chassis for evaluation—probably because it would look better than a butchered Ford body. At the time, several manufacturers in California had been marketing in the enthusiast magazines replacement sports-car bodies to be placed on modified car frames, and the use of a suitable one would also allow engineers to study how fiberglass would stand up to the rigors of the road.

It became clear that the lowered height of the car and the thinner body cross-section would also play havoc with the placement of components such as the radiator. If a full-size radiator was placed vertically, it would protrude beyond the established height for the hood. To make it work, the assembly was placed at an angle, but with the motor and cooling fan further back than normal, a way had to be found to pull air through the core. The solution

An advertisement from 1953 for a fiberglass car body by Glasspar Company similar to what may have been used on the "Burnetti" engineering testbed. *Alan Tast collection*

An early prototype interior, summer 1954. The chrome shifter knob would not make production. *Ford Motor Company*

was to place a deep shroud between the radiator support and the fan, creating a tunnel for the fan to suck air past the tubes and fins.

Even though the Corvette and the Kaiser Darrin were laid up in molds, Ford body engineers reportedly never considered using fiberglass for their car for two reasons. First, with an anticipated production run of 10,000 bodies for the model year, it would be more cost-effective to stamp the body panels out of steel. The method of producing fiberglass bodies in fixed molds, it was determined, would take too long to keep up with anticipated demand, and working with steel stampings was a proven process to the automaker.

Second, the engineering staff had very little experience with fiberglass, and the tight developmental and production schedule precluded experimentation with an unknown-to-Ford technology. Executive body engineer Clare Kramer and chief body engineer Henry Grebe also had in mind one feature for the car that everyone else wasn't providing that would require the rigidity and durability of a steel inner structure: roll-up windows.

Deadlines and Details

Work on the clay was to be completed by May 1, but last-minute changes and final refinements would delay its showing to the "brass" until May 18. After receiving a coating of "Di-Noc" to provide a paint-like finish, the mass of clay, wood, plexiglass, aluminum foil and metal was rolled out for review by Crusoe and his staff. The decision was made to proceed with work on the car.

As summer wore on, evolution of the car's features were fussed over. First, the instrument panel was revamped. In the original drawings and on the clay model, a hooded dome shrouded the collection of seven gauge faces—a large speedometer head just above the steering column, flanked by a medium-sized clock and tachometer on each side, and ringed on top by four small gauges for the ammeter, oil pressure, water temperature, and fuel level. Along the engine-turned band running across the middle, rotary and pull-knobs were placed for lights, vents, choke, radio, and heater controls. The radio, with push buttons and a rectangular dial face, plus the heater control head with a pair of sliding levers, were placed toward the

Another view of mid-1954 prototype, illustrating the adjustable steering wheel's positions. *Ford Motor Company*

front of the passenger seat, crowding out the glove box. After reviewing the layout and deciding that producing the original configuration would not fit into the proposed budget for the car, another part from the full-size '55 Ford was pulled for use: the Astra-Dial speedometer, a half-ellipse with a pale green transparent shield that allowed light to pass through the calibrated face. Designed by John Najjar (while others credit Ash) and patterned after the more rounded assembly used for the upcoming '54 Ford, its bottom was strung with turn-signal indicators in separate outboard pods and a combination of gauges and "idiot lights" in between, a compact unit that could be modified for the new car by simply changing the plastic speedometer face to add 30mph to the scale.

By using the revamped cluster, though, a new place for the desired tachometer and clock were needed. Taking a cue from the original layout for the instruments, designers moved them into the roll of the dash, flanking the head assembly. A reconfiguration of the knobs, radio, and heater controls allowed these to slide toward the driver, and the glove box could now be accommodated.

The Hardtop

Another advance in the design of the car was in the way the cockpit would be closed off. Originally, a soft-top frame was called out that could be collapsed and stored in the trunk. But, after reviewing comments from the survey, an interesting innovation developed, with some nefarious "lifting" of ideas—again, from the Mark II. William Clay Ford, son of the beleaguered Edsel B. Ford (who was instrumental in the 1940 Continental but derided by father Henry, Sr.), recalled for Boyer in his book the event that perhaps started the ball rolling for the hardtop: "The idea for the blind quarter roof came when Product Planning Manager Chase Morsey came to the Continental Division for a sneak look. We were months ahead of the T-bird in clay, and he 'borrowed' our roof line for a car that was to precede the Mark II by a year." Passing this on back to the styling staff, Boyer stated that George Walker echoed the idea and suggested it be put to use on the two-seater. Hershey, on the other hand, doubts the Walker connection.

The result was a removable, lightweight fiberglass hardtop that would latch down to the body and windshield header. It gave the car a "formal" look and would help in the fight to keep out wind, moisture, and cut down on road noise with its fixed rear window and rubber weatherstripping. The top could be left off, it was reasoned, in warm, dry periods of the year, and the canvas one brought out with the threat of inclement weather.

General Motors' Firebird I experimental turbine car of 1954. This was slated to be named Thunderbird, but Ford had registered the name with the Automobile Manufacturers' Association just days prior to GM's application. *Copyright General Motors Corp., used with permission*

The Car Gets a Name . . . and Loses It

Though the little car was on a roller-coaster ride of on-again, off-again priority, no formal attention to its name was given until June 1953. Hershey asked designers to submit names for the car. With lists of names provided by the staffers, one grabbed instant attention. Submitted by designer Alden "Gib" Giberson (who, like Hershey, had a southwestern background), the moniker Thunderbird was a perfect fit. Used throughout the Southwest for places such as a hotel-casino complex in then-developing Las Vegas, it conjured up power and flight, and the tie-in with American Indian legends gave it a mythological heritage. Hershey, familiar with the mythological creature, took a liking to it immediately.

A nameplate, similar in style to that used for the 1957–59 (and 1961–62),.was made for the car before the end of June and placed on the front fender just behind a revised set of three louver blades. Giberson was also given the chore of developing an emblem to emulate the name. After a variety of ideas were sketched out, a winged Ford crest was placed on the clay, but sometime during July, the nameplate disappeared-perhaps a jealous stylist's prank. It would be lost until the beginning of 1954.

As the program kept going, other names were bantered about for use. Ford's advertising agency, J. Walter Thompson (JWT), was even consulted to develop a list of suggestions. The 150-name list did contain many that would go on to be used with other Ford products, but the Giberson suggestion was still deemed the most appropriate.

The Design That Almost Didn't Make It

While the developing sports car was in the "fussing" stage, its future was not essured. A Corvette was finally procured in July for close scrutiny, revealing what was considered to be major quality problems in its construction and trimming. Crusoe apparently was satisfied with the Ford two-seater's progress, but a commitment for final release into production was not forthcoming. His indecision would delay the final go-ahead until his annual trip with Walker to the Paris Auto Show. During the period between May and September, weekly progress reviews were held to view refinements to the design on Fridays, with no firm commitments. To cover their bases, sensing that Crusoe might change his mind on the current proposal, Maguire asked Woods to start work on a new car should the winds of approval change direction.

Thankfully, the visit to the '53 Paris Auto Show yielded the green light so long awaited. Crusoe and Walker also took Maguire along. With the '54 models on display, Crusoe finally decided that the time was right to spring the new Ford into production. With a phone call from Paris to Dearborn, from Maguire to Woods, the juggernaut again began to move. First, Maguire instructed, stop development of the alternate two-seater. Second, Woods was to begin getting the car from styling to engineering for the prototype and production phases.

A Change in Direction

With the return of Crusoe and company from Europe, a change of direction was dictated for the still-unnamed car. As feedback from the marketplace started to roll in on the Corvette and the Darrin, complaints of lack of creature comforts became obvious. Discussion among the product planners now was focusing on a more luxurious car, one that would attract not the road-course jockeys as much as the country-club set. With this approach, cer-

The Oldsmobile F-88 was a GM Motorama concept car for 1954. Appearance of two-seaters other than the Corvette led Ford to seriously believe that GM was preparing production versions for other divisions. *Courtesy Oldsmobile History Center*

Additional 1954 Motorama cars included the fastback Corvair and hardtop versions of the Corvette. Appearance of the Waldorf Nomad (nicknamed for its unveiling at the Waldorf-Astoria) led Ford planners to consider a similar version for the T-bird. *Copyright General Motors Corp., used with permission*

tain additions and concessions would have to be made. Package size could allow the addition of niceties such as power brakes, power steering, power windows, and power seats, but other features would have to be reworked.

First, the convertible top: The removable assembly originally contemplated did not lend itself to convenience. A better option, suggested by engineer Bob Hennessey and developed with Paul Olson, was something similar to the Jaguar XK-120's double-hinged frame, which stowed behind the seat. Since the seats were being changed from a pair of buckets (the original proposal) to a full-width bench, the assembly could be easily hidden. While this would differ from the American practice of providing a well for the top bows, it allowed the now-fixed body design to remain unaltered.

Second, the addition of power assists, hardtop, and other "bloating" required a change in brakes, suspension, and drivetrain to accommodate the weight gain. From the original target of 2,525lb, the car gained 312lb by the time it reached preliminary approval status. The final version, though, fully equipped, was bogged down with another 363lb, tipping the scales at about 3,200lb. The power curve for the '54 Ford's 239ci Y-block did not provide the snappy performance required, so in its place the 256ci police version, also the standard Mercury engine, was used.

Third, as the car was now scheduled for introduction to the public at the Detroit Auto Show toward the end of February 1954, a name had to be picked. This was passed around through December, and at last the Giberson suggestion was brought back to the fore. But, before the finalist was selected, a short list was drawn up with such names as Runabout, Arcturus, El Tigre, Coronado, Apache, Beverly, Eagle, Falcon, Country Club, Tropicale, and Savile. Of the batch, Ludvigsen would write over fifteen years later, Savile was Crusoe's favorite until Hershey provided the Thunderbird title.

The cover of "Sports Car" brochure released during spring 1954 to promote the Thunderbird. Rendering of front illustrated truncated headlight doors, rear-view artwork had "1954" license plates, and the engine drawing featured a "high-hat" air cleaner. *Alan Tast collection*

The rush to adopt the name had begun—and with it, Ford one-upped GM when it registered the name in early January with the Automobile Manufacturers Association (AMA). General Motors, unknown to Ford, had planned on naming an airplane-styled turbine-engined experimental test bed the Thunderbird, but was beaten to the punch by about two weeks. The result was that the experimental car was renamed to match the emblems already painted on its fins and sides: Firebird I.

Though not credited in most accounts, it would not be fair to neglect another group using the title: the United State Air Force's aerial demonstration squadron based at Nellis Air Force Base near Las Vegas, Nevada. Formed during 1953, the flying ambassadors in blue for the Air Force were a highlight of air shows across the nation with their red, white, and blue jet fighters that featured graphics of a blue-winged bird on their bellies. Their presence in the media certainly would have played into Ford's decision to use the name: After all, Corvette was the name for a classification of light Navy warships that were fast and agile, so a military-styled bit of "name-dropping" was perhaps a justifiable tit-for-tat.

The Stage Is Set

As the date for the Detroit Auto Show approached, engineering was now proceeding at the rapid pace that only a few months prior had been seen in styling. Drawings for the many subassemblies, stampings, and hardware were being produced for release to subcontractors to begin tooling up for delivery of parts by August. While the shared components with the new '55 series would help speed up the schedule, quite a few details had to be worked out. By the middle of February, line drawings were being hardlined for preliminary review by Ford and Budd Co. planners and engineers.

As the final days before the introduction wound down, a fiberglass copy of the car was readied for press photography and the display. On February 15, the Monday before the event, a Seafoam Green model was wheeled into the styling rotunda for the cameras. Ornamentation did not call attention to the "new" name; in fact, there was no sign of "Thunderbird" on the car—no script was yet prepared. The nameplate that appeared on the static model, though, provided a hint of what the new high-end Ford would be called: Fairlane. (The Fairlane nameplate was used to gauge public reaction to a name that would be used on Ford's 1955 upscale offering.) The Ford crest had been redesigned to feature a three-pointed gold tiara above the Ford name and a griffin-and-ball-encrusted tri-color shield; a small version was placed on the hardtop, and larger ones were used above the Fairlane script on the nose panel and gas door lid, placed in the rear deck lid. The 1954 Y-8 emblem was placed behind the redesigned fake louver casting, and full wheel covers from the current Ford were also used. A bit of subterfuge was also accomplished by showing the car with a flattened headlight casting that surrounded the sealed-beam bulb assembly. The final proposal for the surround, with a pronounced, raked hood, would come again from the larger brother Ford, but would not appear until late spring.

Two days later, on February 17, Ford's general sales manager, L.M. Snead, held a press conference to show off the Thunderbird. Although it had been dictated that the car would be designated a "personal" car, reference to its

During mid-August 1954, styling consultant George Walker suggested using a "Fairlane" stripe on the T-bird to foster identity with the higher-trim, full-size Ford. Within a week of this photo session, Ford division Chief Stylist Frank Hershey and others would successfully lobby Henry Ford II to have the spears removed. *Ford Motor Company*

sportiness was not missed by the press or by the car's promoters. Press releases from Ford included comments such as, "The Thunderbird is a new kind of sport car" and, "It provides all of the comforts, conveniences and all-weather protection available in any of today's modern automobiles." As part of the introduction, writers were treated to a brief history of the origin of the Thunderbird legend and name, provided to Hershey by Giberson a few weeks before.

The car was a smash! Magazine editors, already lamenting about the question of what a true "sports car" was and what the public was expecting, prepared copy for their April and May long-lead deadlines to describe the car due to be available in the fall. But, for the statistic-hungry motor-head, no performance data was available on the Thunderbird in comparison to the Corvette or other two-seaters. The release of data was delayed as working prototypes would not be completed until later in the spring, and even then such information as top speed, braking distance, and fuel economy would at best be up to educated speculation by outsiders.

The Prototypes Take Wing

Publicity around the new car was taken advantage of to the hilt. Ford, eager to gain an international audience as well as enhance its performance image, entertained famed World Champion race-car driver Juan Fangio in late March or early April for a day of demonstration driving at the Dearborn test track, across the road from Greenfield Village to the south. Although Fangio was not allowed to drive the car (apparently the only working prototype at the time), reports had touted that the racing veteran was impressed with the thrashing given the car. Pictures taken of Fangio and the driver by Ford's publicity staff and used in magazines such as the June 1954 *Motor Trend* showed the car fitted with Fairlane-style "eyebrow" headlight doors, a prototype air cleaner that was similar to the one illustrated in the first four-page brochures published for the Detroit show and dealers, and a quilted hood liner, which would never see production.

With the scheduled late-summer production start-up a few months away, drawings, samples, and test parts were flying around the Detroit area and to major subcontractors across the Iron Belt at a furious pace. By the time August rolled around, everything was in place for hand-assembling a small number of preproduction cars, which would be used for evaluation of the assembly process as well as road testing.

But, before the absolute final okay was given to the production of the Thunderbird, one more curve ball was thrown by management. The T-bird was from the start a very clean, straightforward design with little ornamentation. On the other hand, Ford's design strategy for its full-size line focused on three trim levels, linked to the price range of each series: Mainline, Customline, and Fairlane.

The engine bay of Raven Black prototype car from summer 1954. Chrome-plated valve covers were not released for production. Finned, cast-aluminum pieces with the T-bird logo would instead be used in conjunction with the Engine Dress-Up Kit. *Ford Motor Company*

The Fairlane was fitted with a simple stainless trim spear, developed by Hershey, which curved down from the top of the front fender and onto the door to create a check mark, then ran aft straight across the remainder of the car's side. (Hershey would say later that he had a hard time selling the "Fairlane stripe" to upper management for the full-size car.) Crusoe, eager to link the Thunderbird and Fairlane lines together for rub-off value, had been lobbying for the installation of the trim on the little car, with no sympathy from styling.

A power play over the side trim erupted from late July to early August 1954 between Walker and Hershey. Hershey, who elected to take a vacation during the end of July, left Dearborn confident that there was nothing left to do with the Thunderbird for final production. However, Walker had "Fairlane" trim prepared for and fitted to the cars, along with wire wheel covers that were supplied by his son, who operated an auto accessory company. By early August, they were shown to Crusoe, who approved of the additions. Upon his return from vacation, Hershey learned of Walker's "meddling" and ordered the trim and covers removed from the car and the promotional literature, which was being printed at that time with the stripe and wire covers. The first run had to be destroyed and started over, but artwork being prepared by JWT for an ad to appear in *Sports Illustrated* got by with the stripe. After viewing the cars and listening to the arguments of the stylists who did not like the trim, it was decided to keep the cars bare with one exception: Crusoe would have one of the sets salvaged for his own car, which is believed to be among the first production cars.

After almost a year and a half of planning, modeling, calculating, and fabricating, Ford's new "personal luxury" car was about to leave the nest.

Chapter 2

PRODUCTION OF THE FIRST-GENERATION THUNDERBIRD

As August 1954 drew to a close, the Dearborn Assembly Plant was gearing up for production of the new 1955 Ford model line. Though production of the revised Fairlane body style would not commence until October, pressure was on to build the new Thunderbird two-seater. From the beginning of August to the beginning of September, workers and managers were slowly intro-duced to the nuances of producing the little car along with its larger brethren.

The assembly process at best was a make-shift arrangement that was integrated with various portions of full-size construction. Since the bodies were being supplied as built-up shells from Budd's Charlevoix and Conners Avenue body assembly facility elsewhere in the area, the major work

Fresh from Budd's Detroit plant, six 1955 bodies-in-white were brought to the Dearborn Assembly/Rouge plant. *Ford Motor Company*

The final inspection line for 1955 T-bird. Workers adjust convertible top assemblies, while the car immediately behind has its hardtop propped up above the hood so that its soft-top can be worked on as well. Full-size cars are on each side of T-bird line. *Ford Motor Company*

required was final bodywork, painting, and installation of running gear and trim. The bodies, brought to the plant on trucks, were fed into the paint line for station wagons, then mixed in with them for fitting of chassis and driveline components. While this was going on, a separate area of the trim department was assembling the instrument panel and seat assemblies. The T-birds were diverted from the car line long enough for interior fitting, then placed back on the final assembly line for inspections and adjustments. Once the fully assembled unit was able to drive away on its own to the satisfaction of the people at the end of the process, it was sent to a separate holding area.

Prototypes and Preproduction Cars

Since at the beginning only three colors were offered—Raven Black, Skyhaze Green (renamed Thunderbird Blue), and Torch Red—three cars were built for styling, engineering and marketing/sales as prototype units. The first T-birds built beyond the prototype cars during August weren't really considered "production" cars because they were intended for use by production-line personnel as "pilot" models so that the workers could "get the feel" of how the Thunderbird was to go together. Interspersed with the last of the '54 Ford full-size cars, the Thunderbird's special requirements must have dealt supervisors and line workers fits!

The disposition of the first three cars, P5FH-100001 through P5FH-100003, was the subject of controversy among historians for many years. In the September-October 1991 *Early Bird*, a former Ford Design Center stylist, Richard Clayton, revealed to Bill Gill of the American Road Thunderbird Club that he had removed the data plate from -001 before it was destroyed in late 1956 (by dropping it from a helicopter), and that -002 and -003 were also reduced to scrap. Early records of the first Thunderbirds were destroyed during 1966, but before they were incinerated, a request for information on the subject yielded some interesting news. A decrepit '55 was found in the Los Angeles area behind a body shop during 1965, a Raven Black car numbered P5FH-100005. Realizing that such a low sequential number may mean that it was one of the first T-birds built, its new owner, George Watts, contacted a friendly enthusiast in Ford, a secretary in the office of the General Consul named Lois Eminger, who also was an active and fellow member in the Classic Thunderbird Club International (CTCI). A search of filed invoice copies led them to believe that Watts' car was perhaps the first one recorded. As he related in the July-August 1966 *Early Bird* magazine, Eminger, dubbed "Mrs. Thunderbird" by Ford officials, was able to locate its invoice, but determined that the four prior numbers were for "Ford sedans, station wagons, etc." This car, which has been restored at least three times since being first "discovered," has often been called the first production Thunderbird. It was used for the road test conducted by *Sports Illustrated* in the fall of 1954, and it showed minor differences from production models.

Eight years after Watts located -005, though, a father and son in eastern Pennsylvania sold to enthusiast Jeff Barnes what turned out to be car -004 (it had been through sixteen previous owners), which was very similar to Watts' in several of the details that distinguished them from typical production cars, and was closely examined in the winter 1975 issue of *Thunderbird Illustrated*. Research by enthusiast Col. Fordham Johnson, which included compiling data on the '55 T-birds for which invoice copies were destroyed as well as interviews with people involved with the T-bird's production, was published in a series of articles in the *Early Bird* during the middle and latter portions of 1982 and, by the mid-1980s, he determined that cars -004 through -010 were all preproduction cars, according to coding on their data plates, but believed that they were reclassified as production units.

Once management was satisfied that problems pinpointed during the pilot phase could be worked out and modifications made in the sequences of assembly, production began in earnest. Full-blown assembly of the T-bird would be phased in slowly until a count of thirty units a day could be comfortably completed—at least that was the original plan.

A Fairlane Town Sedan precedes a T-bird past the chassis inspection station. *Ford Motor Company*

Countdown to Launch-Time

As the first cars were being assembled, promotion of the new image-builder was heating up. Even though the automotive and general press had known about the car since late winter 1954, introduction time for production cars in late October would require that most dealers (and especially those in major urban markets in which most would probably be sold) would need a new T-bird in their showroom in as short a time as possible.

During September and October, a push was made to get the cars in place for the scheduled introduction date of October 22. As lead-ins to "T-day," ads were placed in major magazines, local newspapers, on television, and on radio. Public relations people and marketing executives made sure that very visible people would get into the car. One report was that movie actress Jane Wyman was so intent on having the first car that she agreed to host a party at her home, complete with her new Thunderbird in the living room!

By December 1954, demand for the car would force planners to double output to approximately sixty per day. When originally introduced, planners had anticipated sales of 10,000 units, but when on October 22 almost

4,000 orders were placed, those figures were tossed aside and reworked to provide for a volume of around 20,000 per year. Suppliers went into overtime to meet Ford's demands, and the Dearborn plant had to rearrange schedules to increase production capacity.

As the number of cars reaching the public climbed, though, so did complaints. The Thunderbird, like any other brand-new product, was subject to flaws. Rain getting into the car with both the hardtop and soft top secured were major reasons why a redesigned set of weather-stripping was introduced into production on January 3, 1955. Other minor items would also receive attention on a warranty basis or be pressed into production as the days rolled on, but three major complaints came from the very top of Ford management: Henry Ford II, chairman of the board, and Lewis D. Crusoe, general manager of Ford Division.

Ford, having been presented with one of the first cars, must have been a proud man driving around the east-central Michigan area with the talk of the motoring public. However, according to Richard Langworth in his book on the Thunderbird, after a golf outing with acquaintances a few weekends after the car was well into production, he passed word down to Crusoe and others responsible for the Thunderbird program that he was getting nice comments about it, but also negative remarks that "the car was too small" to carry golf clubs, and the lack of a rear seat meant that you couldn't drive your friends around the estate. Later, he would also pass on another friend's comment that the convertible top assembly was too awkward to work manually, and decree that a power-assisted top be developed. Perhaps luckily for first-generation owners today, that order was never followed through, except to revise the top linkage for easier operation by mid-1956.

Crusoe had also been getting wind of comments about lack of trunk space and the desire for more passenger room from the person who would succeed him as general manager of the division, Robert S. McNamara, and that something would be done about it. At the turn of the year, Crusoe would become executive vice president of Ford's Car and Truck Division with McNamara stepping up the ladder. A meeting between the two during the transition phase yielded the decision that a four-seat version of the Thunderbird would be one of the projects that would come from the division under McNamara, who saw the car from the perspective of sales and profits, and not the romantic, loss-leading showroom magnet that Crusoe so desired early on. The T-bird was leaving its mark as an upscale Ford, and with the new Fairlane series and models such as the Crown Victoria improving the division's standing in the low-to-mid-price range, its usefulness as an attention-getter had, in McNamara's eyes, been played out.

As the year progressed, reaction to public demand for the car pushed Ford into offering new colors. By January 1955, special orders were being taken for Snowshoe White bodies, and Ford's traditional spring colors promotion would add Goldenrod Yellow to the palette. Also becoming popular was a stainless steel gravel guard placed on the front edge of the fender skirts, eventually becoming standard on the car by May 1955.

But changing the color of the package or some of its trim could not cure the car's biggest drawbacks: an overheated passenger compartment, lack of trunk space, and poor visibility toward the rear for the driver when the hardtop was on. The solutions to these derisive traits would result in a package that would be given the distinction of being called the 1956 Thunderbird. But until that car was made available in the fall, people would have to put up with the T-bird's little problems.

Enamel paint is "baked" on T-birds in this heat-lamp tunnel. *Ford Motor Company*

Racing for Glory

Although T-birds weren't designed for competition, the temptation to modify them for racing (or simply running them in street trim) proved too great. Sporty looks, two seats, big engine, and small chassis—from the outside, it looked pretty credible for going head-to-head with cars such as the Corvette and Jaguar. However, looks could be (and were) deceiving.

During 1955, attempts to run the T-bird in road and stock-car racing were doomed. On the first day of competition during the Daytona Beach, Florida, SpeedWeek, in the Production Sports Car Class, under $4,000, Flying Mile runs, T-birds with three-speeds and higher-ratio 3.31:1 rear ends (normally intended for Ford-O-Matic cars) driven by Bill Spear and John Littlejohn posted speeds of 121.992 and 121.826mph, respectively. Even "Uncle Tom" McCahill, automotive critic for *Popular Mechanics* magazine, entered a modified T-bird (which he claimed was the first one sold); driven by Joe Ferguson, it came away with winning times in the flying-mile competition, hitting the traps at 124.633mph. Another T-bird came in second at 123.401mph. The next day, in standing start mile runs, Ferguson again came out on top, along with two other T-birds, in the American Sports Car Class.

There were few successes for the model after playing on the beach. The little T-birds were no match for Corvettes and Jags when it came to handling in corners and braking, although the T-Bird's straight-line acceleration wasn't too bad. Early failures were seen by many as an indictment against the car.

Members of the racing fraternity and their suppliers were not quick to accommodate the needs of T-bird racers with heavier suspension components, which was what it really needed to be competitive. Speed shops, on the other hand, had Y-block equipment to outfit the T-bird and other Fords with multiple carburetors, magnetos, and other speed parts. Quick to gain notice as a potent add-on was the McCulloch centrifugal supercharger, which the company regularly flaunted in magazine ads appearing in *Hot Rod* and other similar publications. Cars equipped with one and even two of the wheezers would run the next year at Daytona on the sand as well as at Bonneville and other places where competition existed.

Greenfield Village and the Henry Ford Museum are barely visible in the background as a T-bird poses at the Dearborn Test Track, formerly used as an airport in the days of the Ford Tri-Motor. *Ford Motor Company*

Competitive use of the 1955 T-bird was not widespread, but some were modified to run in such events as Daytona Speed Week. This 1955, pictured at the 1956 Daytona event, used a pair of McCulloch superchargers in a two-stage arrangement, with spark provided by a magneto. *Petersen Publishing Company/PPC Photographic*

The last 1955 T-bird built at Dearborn is placed on rollers to check the front end for vibration as a worker finishes re-installing a headlight door. A 1956 Sunliner can be seen in background. *Ford Motor Company*

Coming and Going

Reviews of the '55 from the press were gushing at first, but soon were tempered by the fact that even though it looked like a contender for Jaguar's place in sports-car circles, it could not match the British car's power or handling characteristics. Although Ford's public-relations (PR) people constantly reminded them that the T-bird was a personal luxury car and not a sports car, the early influence of sports-car design created certain expectations for the Ford flyer. By spring 1955, people were attempting to run with the car in competitive events, only to become disappointed in the car's inability to corner and brake as well as the foreign jobs dominating the tracks. The 292ci motor could propel the car down the straightaways in competitive fashion, but the lack of performance-class steering, braking, and suspension meant that drivers either had to back off on the accelerator or run the risk of propelling themselves off the course.

Whether it was road racing, straight-line "controlled-acceleration contests" (i.e., drag racing) or good-old-boy stock-car racing, Ford's image was not being helped by an anemic "personal" car when the public was expecting a factory hot rod worthy of succeeding the flathead V-8's performance reputation with the younger generation. Aware of this, Ford made continuous emphasis in Thunderbird advertising about its elegance, style, and grace, hoping to draw attention away from the horsepower-crazy press and its fawning admirers at the newsstands, speed shops, and drive-ins. The car wasn't being marketed at reckless youth, but at their mellower and saner older brothers, fathers, and mothers.

The car was selling better than Ford's product planners had originally predicted, with *Motor Trend* noting in its June 1955 issue that by April 3 of that year, 5,925 T-birds had been sold and, more telling, that a two-month backlog of orders had yet to be filled. When compared to the Chevrolet Corvette, which was now in the third year of its styling cycle but finally sporting the revolutionary 265ci V-8, the T-bird was a runaway success, and certain-

ly hurt the fiberglass bow-tie flyer in sales. By the end of the 1955 model year, 16,055 Thunderbirds had been produced, while only 674 'Vettes had been built.

Even more telling, several Corvette-inspired (and surely Thunderbird-inspired, as well) competitors came and went by the fall of 1955. The Howard "Dutch" Darrin-designed KFD-161 would go down in flames, even after additions of a fixed fiberglass hardtop and modifications to the anemic 161ci Willys F-head motor including a supercharger or, in some of the last fifty built by Darrin himself, a Cadillac V-8, failed to excite sales or appeal. Of course, the demise of the Kaiser-Frazer Co. as an automobile maker had the public shying away from an "orphan" car such as the KFD-161 Dragon. It is interesting to note, however, that between Kaiser and Darrin's private efforts, the car did sell over 500 copies, though this dragged out through 1958 with the bodies left over and acquired by Darrin.

The Nash-Healey, which was one of the cars used to compare against the Thunderbird back in 1953, was gone—victim of a high ($6,000) price tag and too much weight for the horsepower. Hudson's attempt to go against the 'Vette and 'Bird did no better: The Italia, an aluminum-bodied sports car with a 114hp Twin "H" six-cylinder motor, could only muster enough interest for twenty-four copies to be built before it got the ax in late 1954.

As much as others tried to copy or one-up the success of the Thunderbird, though, it was quite clear that the Crusoe's early insistence on developing the car as a "user-friendly" boulevard cruiser, rather than an all-out sprintster, was right on the money. McNamara could breathe easier, and the public couldn't wait for more.

Without a well to hold the spare tire, almost half of the usable trunk space was lost, resulting in owner complaints. The car pictured at the 1994 CTCI Convention in Dearborn is an early model with "doughnut-style" exhaust outlet inserts. A drawback of the high-mounted exhaust outlets, which haunts seldom-driven early T-birds, is that they trap moisture in the tailpipes and mufflers, promoting premature rust-out in stock steel systems. *Alan Tast photo*

An early production 1955 with a Ford-O-Matic and a T-bird emblem on the ashtray face. The emblem moved to the dashboard by the middle of September 1954. *Alan Tast photo*

A preproduction 1955 T-bird was modified with a Boeing gas turbine motor. Turbine research was conducted by all of the Big Three during the 1950s. The large opening in the fender is an exit for the exhaust. *Ford Motor Company*

Though not in direct competition with the T-bird, cars such as the 1955 Pontiac Star Chief convertible reflected the move toward sportier styling to create exciting automobiles. *Pontiac Historical Services*

Considered by *Motor Trend* as the best-looking car of 1955, the hemi-powered Chrysler 300 was a cross between a New Yorker and an Imperial; it rivaled the T-bird in the personal luxury market. *John Lee photo*

Chapter 3

MINK COAT FOR FATHER

The success of the '55 Thunderbird certainly took a lot of Ford's upper management by surprise. Though nobody would say it publicly, underestimation of the 'Bird's acceptance was a welcome relief. But, after the car had been in the hands of the press and the enthusiasts, it was clear that some fine-tuning was needed to increase its appeal.

Primary complaints weren't about performance or handling (at least in the eyes of Ford's executive staff, though the likes of Walt Woron and Tom McCahill would disagree), they were with passenger comfort and convenience. From the start, the Thunderbird was hindered with several unkind traits (at least from a non-sports car aficionados perspective), due to the very nature of the car's design. First, it suffered in luggage capacity, its spare tire obstructing almost a quarter of the available room in the rear; Mom couldn't bring home groceries in sufficient quantity or pack enough bags for a long weekend outing, and Dad couldn't comfortably throw in a bag of golf clubs (never mind two bags if he brought along a friend) in the back (Hershey pointed out that

Photographed in spring 1955, this often-used publicity photo of Ford Division Vice President Lewis D. Crusoe's personal Raven Black 1955 Thunderbird illustrates the Huddlestone-Whitbone continental kit fitted to the car to increase trunk space. This car also carried one of the prototype sets of Fairlane spears which almost made it into production. *Ford Motor Company*

A brand new T-bird poses in the shadow of the Dearborn Assembly Plant in the spring of 1956. *Ford Motor Company*

from the start the car wasn't intended to be designed around "momma" with features such as a large cargo area, but was supposed to be a sports car; instead, he lamented, it ended up as a boulevard cruiser). Second, if you left the hardtop on, it created a huge blind spot for the driver to his immediate rear, making it virtually impossible to see anyone to either side of the car. Third, the confined cockpit and its proximity to the rearward-placed motor was a veritable heat-sink with no air movement, which would make long trips (especially on moderately warm to hot days) very uncomfortable. Fourth, unless you didn't mind leaving the hardtop on most of the time, the clumsiness of the convertible top assembly was a sore spot for those who were becoming accustomed to touching a button or flipping a switch to raise and lower their car's top.

Fine Tuning

To fix all these problems, the design and engineering teams began work before the '55 even hit the streets. Rhys Miller, who had been working as a design consultant with "Buzz" Grisinger for Kaiser-Willys during 1953–54 (and previously was one of the four outside consultant designers asked to submit designs for the Continental Mark II in early 1953, along with Walker, Vince Gardner, and Wally B. Ford [no relation]), was approached by Hershey in late summer 1954 with a job offer to lead the Thunderbird design studio for the '56 and '57 facelifts. Said Miller, "No work had been done and everything was behind schedule. I knew very little about the car, having only seen preproduction photos. The offer was very interesting, but I told him I had a partner and a business and I would have to discuss it with [Buzz], which I did. Buzz

33

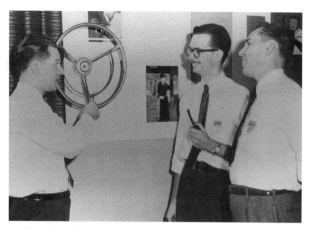

Staff stylist Maurice "Mauri" King points to a 1956 Ford "Lifeguard" dished steering wheel (developed in Rhys Miller's Thunderbird studio) during 1955 while other Design Center staff members look on. One of the "behind-the-scene" people who worked on the first- and second-generation T-birds, King, who came to the United States in 1954 from Ford's operation in Dagenham, England, would go on to play a major role in the development of the English Ford Cortina and Capri in the 1960s. *Ford Motor Company, courtesy Bradley King*

A publicity photo from mid-1955 served to demonstrate three major parts of the 1956 Lifeguard package. Seat belts, the dished steering wheel, and a foam-backed instrument panel cover (though not the same as the production version) were promoted heavily, but public reaction was lukewarm. *Ford Motor Company*

thought it was a good move and might work out for both of us to be at Ford Motor Co. I took the job about October 1, 1954. Buzz followed me about two weeks later, after I informed Frank [Hershey] that Buzz might be interested in coming to Ford. He was hired by Gene Bordinat to head the Mercury advanced studio [and] stayed at Ford until his retirement in 1970, after being chief designer of Lincoln-Mercury Division for ten years."

Miller's "studio" in the design center, as noted earlier, was in the basement "where all the shops were, metal, fiberglass, plaster, woodworking, etc.," he notes. "My space was probably about 30ft by 30ft and adjacent to the wash rack where the company cars were washed. Anyway, they moved two new T-birds in [for the '56 and '57 programs—these were the first and second prototype cars mentioned in Chapter Two], and we built modeling platforms around them and went to work. My 'crew' consisted of two new-hire, first-job designers, one layout man, and three clay model men. It did occur to me, when I had a moment to think about it, that we were not getting very much attention and didn't seem to be taken very seriously. I understood more later on when I learned more about Bob McNamara's attitude about the two-place 'Bird. He was trying to kill it as it was being born."

The '56 and '57 would be developed in parallel, with the latter to receive more extensive work as time and budget allowed. Developing both cars at the same time would save time and money, both of which were at a premium by fall 1954, and the '56 needed to be finished quickly to meet engineering and production release dates. Said Miller, "My

plan was for a quickie solution on the '56 and then explore the possibility of moving the spare back inside and changing some sheetmetal for the '57—if we could afford it with McNamara pulling the purse strings tighter."

The convertible top, which on the original '53 proposals was to be a detachable framework that could be stowed in the trunk, had already been rejected, and the existing flip-down frame could not be made a power-operated one (such as on the upcoming '56 Corvette) without a major expenditure of funds to engineer the hydraulic lift system and modify the body for a flipper lid and top well. Though studies were made of how to do it, the decree by McNamara to abandon the two-seater for future production past the '57 model year ruled out that solution.

It was easier to justify the expenditure of money and time to fix the remaining drawbacks because they could be developed in a short amount of time and either carried over into the '57 or eliminated. The '57 T-bird would be in design for a while after the '56 components were released for engineering and production.

Solving the overheated cockpit would be a little tricky to do. Creating a flow of fresh air into the cavity below the instrument panel was theoretically possible with the existing ductwork that ran from the inner front fenders into the body, but the front bumperettes and lack of room to increase their size negated this. The solution was to place a door in each side of the body in the area of the kick-panel, and allow the driver or passenger to open or close them as needed to catch fresh air as the car speeded along, and force it into the lower area near the floorboards.

Indecision on the spare tire and hardtop would drag on beyond the established deadline to place the changes into production for an October 1955 release date.

Still not given a place to stow the spare tire inside the trunk, designers moved it outside and sheathed it in sheet metal and a chromed "horseshoe" bumper guard. This 1956 has a late-style Burtex trunk mat, indicating production after June of that year. *Alan Tast photo*

"Continental" Spare

Around the beginning of 1955, aftermarket suppliers were reacting to the public demand for more trunk space. Manufacturers such as the Hudelson-Whitebone Co. of Champaign, Illinois, a popular supplier of external rear wheel carriers, were offering in the enthusiast magazines a version for the Thunderbird that would move the bumper/exhaust outlets rearward enough to allow a bracket assembly mounted to the car's frame to hold the extra tire and wheel. A formed set of sheet metal pans covered the gap between the bumper and body, and created a "Continental" look for the car, harkening back to the shrouded assembly on the bustlebacked 1940–48 Lincoln Continental. Several other versions by other suppliers would also crop up, some with chrome-plated tubes between the body and exhaust outlets, others with louvered pans, but the concept was the same: Move the wheel outside for more trunk space inside.

Having complained to his staff already about the lack of storage in the trunk, Crusoe had by April 1955 one of the Hudelson-Whitebone kits fitted to his personal Raven Black '55, which was already customized with one of the Fairlane-stripe sets left over from the August '54 proto-type cars. But the designers had come up with one better than what the aftermarket was offering. According to Miller, in late October 1954 work was being done on the rear end and hardtop revisions. Grisinger, he said, had just been hired on, but his office space on the main floor was not yet ready, so for a few weeks he set up shop in the

Family ties. The 1956 Ford Fairlane Crown Victoria would be less successful in sales than its predecessor. Many of its components were used in the 1956 and 1957 T-birds. Pictured here is a Peacock Blue/Snowshoe White example with Sports Spare Wheel Carrier owned by Lin and Deb Hoskins of Trumble, Nebraska. *Alan Tast photo*

Aaah, relief . . . With the fender vent doors open, passengers could dissipate the buildup of heat from the motor and transmission. For 1956, the Fairlane crest moved to the fender, displacing the V-8 ornament. *Alan Tast photo*

basement Thunderbird studio and assisted the team. "I was satisfied with the bumper section and bumper tip exhaust outlets, but we were having trouble with the center section that carried the tire," noted Miller. "Buzz was sitting by himself and doodling some sketches. Finally, he called me over. 'What about this,' he asked, showing me the sketch. 'Looks good to me,' I said. I called the layout man over and we worked out the sections. It was given over to the clay modeler, and in a short time we had our completed bumper and Continental tire carrier."

The final scheme selected would be a vast improvement over what was cropping up on the streets across America. By slicing out the center of the rear bumper and adding a "horseshoe" extension in the middle, the

This photo of two women with their pink 1956 T-bird, camping trailer, and the brand-new World Headquarters Building in the background appeared in the January 1957 *Ford Times* magazine. Though not the first choice by many for towing, vacationing people in America and Europe could be found pulling small trailers with V-8-powered little 'Birds. *Ford Motor Company*

bumpers could maintain their close relationship with the body, and protect the spare assembly, bolting to a bracket which would allow the unit to pivot backward for access to the trunk and removal of the wheel.

But, as the laws of physics state, "For every action, there is an equal and opposite reaction," which in this case was that the cantilever created on the frame would require that the frame be reinforced. Chassis engineers came up with a stop-gap measure that would be introduced into production as a running change in early production through November, when heavier frames could be made available: weld 2in-wide straps of steel on the bottom of the frame as reinforcing plates. The strapwork would add about 300lb to the weight of the car, but the heavier frames would cut that figure back to a limited extent.

The "Hole" Story

As the deadline for hand-off to engineering and production was nearing, the other major flaw had yet to be eliminated: the blind-spot in the hardtop. In the studio, almost a dozen mockups were made of alternate solutions with wraparound rear windows. The primary solution centered around a thinned-down C-pillar, with a fixed quarter window similar to what would be found on the soon-to-be-released Continental Mark II. The window, which required a frame around the outside to support weatherstripping and to hold the glass in place, would improve visibility, but would also increase the cost of production of the hardtop, not to mention the warranty problems and customer complaints that the windows could easily be broken when the

hardtop was placed on the ground.

Finally, before the end of January, the answer was in hand, and one of the most-classic touches and distinguishing features of the 1956–57 Thunderbird was born: the porthole. To whom should go the credit for the device? The popular story is that designer Boyer, who served in the closing days of World War II as a naval aviation cadet in California, remembered them from his time in the service, and had a set of inner and outer trim rings fabricated for a '55 hardtop out of chrome-plated brass, later mounting them on a boat he owned.

Another story comes from a staff stylist, Maurice King, an English gentleman who had come to Dearborn with his family in 1953 after working for Ford's operation in Dagenham, England. As related by his son, Bradley: "One day in April 1955 my father was working on rendering the bodies of Thunderbirds. There was a circle template on his board placed on a drawing of the car, which was in the way. As father related to me, he moved the template over the side of the roof, thought for a second, and drew a circle roughly where the porthole would be."

Miller, though gave this account: "We tried several workouts on the hardtop for better visibility. My first suggestion being for a circular window or porthole as it became known. Frank [Hershey] told me that they had already considered that but it was not deemed to have adequate vision. I had one put on one side of the top to compare it with subsequent designs. If we made a regular quarter window out of it, it became too weak for a top that had to be handled on and off. We even tried elliptical windows and vertical slot windows. The elliptical window was used some years later on the Continental Mark IV and V. However, when compared to the neutral shape of the circle, the porthole was the unanimous choice of both designers and management. We had created nothing new with the round window [it had been used as early as 1900, and even Raymond Lowey, the famed industrial designer, had one installed on his customized '40 Lincoln Continental]. However, the public thought it was great and everybody was happy."

"Lifeguard" on Duty

The '56 was improved animal with better ventilation from the side vents, the addition of glass wind deflectors to substitute for the lack of vent windows in the door assembly, the porthole top option, the Continental kit, rerouted exhaust outlets through the ends of the rear bumpers, and lengthened rear springs to improve the "truck-like" ride of the 102in wheelbase. Along with changed body ornamentation that prominently displayed the Giberson-designed turquoise-and-chrome Thunderbird logo as well as the gold-crowned Ford crests behind the carried-over check-

marks, design changes would play second-fiddle in Ford's overall campaign to promote safety during 1956. McNamara, a practical man, had felt that the growing horsepower race would lead to an imposition of federal regulations that would stunt the growth of the industry; congressional hearings were already underway to explore the rise in traffic fatalities, and threats of sanctions against automobile manufacturers was a real possibility. To stave off the wolves and, it was hoped, portray Ford as a responsible corporate citizen, 1956 was decreed to be the year of "Lifeguard Design." During the developmental phase of the '56 programs, Ford engineers worked with researchers from Cornell University in developing a safer automobile. Ford even provided a '55 Fordor sedan for Cornell to radically modify into its Safety Car (which can be seen today at the Henry Ford Museum). Researchers determined that most accident injuries came from impalement of the driver on the steering wheel, the sudden impact of bodies with unpadded or fixed objects, and the inability of door latches then in use to lock securely and retain occupants in a crash. The end result was the Lifeguard Design packages available across the board for all Ford, Mercury, and Lincoln

Not all of them come out perfect the first time! Cars that received small dings, scratches, and other blemishes in their finish were sent to a repair area for touch-up before they were released for shipment to dealers. This 1956 T-bird had been masked off for paint repair and was being fussed over by workers in this March 1956 photo. *Ford Motor Company*

lines. While such goodies as a padded dash and seat belts would be extra-cost options, many features became standard on all lines: a crash-absorbing dished steering wheel, revised door latches that were less-prone to popping loose on impact, and a hinged interior rear-view mirror that would swivel out of the way if needed. The Thunderbird would not be left out of this campaign. Miller even noted that work on Lifeguard features consumed much of the studio's time and effort. Even the December 1956 *Ford Times*, the division's monthly pamphlet/magazine sent to favored customers, which focused on travel as well as the newest Ford products, carried the story of a T-bird owner and passenger who walked away from a roll-over thanks to the ruggedness of the fiberglass hardtop's construction, along with other Lifeguard features.

By the beginning of March 1955, the '56 Thunderbird was complete. "We redesigned the seat covers and side panels, put in a safety deep-dish steering wheel, padded the instrument panel, installed lower-cowl side vents, and we had the '56," quipped Miller. A photo series with all the changes in place for the '56 Thunderbird was conducted on May 4, 1955, with the porthole top. The next day, however, another photo session with styling mockups of the '57 and early full-size clays of the 1958 project reveal that the quarter-window hardtops were still much in evidence on the clay-and-fiberglass models. Also around that time, photography work for the '56 shop manual would also reveal that one of the quarter-window cars with a squared-off window frame was in the photography studio to be used to illustrate adjustments to the side glass. And, to make matters even more confusing, an illustration in the brochure for the '56 Fairlanes would show a quarter-windowed T-bird in profile. Though it is a loose sketch done in charcoal, and not intended to draw

Horsepower Race

Drivetrain choices for the Thunderbird in 1955 were limited to the Mercury's 292ci, 4bbl motor (offered midyear in full-size cars under the auspices of a Police Interceptor option), with horsepower dependent upon transmission choice (the Ford-O-Matic-equipped ones pumped out a few more). The M-code 292ci was carried over, but only with a standard-shift transmission. To get an automatic or any of the stick models, people had to pay extra for the P-code 312ci version, which differed by 0.05in in bore and 0.14in in stroke, as well as by 13–15hp, depending on if it was a stick or Ford-O-Matic.

For some people, a 225hp T-bird would not be enough. Even in the '50s, cries for "more power" could be heard. The answer was developed in late 1955, in part with help from Ford's hired gun in the Los Angeles/Long Beach, California, area, race-car builder Pete DePaolo. Ford had decided to get into sanctioned racing as a way to improve its image with enthusiasts, acting on the "win on Sunday, sell on Monday" adage. With help from Ford's engineers and others in the organization, DePaolo would prepare race-ready Fords, Mercurys, and T-birds to compete in many '56 events, including Daytona SpeedWeek in mid-February and various stock-car events. Although most of his crews' attention would go to the full-size sedans and convertibles to be run on the dirt and paved tracks of the Southeast stock-car circuit, there were a few Thunderbirds prepared for the rigors of flat-out controlled-speed contests.

The end result of all this effort would come to fruition in the release in late April 1956 of a bolt-on package (B6A-9000-B) for the 312ci engine that would bump it from 215–225hp to a then-impressive 260hp via the use of a dual four-barrel carburetion system (relying on the old standby "teapot" Holley design), a longer-duration camshaft, and distributor parts to modify the existing single-point unit. It was strongly noted that preference would be given first for racing applications until supplies could be built up, and that they were for stick-shift applications. By July, supplies were sufficient enough to warrant the release of Product Service Letter P-311a, which gave installation instructions for the package.

Since they were only offered as dealer-installed or over-the-counter for others to install, no special effort was made to introduce the kits in production, in part to hold true to the "responsible" image Ford was building. However, the end result of the safety versus horsepower battle was that padded dashes and seat belts didn't sell; multiple-carburetor motors with hot cams did! Chevrolet ran away with full-size sales from Ford (but not without a fight),

attention away from the page's text describing the full-size Fairlane, it does stand out as "one that got away" before the final decision for the T-bird was made.

The Lifeguard program would earn kudos from such organizations as the American Automobile Association (which was screaming by the late summer of 1955 for auto manufacturers to tone down the horsepower war, and itself pulling its sponsorship of racing events) and provide Ford with *Motor Trend* magazine's first Car of the Year Award for its safety promotion. However, people just didn't care about how safe a car was; they wanted to know how fast it could go! Chevrolet, in its second year of producing a low-priced overhead-valve V-8 motor, offered the 265ci "small block" in a variety of induction packages from a single 2bbl carburetor up to the exotic twin four-barrel power pack that would find its way onto many Corvettes, Bel-Airs, and Del-Rays. Ford had to respond, and in a big way.

A private-owner entry in one of the 1956 Daytona Speed Week competitions. *Courtesy Petersen Publishing Company/PPC Photographic*

while the Thunderbird still outsold the redesigned Corvette almost five to one. The 'Vette became more civilized, with roll-up windows and an optional power-operated top, but it was still more of a sports than touring car. Thunderbird still led in the way of power assists, but Corvette was about dead even in options.

After all was done and said, the '56 T-bird would yield to its new sibling, a restyled '57 Thunderbird that would herald the best (and worst) to come.

Musical Chairs

With the success of the Thunderbird also came some failures, perhaps the biggest of which was the loss of the Ford Division chief stylist and the T-bird's primary design father, Frank Hershey. In March 1955, following the appointment of George Walker to the position of vice president of styling by Henry Ford II, Hershey had decided that since he was at odds with the rarely present Walker no chance for advancement or the fostering of his ideas was left, so he accepted a job offer from Kaiser Aluminum and Chemical in California, which was attempting to develop a design department that included automotive bodies and other products. (He remained at Kaiser through 1964.) Rhys Miller, who had taken over as head of the T-bird design studio on September 1, 1954, to handle the '56 and '57 facelifts, was promoted during the same month to head Ford Advanced Design; however, the long hours on salary due to demands by management to see one variation after another created a burn-out situation. "We worked three or four nights a week plus Saturdays and some Sundays," recalled Miller. "The hourly paid clay modelers were making more money than I was." Maguire's penchant for trendy, flamboyant design also did not sit well with Miller. After leaving Ford at the end of September 1955 to work for Chrysler under Virgil Exner to head Chrysler's small car design group, he would join Hershey at Kaiser in October 1956. Said Miller of leaving the T-bird studio, "I was somewhat reluctant to make this change. I had become attached to the little 'Bird. However, the '56 facelift was completed and released for production, and the '57 was 90 percent finished. Then too, I had been given the word by McNamara that the two-place 'Bird was finished, and I would be starting work on the '58 four-place. I hated to see the two-place dropped and voiced my opposition to it, to McNamara, two or three times. I was for giving the buyers a choice, as long as we had the tooling for the two-place, keep it and have a four-place, too. McNamara was adamant that we couldn't afford the parts inventory for both cars, etc."

Hershey's departure would then leave Walker with the opportunity to place Bob Maguire in charge of the division's styling efforts. Picking up where Miller left off in the Thunderbird studio was Bill Boyer, whose responsibilities would now include completing the final details for the '56 and '57 T-birds, as well as the upcoming "195H" program for the four-seat Thunderbird.

Ford's entry in the 1956 SpeedWeek was this highly modified 1956, prepared by Pete DePaolo to gain publicity and performance exposure. DePaolo's staff improvised the headlight covers from aluminum mixing bowls shortly before competition began. *Courtesy Petersen Publishing Company/PPC Photographic*

The car prepared by DePaolo and driven by Chuck Daigh was fitted with this prototype version of the 260hp dual four-barrel carburetor package, which would become available through dealers later in the spring of 1956. For reduced weight on the beach at Daytona, the radiator fan, shroud, heater, and fresh-air ductwork were removed. *Courtesy Petersen Publishing Company/PPC Photographic*

Going for Broke

By late 1955, Ford's archrival, Chevrolet, was helping specific teams with factory assistance in setting up Corvettes and full-size cars for competition—and claiming bragging rights in its advertising. Not about to be left in the dust, Pete DePaolo of Long Beach, California, was retained to develop a stable of race-ready Ford products for running in 1956 events, starting with Daytona SpeedWeek. Among the cars built were a pair of '56 T-birds, including one with the new 260hp dual four-barrel package. Stripped of interior, bumpers, windshield, and any unnecessary components, the car was sent to Daytona emblazoned with large white lettering that left no doubt who sponsored the car or what model it was.

The T-bird that received the most attention was one driven by Chuck Daigh. Competing in the standing-mile race, Daigh's first runs and passes by a few Corvettes were disqualified when motor tear-down revealed an overbore condition in the affected cars. Even though the T-bird set an unofficial record of 92.142mph, all cars were allowed to rerun the event with "legal" motors, and Daigh again came out on top with an average speed of 88.779mph. Adding to the victory, another T-bird driven by Bill Norkert would score an average of 87.869mph for second place.

Later, during the flying-mile races, it would be close, but no cigar: Corvettes would post the two-best times, but T-birds claimed the next three. Interestingly enough, one of the Corvettes would be found before the race with a "misplaced" engine block in the trunk, which was promptly removed before it was allowed to compete, according to an article in the May 1956 *Motor Trend.*

Daigh's success gave Ford something to brag about. Advertising drawn up immediately following SpeedWeek would play up the feat of his run from zero to 150mph in 40.5sec for the June 1956 *Motor Trend* in an ad titled "Mink Coat for Father." By the time the magazine hit the stands, the dual-four barrel package used by the DePaolo T-birds was available at dealerships over the counter, and with a three-speed and 3.73:1 rear axle, aspiring hot rodders could come close to duplicating Daigh's performance at local drag strips and abandoned airfields.

The Ford-sponsored T-bird, driven by Chuck Daigh, kicks up sand as it starts down Daytona Beach for the "Standing Start" acceleration contest. *Ford Motor Company*

Chapter 4

THE SILENCING OF THUNDER

Even as the 1955 Thunderbird was spreading its wings, the decision was being formulated that its metamorphosis would end with the 1957 model year. With his newly gained power to call the shots in January 1955, Robert S. McNamara would begin to leave his stamp of authority on the Ford Division in a big way, but not without hesitation and resentment from those under (and above) him. Within the mind of the accountant, all was profit or loss, and the bottom line for McNamara was that the two-seat Thunderbird was a loser, sales wise. The car, which relied on sharing parts with the full-size Ford, would by its third year be a burden on the Dearborn Assembly Plant line. With the restyling of the full-size Ford and Fairlane 500 line-up, the T-bird wouldn't share components such as speedometers and other dash components, and McNama-

ra wasn't about to commit funds for a complete restyling of a car he couldn't justify to himself, Henry Ford II, or the board of directors. As the gray winter skies over the Motor City would lighten with spring 1955, a more ominous cloud was forming over senior management that would help to spell the end of projects such as the Thunderbird. That cloud would be the Edsel.

In-fighting over the new Special Products Division and the "E-car" would sap strength from the company as a whole, and the Ford Division would not be left out of the scrape. McNamara was set in his ways about letting the two-seat Thunderbird die and introducing a sellable four-passenger T-bird, which could help to do two things: make money for the division and kill the Edsel. A four-passenger T-bird would be direct competition for the up-

Though it was ready for display in 1955, the Mystere was held back for a year from the show circuit due to all the design features that were taken from it for the 1957 Ford/T-bird. *Ford Motor Company*

One of the first clays to be photographed in spring 1955 was this study using 1957 full-size detailing on the driver's side (notice different passenger side headlight shaping). Though the original concept was to carry a "family line" theme between full-size Fords and T-birds, extensive tooling costs for the fenders plus the decision to suspend two-seater production after the 1957 model year would kill this proposal. *Ford Motor Company*

per-end E-car, which would exist between Mercury and Lincoln, while a two-passenger T-bird would only have to butt heads with the Corvette. On the other hand, notes Hershey, the executives were making a big mistake by dropping the two seater. "They were going from a two-passenger to a four-passenger car and still calling it a Thunderbird. It was decided that a four-passenger car could not be made to look like a two-passenger car. So, they decided to make a whole new design, which had no relationship to the two-passenger Thunderbird."

It must be remembered that during 1955, the 'Vette was on the way out, or so the rumors were around Detroit; by the end of production, around 700 would have been built. Nobody anticipated that the '56, '57, and later models would experience a healthy upswing in popularity in mid-1955, but the combination of restyling and intervention by Zora Arkus-Duntov turned around the fiberglass flivver and cultivated a loyal but low-production following, something McNamara's logic could not justify. Production volumes for the Corvette would reach over 10,000 by 1960, an annual number that in McNamara's view of the world was not justifiable for a competing model.

Family Lines

The Thunderbird was already quite a ways into the design process for its third facelift by early 1955. Proposals for the car were started during the fall of 1954, with stylist Rhys Miller leading a team of designers on both '56 and '57 facelifts. "I was asked to come up with a design that had a family tie-in with the '57 Ford," stated Miller. When McNamara decided in meetings with his product-planning committee that the '57 T-bird would be the last two-seat Ford under his reign, it became apparent that monies necessary for a major redesign or even a new two-seater would be out of the question, and that remaining funds for the proposed facelift would be tight. Thus, the final evolution of the '57 Thunderbird would be a function of trying to make the most of what was available from the 1955–56 T-bird and developing '57 Fairlane series.

Formulating design cues for the new full-size cars would be a styling exercise, the Mystere, that was developed by Hershey, L. David Ash, Damon Woods, and, according to some accounts, John Najjar (Najjar denies working on the project) during the latter half of 1954. Named after a French jet fighter, the Mystere had all the makings of a wild concept/show car of the time: big tail-

Pictured a few weeks after "Dagmar" bumperettes had been documented and rejected, a 1957 Studebakeresque front bumper is evident, along with the developing front wheel cutout, wide-vee nose panel ornament, and the quarter-window hardtop being considered for the 1956. Notice the door handle/fin integration and the tall rear canard. Behind the car is Crusoe's 1955 T-bird. Quarter window treatment for the hardtop had already been abandoned, but was still being used on mock-ups. *Ford Motor Company*

fins, a large plexiglass bubble canopy for a roof, quad headlights, low silhouette, and a feature line that mimicked the '55 Fairlane's check-mark trim in an exaggerated fashion. Before the concept car could be finished and put out for display (originally slated for late summer to early fall 1955), so many ideas were taken from it that to release it for public viewing would give away the '57 Ford line's distinguishing features; so, it was held back a year, and work progressed on the '57 Fords and Thunderbirds.

The major cross between Ford and Thunderbird was the low, canted fins on the rear quarters; to allow use of the Fairlane's rear taillights, the T-bird adopted the chic wings. States Miller, "[Following finalization of the '56 design] we were able to more or less concentrate on the '57. We removed the sheetmetal from the back of the doors rearward, built an armature for the clay and started a whole new rear-end design—fenders, trunk deck, bumper, and taillights. By lengthening and reshaping the deck lid and quarter panels, we were able to once again slip the spare tire back inside where it belonged and still have space for the golfers and shoppers. Engineering also helped by relocating the fuel tank." The end result looked natural enough, but much trial and tribulation was expended over how to treat the rear of the car. Several clay-and-fiberglass proposals were developed for review at the weekly review sessions during late fall and winter 1954–55, each examining either a trim deviation or re-contouring of bumper or body panels. "As fins go, I think

The front-end proposal for the 1957 developed during the winter of early 1955 examined filling in bumperettes with bullet-shaped cones, wheel-cove molding, fender ornaments, and a 1956 Thunderbird Special Y-8 badge. *Ford Motor Company*

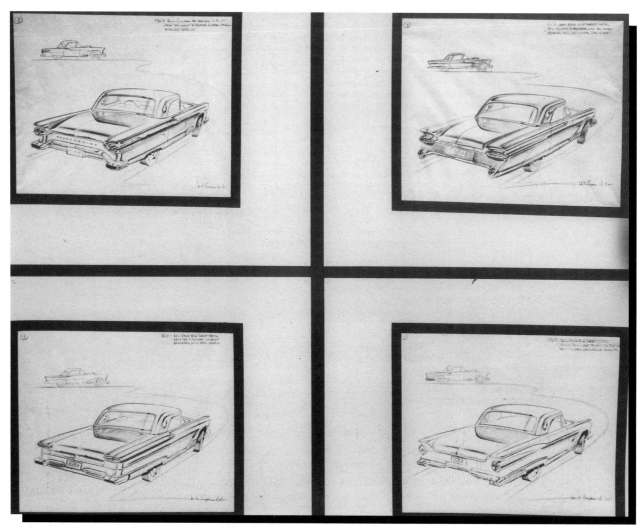

From a photo dated July 7, 1955, this collection of four rear end sketches by Bill Boyer illustrates the continued presence of the front fender cutout and different rear bumper/deck lid treatments. The upper right-hand sketch reveals what would become the final choice for bumper and trunk. Studio head Rhys Miller notes, though, that final approval of the rear end was given in March 1955. *Henry Ford Museum & Greenfield Village*

we worked them in successfully and kept a product relationship with the full-size Ford," Miller noted. "We had one workout with the door handle integrated into the front part of the fin, a very clean workout, but that was vetoed by the cost people." Styling sketches abounded for proposals to alter the taillight and bumper treatments dating through May 1955, but the McNamara directive stifled creativity beyond the dream stage.

Since revamping the car had to be done on a budget, the front did not face the same amount of change, but what was done was quite handsome. With little funding available to change the front sheet metal, the easiest thing to do was develop a different bumper assembly and fill the existing grille cavity with a larger piece of stamped mesh. "Engineering wanted more cooling but wanted to spend little or no money," remarked Miller. "Consequently we

This color rendering by Maurice King dated August 15, 1955, shows porthole top and ribbed aluminum appliqué in wheel cove. *Courtesy Bradley King*

were trying various ways of restriking the front bumper—lowering it in the center to allow for a deeper grille opening and more cooling. I could see this was not going to work and look like anything. I was very vocal about this

Photographed on August 8, 1955, the final front end proposal is evident, while the rear end carried pods. The rear of this clay was also used in development of the 195H/1958 T-bird proposals. *Ford Motor Company*

Photographed in early 1955 (note snow in background), the side trim had been studied for two-toning including use of the crossed-flag emblem on the front fender and hash marks similar to what would be used on the 1958 T-bird. The fender cove had been officially dumped by September 1955, though, when it became known that the 1956 Corvette would use a similar device as a major styling feature. *Ford Motor Company*

and kept showing new bumper designs and kept getting shot down every Thursday, which was show day for management. Bob McNamara was now hitting his stride and throwing a lot of weight around."

The bumper was reworked to provide deeper ends to house the turn signals and hide the place where the 1955–56 units were located. This allowed designers to better mock the '57 Ford's new rectilinear turn signals and rear bumper profile, integrating the two in a loose fashion.

One design theme that was left on the drawing board, though, was the use of a recessed scallop behind the front-wheel opening. This motif, which Miller said was favored early on by Hershey, was very close to production approval by late August 1955, with a ribbed-texture stainless steel insert. Drawings and photographs tracing the evolution of the '57s design point to this "chin" being seriously considered, but advance-release photographs (and probably a sprinkling of "industrial-espionage" photos) showed a dramatically restyled '56 Corvette with a similar-looking cove that ran farther back into the door and a fixed-side-window hardtop. Rather than run the risk of being called a "copy-cat" by its competitor, executives decided to abandon the T-bird's proposed "chin" around the end of August and retain the existing profile.

Interior-wise, the story was one of making do as well. The instrument panel from the 1955–56 T-bird was by now dated, since the '56 and '57 full-size Ford would both use a hooded visor in place of the see-through Astra-Dial speedometer head. A rework of the '56 Ford's instrument cluster was adapted (the '56 Ford's cluster was actually patterned after the '53 T-bird proposal, but modified to work for the full-size car), but the instrument panel stamping had to be cut up for it to work. Interior stylists made a silk purse from a sow's ear by hiding the cobbled assembly under a vinyl-covered foam dash pad. The pad would now be standard on the T-bird instead of the bulky half-dash unit offered the year before. To update the door panels, a new rectangular pattern was formed with alternating areas of Thunderbird outlines. Seat upholstery changed in '56. The previous year's two-person theme was de-emphasized by connecting pleated inserts with a bridge of material. It was again a simple pair of inserts, but would waterfall across the back and lower cushions.

Opting Out

Making the car appealing also meant providing it with accessories for convenience or pure vanity. Other, more "gimmicky" options would prove popular and novel, as well. One such item was the Volumatic radio, which through 1950s state-of-the-art electrical engineering would automatically increase the volume of the car's radio as the accelerator was depressed between 10 and 60mph. A stylish rear-deck antenna, which was designed to be mounted in the center of the rear deck lid, also gave a sporting elegance to the car's looks. Many of the same options that were available in 1956 would also be carried over, such as power-assisted windows, steering, and brakes.

For '57, one option that would have people talking was the Dial-O-Matic power seat. Adapted from the new Mercury, a dial/switch assembly under the dash would provide up to five vertical and seven horizontal positions for the four-way seat track. The theory was that a person would get into the car, select their specific "fit," and let the Dial-O-Matic do the rest. When the ignition was turned

This public relations photo of the 1957 T-bird taken during midsummer 1956 reveals that preproduction hardtop clamps behind the door are taller than the production versions. This appears to be a base-model car with "dog dish" hubcaps and no radio antenna or exterior rear-view mirror. It does have the optional fender skirts, wide whitewall tires, and a porthole hardtop. *Ford Motor Company*

14in-diameter wheels also lowered the car's stance slightly, but when it was all put together, the changes weren't overwhelmingly spectacular. That department would be covered by the choices in powertrains.

As the model year progressed, engine/carburetion offerings would cover the entire range from mild to wild. On the lower end, a person who liked the economy and simplicity of a 2bbl 292ci engine would be completely satisfied with the T-bird's standard C-series motor. It was rated at 206hp at 4500rpm, with the torque curve peaking at 297ft-lb at a more leisurely 2700rpm. Using a new Ford-designed 2bbl low-profile carburetor and low-compression heads rated at 9.0:1, it could run on regular gasoline. As the base model T-bird its transmission choices were limited to either the manual three-speed or overdrive.

The more popular choice, though, was its larger brother, the D-series 312ci/4v. Topped with a new low-profile Holley four-barrel carburetor, its output was channeled to either of the three gearboxes available, including the Ford-O-Matic, which was now a fluid-cooled assembly (the '56 T-bird's automatic received the updated cooling system in June of that year as a running change), instead of relying on a stream of air being pulled in through a duct and across a finned torque converter. Unlike the past two years' offerings, no difference in compression ratios was deemed necessary for standard or automatic transmissions—the D was given a 9.7:1 ratio and rated at 245hp at 4500rpm.

Bordering on the T-bird's wild side were three high-performance versions of the venerable Y-block, each developing a legend of their own: the E and F-series motors. The E was an evolutionary step from the 260hp kit offered over-the-counter in '56, but available from the factory for 1957 and tweaked to gain an additional 5hp through a reworked dual four-barrel manifold, camshaft, and valve springing. Using the same block and internal components as the D with exception of the valvetrain, a recalibrated distributor, and relying for the last year on the "teapot" high-profile Holley carburetors used on Y-blocks from the early to mid-1950s, the E was regarded as a strong competitor for Chevrolet's reworked small block, which was now up to 283ci and, like the Ford motor, in varying carburetion choices from 2bbls to twin four-barrels. Registered horsepower and torque output were pegged at 265hp at 4800rpm and 336ft-lb at 3400rpm, making it the more powerful of the popular engine choic-

off, the seat moved to its rearmost position. When the car was started again, the last-selected position would automatically be recalled. However, as salesmen, drivers, and managers would soon learn, the Dial-O-Matic had one flaw: Whenever a car equipped with it stalled, the seat immediately pulled back to its lowest and most rearward position, forcing drivers to stretch their legs to reach for the foot pedals. The option was dropped by the end of the model year, but the more reliable four-way unit was offered throughout the period.

From Mild to Wild

Continuing development of Ford's high-performance image would not be lost on the T-bird. As part of Crusoe's meeting with McNamara at the end of 1954, before their promotions, upgrading the '57 T-bird with an independent rear suspension and better braking had been considered. But, with the "freeze" being placed on two-seater development, improvements were limited to beefing up braking and suspension components. The company's switch to

A variation on an often-reproduced press release photograph, which usually has a woman and man in the 1957 pictured. During the sitting on the patio of the Styling Rotunda, a professional model and one of the Ford studio interior stylists, John Foster, frame in the two sons of product planner Tom Case, Tom (age 7) and Andy (age 4). The Case family traveled as a foursome in company-owned 1955–57 T-birds, covering more than 60,000 miles during the three years of two-seater production. *Ford Motor Company*

Finally, a new fuel tank arrangement allowed for a spare tire well in the trunk of the T-bird, as evidenced in one of the "F-code" 'Birds from the collection of Chicagoan Jerry Cappizi. To accommodate the spare and gain more trunk room, the rear of the car was stretched 4in. *Alan Tast photo*

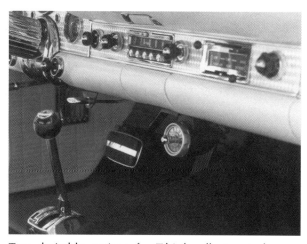

Two desirable options for T-bird collectors today are shown: the underdash control for the "Dial-O-Matic" power seat and the signal-seeking Town and Country radio. The "memory seat," though a novel idea, would not be carried over into later production. *Alan Tast photo*

The two-four-barrel air cleaner of the "E-series" motor had two raised domes, allowing the filter element to fit under the low hood and around the "teapot" Holley carburetors. "Es" were also provided with remote fuel filter canisters, often called "trash cans" due to their corrugated cylinder shape. *Alan Tast photo*

es in the early catalog. Like the D motor, the E could be had with any of the three transmission choices.

As the end of 1956 drew closer, cries from weekend boulevard-racers and all-out stock car/dragster aficionados to wring out more from the Y-block would result in a hotter E motor, in the form of a 285hp package. Announced to the press in October 1956 and appearing in magazines such as *Motor Trend* by December 1956 in its "Spotlight on Detroit" section, the Super-E was developed with the assistance of DePaolo Engineering, Ford's high-performance consultant in California, and offered as a dealer-installed or over-the-counter upgrade for the dual-four motor. Included in the kit was an Iskanderian E-2 camshaft with a longer

duration and higher lift, plus dual valve springs, which were originally slated for the most-radical engine to be developed by Ford to date: a supercharged 312.

Great Balls of Fire

During the mid-1950s, various attempts were made to increase the power and torque output of production motors. Borrowing on a technology developed during the 1930s and refined during World War II for high-altitude use by bombers and fighters, the McCulloch Co.'s Paxton subsidiary was pursuing the installation of its centrifugal supercharger in production-model automobiles. Paxton established a facility in Detroit during 1953 to provide a local contact for the California-based operation, and landed a production deal with Kaiser-Frazer for fitting super-

Preceded by a Fairlane 500 Sunliner convertible, a T-bird is about to be lowered onto its frame/chassis. From here workers will install the radiator, fan and shroud, hood, and make connections for brake and transmission coolant lines, throttle linkages, etc. *Ford Motor Company*

chargers on its full-size 1954 Manhattan sedan. This was a car that needed help: With an F-head six-cylinder that was by all rights obsolete in the wake of low-priced overhead-valve competitors, the added boost of the blower would give it a new lease on life, but not enough to help save the dying company. The next to benefit from the technology was Studebaker, which was also struggling against the Big Three to compete in the horsepower race and attract buyers. Studebaker President James J. Nance authorized installation of a supercharger on the '57 Golden Hawk, Studebaker's four-seat retort to the Corvette and Thunderbird (at least in the power department), and raised its advertised horsepower to 285hp.

As the independents were attempting to match GM, Ford, and Chrysler with add-on performance enhancers as

a low-cost method to wring more out of either antiquated or poorly designed engines, the big boys were also playing one-upmanship: Chrysler was gaining a reputation with its Hemi motors in such cars as the Chrysler 300 and Dodge's Red Ram-equipped D-500; Chevrolet was touting its new mechanical fuel-injection system developed by GM's Rochester subsidiary, along with sister division Pontiac, who with "Bunkie" Knudsen at its helm, was attempting to shed the stodgy, straight-laced image associated with the nameplate and present a fresh face as an upper-range "gentleman's hot rod" with offerings such as the limited-production Bonneville and its fuel-injected motor.

Ford engineers could not sit on their hands and ignore the escalation of the horsepower race. Two factors would force them to respond (and respond quickly) to the chal-

To compete with Corvette and T-bird but offer more passenger room, Studebaker offered the 1957 Golden Hawk, a Paxton/McCulloch-supercharged hardtop. Just after the release of the Hawk, Studebaker's James Nance defected to Ford to serve as its new vice president-marketing. Along with the advice of outside consultant DePaolo, a revised version of the Paxton/McCulloch-supercharger would be used on the T-bird and full-size Fords by February 1957. *Alan Tast collection*

lenge: the development of the Rochester fuel-injection system for the Corvette, and the hiring of Studebaker's Nance as Ford's new vice president of marketing. Consultant DePaolo, aware of the benefits of adding forced induction via McCulloch's variable-speed (VS) blower after seeing them in use on private-owner Thunderbirds and other cars, was convinced that it would be the easiest route to take to upstage Zora Arkus-Duntov at Chevrolet. Nance, having had firsthand knowledge of how such a package had enhanced Studebaker's image, pushed for a blower-equipped Ford and T-bird from the executive end. With two major influences speaking for the introduction of a supercharged Ford V-8, the decision was made to enter into a contract with McCulloch/Paxton by the end of 1956.

Using a low-compression 312ci motor as the starting point, a host of modifications were required to make the package work. An oval-shaped can was placed low on the passenger side of the engine bay as the filtered air intake and was connected to the input side of the supercharger via a large, flexible hose. The incoming air would be compressed within a series of chambers containing large steel balls that were positioned by high-strength springs. As the compressor was turned faster by a V-belt linked to the crankshaft pulley, the balls would be flung farther away from the center of the assembly and compress the incoming air until it reached the outlet port at the circumference of the aluminum housing. From there, the high-pressure air would rush through another large hose into an aluminum "bonnet" that surrounded a teapot Holley four-barrel carburetor adapted from the '56 Lincoln, which had a higher volume capacity than the redesigned low-profile four-barrel. A modified four-barrel intake manifold was developed to accommodate the carburetor and bonnet assembly. The low-compression cylinder heads were fitted with higher-rate valve springs, higher-strength rocker arms and pushrods, and a re-engineered camshaft. Strangely, though, no special work was done to the exhaust manifolds and no effort was made to enlarge the diameter of the exhaust piping. Installation details for the T-bird would differ from the full-size cars to allow for placement of an oval-shaped air cleaner can.

Rated in sales literature at 300hp (with no rpm figure or torque data) with the McCulloch VR-57 centrifugal supercharger, the package would become known as the F-series motor. With the F you could get any of the transmissions, but this would not happen until June 1957, when a toned-down version of the motor would be released for large-scale production.

Initial release of the supercharged motor was planned to coincide with the period a week prior to the beginning of Daytona SpeedWeek, an orgy of go-fast driving that was receiving major media coverage and capturing the attention of the general public. It would be here that bragging rights would be claimed by manufacturers for the course of the model year, based on the standing start and flying-mile dashes across the sand, a road course at New Smyrna Beach's airport, and another course for stock-car racing.

In the end, Ford would capture a lot of PR mileage with its fielding of specially prepared Fairlanes/Custom 300s, T-birds, and Mercurys, but it would also draw the attention of an ever-concerned U.S. Congress, insurance companies, and safety-conscious individuals who saw the worship of all-out automotive performance as a major factor in the ever-increasing death tolls on the nation's highways. This fact also caught the attention of high-level management, especially McNamara, who didn't really care for the high-performance approach to automotive marketing and would be the first to kill the company's ef-

One of the fourteen "D-series" T-birds, which was fitted with Phase I VR-57 superchargers and sent to Daytona Beach in early-February 1957. Ordered without a heater or other power-robbing options such as power steering or power brakes, the cars were built purely for competition. Sharp eyes can see the smooth-style front housing and clamp typical of the early blown cars. *Alan Tast photo*

Most-common of the 1957 motors was the single four-barrel "D-series" 312ci Y-block. Chrome-plated items from the dress-up kit included the famous finned, aluminum valve covers; air cleaner cover; and oil filler cap (the heater housings and fan shroud were plated in later years by the car's owner). *Alan Tast collection*

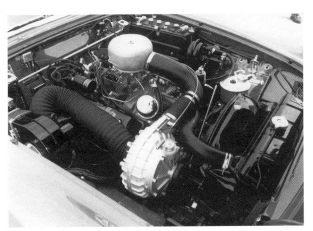

A good view of the Phase II VR-57A blower in the "F-series" 'Bird of Jerry Cappizi. The bolted-together ribbed housing, is a key identifier. *Alan Tast photo*

The last 1957 T-bird is photographed on December 13, 1957, with Dearborn Assembly Plant Manager Lee My-natt behind the wheel. *Ford Motor Company*

forts in racing if he had a chance. So, when the board of directors of the AMA—of which McNamara was a sitting member—announced on June 6, 1957, its recommendation for all car manufacturers to end their sponsorship of racing and high-performance activities as an effort to gain favor with Congress and the insurance industry, McNamara grabbed at the opportunity to stop Ford's involvement in this sector of the business, and the touting of superchargers and dual-fours came to a screeching halt.

Before it could close the chapter on the supercharger, though, Ford had a commitment to use up its supply of blowers. The first run of fourteen VR-57-equipped T-birds built in late-January 1957 were dubbed "Phase I" due to their construction with a stainless-steel clamp holding the two halves of the main body together and other minor dif-

ferences. This first run brought to light problems with the unit's design. A second run of 197 blown T-birds would use the redesigned VR-57A "Phase II" supercharger, which used bolts around the circumference of the casting to hold it together, as well as a redesigned bonnet with an inlet air flap being anchored by rivets instead of drive nails, along with other changes such as the switch from a metal fuel-filter canister to a more traditional glass bowl type, fuel pressure relief lines and balance tubes, and revised throttle and control linkages.

The irony would be that although the cars would be built, it would happen starting on June 10, less than a week after the AMA ban and NASCAR's directive of May 1957 that restricted stock cars to the use of only four-barrel carburetors (a harbinger to the use of restrictor plates

Porthole hardtops for 1957s are trimmed by workers in a portion of the Dearborn Rouge plant. *Ford Motor Company*

and other attempts to "slow down" Grand National racing in the 1980s). Adding water to the firemen's efforts was Ford's internal edict of June 21, 1957, that canceled high-performance development programs and directives from such bodies as the sponsors of the Bonneville National Speed Trials, which decreed that a minimum of 500 cars would need to be built for a given model to qualify for newly created production-sports-car classes. The thunder had been silenced.

Warranty problems with the supercharger may have also done in the option as well. On January 29, 1958, dealers were instructed through Product Service Letter P-372 on how to replace Phase I superchargers with Phase II units. As late as July 22, 1958, Ford issued as part of Management Service Letter M-178 an item for dealers' service departments. At the time, dealers were contending with repair procedures on the Phase II unit, and sending them back to Los Angeles to the manufacturer for rework. Ford's directive was to either repair defective superchargers in-house or acquire replacement units from their regional parts depot.

Paxton, on the other hand, began to offer the VR-57 as an aftermarket item once its exclusivity agreement with Ford expired; by November 1, 1957, it was offering kits for use on the '58 Ford and Edsel's new FE-series (352ci and 361ci) motors, along with a limited number of setups for non-Ford cars, including the '57 Chrysler 300-C and the Chevy Corvette.

Death of the Two-Seater

As the 1957 model year dragged on toward its traditional close in September-October, production of two-seat Thunderbirds was known to be doomed. The popular press by summer was announcing that production of a four-seat replacement with the Thunderbird name was to reach production by January 1958. The Continental Mark II, which never caught on in the volume needed to keep the hand-built car alive, dropped out of production by the middle of May 1957, and it was predicted by some that the T-bird would meet the same fate.

McNamara was also adamant to planners, designers, engineers, and suppliers that the car was "dead" as a two-seater as early as January 1955. Even so, Miller tried to persuade him to reconsider in April or May 1957 and "got a very final no!" he stated. An effort by T-bird product planner Tom Case in September 1957 to determine if two- and four-seat T-bird bodies could be built simultaneously in Budd's Detroit body-assembly operation would quickly lead to a "dressing down" of the young executive by his senior. As related to Richard Langworth in his book *The Thunderbird Story: Personal Luxury*, Case placed a call to a vice president with Budd about the feasibility of dual production, and the Budd executive contacted Ford's vice president of manufacturing, Del S. Harder, about Case's request. Harder, thinking that there may have been second thoughts about the death of the little 'Bird, then spoke with McNamara, who in turn called in Case within the half-hour and said, "Tom, it's dead. I don't ever want to hear of it again. I don't want anybody to do any more about it."

So, with the front wheels in the crusher and the rear being pushed in, the '57 T-bird was bowing out in a prolonged death-throe. Since introduction of the '58, which would be built at the newly opened Lincoln plant in Novi/Wixom, Michigan, would not be until early 1958, it was decided to keep the Thunderbird name in circulation by overrunning production of the '57 version well into the '58 model year at Dearborn. Production of the '57 full-size car ceased at Dearborn Assembly Plant (DAP) around the end of August, with changeover for '58 full-size production being completed by the beginning of September, following Labor Day. The full-size line would be unveiled in dealers' showrooms on November 4, so an accelerated build schedule for the Fairlane series would force a decrease in production of the '57 T-bird. It also meant that short-

Advertising from November 1957 for the "Birdnest," which failed to catch on as hoped. *Alan Tast collection*

ages and eventual exhaustion of '57-style stocks of black-tipped turn-signal levers, window-crank handles, and other parts would lead to substitution of '58 full-size parts. Many T-birds were given a trim-deviation number on their data plate to note that white-handled cranks, levers, and the like were fitted. Also, as the paint lines changed their colors for the new year, T-birds also changed their plumage: Torch Red (R) replaced Flame Red (V); Gunmetal Gray (N) became a shade lighter and was given the H code (creating real problems for body shops to this day); and Azure Blue (L) replaced Star Mist Blue (F) (which would be reinstated into four-seat production).

Fuel-injected Pontiac Bonneville convertible was one of the first dedicated attempts in the midprice range—after the Chrysler 300—to develop a personal-luxury performance car. Limited to 2,000 copies, it gave "Bunkie" Knudsen his image car with which to attract younger buyers, and helped confirm McNamara's decision that a four-seat T-bird was the only way to go. *Pontiac Historical Services*

The two *Battlebirds*, #98 with the 312ci motor, and #99 with the Lincoln 430ci motor, prepare to take to the track at New Smyrna Beach for the road-racing portion of SpeedWeek. Cars would also compete on the beach in Flying Mile and Standing Start Acceleration events. *Petersen Publishing Company/PPC Photographic*

Promotion of the Ford line for 1958 in sales brochures, magazines, and television all included the two-seat Thunderbird, but did not give it the same prominence that it received in the '57 run. It was if the car was being given lip-service, but it was a marketing strategy to keep the name "Thunderbird" in front of the public. As late as December 1957, a bronze-colored two-seater could be found in Ford's full-line sales literature.

Final Assembly

Friday, December 13, 1957, was to workers at Dearborn Assembly Plant a rather unlucky day: It was the final day of Thunderbird production at the facility, and the end of the two-seater that had been introduced to them just over three years before in August 1954. The last serial number to be assigned to a production '57 T-bird would be E7FH-395813, painted bronze and equipped with a hardtop,

The 1957 Fairlane 500's most expensive model, and one which would greatly influence the 1958-66 Thunderbird convertible, was the Skyliner retractable hardtop. This prototype was photographed near Ford's newly opened World Headquarters in July 1956; the Skyliner would not reach production until early 1957. *Ford Motor Company*

white soft top, and most of the power and appearance options. Invoiced to the dealership of Russ Dawson, Inc. of Detroit, it was sold to Theodore Nutter of Farmington, Michigan, according to a story in the May-June 1969 *Early Bird*. A twist of fate would follow the car, as one of Ford's designers, David Holden "Bob" Koto, would become the car's third owner. Koto was head of Lincoln-Mercury's preproduction studio during the late 1950s, involved with the design development of Mercurys and Lincolns through the '60s, and would work on the GT-40 as part of the Corporate Products Studio from September 1963 through November 1964, as well as the '67 Thunderbird's development. The car would remain in Michigan and suffer the ravages of winter driving on salted roads to the point where it was pulled off the road at the end of the 1970s, according to his account in the November-December 1994 *Early Bird*.

As the last '57 T-birds made the migration from factory to dealer to owner there were mixed emotions over the death of the quasi-sports car. Many were of the opinion that the two-seat T-bird would become something to hang on to, since the new version would be a four-passenger model. As the inevitable end of production came, some were even buying them on speculation that their value would go up in the years to come. In fact, the little car's resale value held very well into the early '60s, and desire for it has never ceased. But, the reasons for its demise—lack of additional passenger and luggage capacity, hence practicality—are also what makes the car a favorite in collectors' circles.

After the Fact

While production was winding down, aftermarket suppliers were still busy trying to solve some of the T-bird's design "flaws" for the public, but with varying success. Owners could find in the pages of *Motor Trend, Road & Track, Car Life,* and other popular newsstand fare suppliers for Continental kits, tonneau covers (which were also offered through Ford), hoists and carts for hardtops, ad infinitum.

One offering worth noting that did not make it big but is a curious oddity today is a Town Car conversion. Atlanta, Georgia, based Sanco Inc. produced a unique way to place the hardtop with its Town Car conversion, which placed the fiberglass assembly rearward on the deck lid and left the cockpit open to the sky above. Held in place with toggle bolts and straps, it offered a formal look for the car, but was little more than a curiosity. According to a blurb in the November 1957 *Motor Trend*, it was being offered through Ford dealers.

The most-publicized aftermarket "fix" for the '57 T-bird's lack of rear seats was entrepreneur William Colgan's "Birdnest." Colgan struck upon the idea of bringing the rumble seat into the 1950s, and public demand for a place to put the kids in the 1955–57 T-bird was seemingly an untapped market. By modifying the '57 T-bird's rear deck lid to incorporate a flip-up seat back, and offering accessories such as a

Interior of the surviving *Battlebird* restored by Gil Baumgartner of Suisun, California, from 1992 to 1994 for "Bo" Cheadle. No-nonsense cockpit reveals extensive modifications undertaken by DePaolo's shop. *Alan Tast photo*

Hilborn fuel injectors on #98 were originally set up to run with a McCulloch supercharger, but problems with it resulted in the 312-equipped car being used with just the mechanical injectors. Note the tube headers and lack of radiator fan or shroud. *Alan Tast photo*

plexiglass windscreen, trunk mat, and hardboard side panels, small children could come along for the ride. But the $298 price tag (without the windscreen, which was an additional $60, or the side boards), plus the expense of painting the deck lid to match, would result in the project dying on the vine by late 1958. Sought by collectors today for its novelty, it was supposed to spawn similar versions for the 1955–56 T-bird, but these kits were never brought to production.

The end of production would not be the final chapter in the saga of the two-seater. Well over forty years later, the devotion lavished on surviving examples by people, whether reliving or fulfilling their teenage dreams, maintaining a piece of American automotive history, or simply enjoying the balance of styling grace and timeless beauty, guarantees that the Classic Thunderbird story will be an ongoing body of work.

Battlebirds

The feeding frenzy of 1956's horsepower wars continued into '57 under DePaolo's direction. From development of the 285hp E-model engine to recommending the Mc-Culloch VR-57 supercharger for the F-model engines, performance packages were being prepared for sale on factory-built units and through dealer-installed kits. To promote the coming packages, DePaolo worked with Ford to build four T-birds for the '57 racing season, starting with Daytona Beach's SpeedWeek. Two C-coded cars were fitted with better suspension and brakes, VR-57 blowers, and 312ci motors that had been stroked to 348ci to compete in B-Production/Sports Car Class. Another two C-code cars went into the Long Beach shops to receive extensive modifications for competition in B-Modified/Experimental-Modified Sports Car classes.

The latter two highly modified cars became known as "Battlebirds" due to their all-out racing stance. Each car was different: One was supplied with a 312ci motor, while the other received a modified Lincoln 368ci motor bored out to 430ci They were stripped of all superfluous equipment and unnecessary inner sheet metal, engines were moved rearward 4in, and aluminum bodywork was fabricated for the lower pans, hood, doors, firewall, tonneau, and a fairing behind the driver. Additional modifications were numerous, including a Jaguar four-speed transmission, Halibrand quick-change rear end and knock-off racing wheels, dual fuel tanks, and other assorted items.

The Battlebirds were set up to use both the Hilborn fuel-injection system and a McCulloch blower, but problems with the 312-equipped car driven by Chuck Daigh soon led to its removal following its failure to duplicate a 200mph flying-mile run; teammate Danny Eames, driving the 430-powered car, took first with an average run of 160.356mph. A few days later, Eames took "99" down the beach again in the standing-mile races, and posted the top two times of 98.065 and 97.933mph in the B-Modified division, while Daigh's "98" (sans supercharger) did well enough for third in B-Experimental.

The Battlebirds also competed on the New Smyrna Beach road-race course, though not with the same success. Drivers were changed, with Marvin Panch piloting "98" in place for Troy Ruttman, and Curtis Turner in the "99" car. In the final race for the Pure Oil Trophy, Panch took second behind a Ferrari driven by Carroll Shelby, but captured first in B-Modified. Turner, on the other hand, was forced out of the race due to overheating and did not finish the race.

The *Wall Street Journal* reported that Ford was rumored to have spent $2.5 million on its efforts at Daytona, as well as having shot 40,000ft of movie film to record its successes. Spending of such a magnitude for "bragging rights" did not go unnoticed by Congress, the AMA, and NASCAR officials, such as founder Bill France. After a spring of racing at courses such as Sebring, the Battlebirds and support equipment were sold to Andy Hotten and Jim Mason of Dearborn Steel Tubing by the end of June (the "production" cars were presented to Daigh and, possibly, Eames; Daigh's car would eventually wind up with a Dallas, Texas, collector). They were raced for '57 and '58 by Hotten around the Midwest in Sports Car Club of America (SCCA) events, and even won the Road America 500 at Elkhart Lake. By the end of the '58 season, the cars were sold off: "99" was eventually scrapped after being mangled in an accident, and "98" languished for many years in the hands of several individuals (including famed driver Parnelli Jones) before being restored in 1993–94 to its Daytona-era configuration by Gil Baumgartner of California for its new owner. Baumgartner conducted a thorough documentation and research program for the car and presented his findings in the September-October 1994 *Early Bird.*

Chapter 5

BEANS WEIGH MORE THAN FEATHERS

At the end of December 1954, Robert McNamara and Lewis D. Crusoe conferred on the direction of the Ford Division in the wake of their promotions upward in the organization, and on March 9, 1955, McNamara addressed the product-planning staff on the 1958 Thunderbird program. The group was given four options: 1) continue with the two-seater; 2) develop a four-seat car to replace the existing package; 3) build both a two- and a four-seat T-bird; and, the worst-case scenario, 4) abandon the Thunderbird program. Product planning would be busy for the next two months in drawing up the data necessary to "package" a four-seat Thunderbird for stylists and engineers, but before the package could be handed over to the Ford Division's T-bird Studio, the popular automotive magazines were beginning to reflect the demands of the buying public: In the April issue of *Motor Trend,* staff artist Don Fell penned a drawing of a stretched '55 T-bird with a Landau-style convertible top and an external spare wheel carrier. Speculation, which was probably being fed to *MT's* editors by people in Ford close to the program, was hinting that if a four-seat car would be built, it probably would be a Mercury (the same thing was said of the two-seater during the initial phases of its development as well).

Later, for the same magazine's "Spotlight on Detroit" column by Don MacDonald in October 1955, the question of a four-seat T-bird would again come to the fore-front: "We can't foresee new personal cars beyond the T-bird, Corvette, and Metropolitan," he wrote, "but many engineering dollars are being poured into expanding this concept. A year ago last June, we talked about a whole line of T-birds; look for at least a four-passenger convertible by mid-1956, a wagon, and even a four-door by mid-1957." MacDonald may have been referring to the clay models that were then under development for a showing in early September, as lead-time for the October issue would have been sometime in August.

Internal Competition and Upheaval

It was no secret that the Lincoln-Mercury Division would have loved to bring the T-bird into their sphere of influence: the Davis plan (which was rapidly being re-shaped into the Crusoe-Reith plan by C. Frances Reith, a "whiz kid" with aspirations of becoming head of his own division) recommended a car line between Mercury and Lincoln. A four-seat luxury car like an enlarged T-bird would certainly enhance the division and complement the Continental Mark II, which would debut in May 1955. But as the plan developed and came to a head in April 1955, it became clear that the midline car would come from the newly created Special Products Division

Chevrolet's Biscayne entry in the General Motors Motorama for 1955 was closely studied by Ford's design and engineering staff—early proposals for the 195H T-bird even used the same 108in wheelbase. With front bucket seats and four doors, the Biscayne provided GM designers with ideas for future cars much like the Mystere did for Ford. *Copyright General Motors Corp., used with permission*

It was said that Ford designer Joe Oros credited the Chance Vought F7U Cutlass, a carrier-based jet used by the United States Navy during the early to mid-1950s, for inspiration in developing what would become the 1958 Thunderbird. Twin jet engines, which bulged out of the fuselage, provided a form that became the pointed lower body sculpturing, while the twin rudders and dual exhaust served as the basis for the separate "pontoons" that housed the taillights. *Jeff Ethell collection*

for the 1958 model year, to be known around the industry until late 1956 as the "E-car." Of course, this would be the Edsel, a model born with the best of intentions and research, but without the support of McNamara, who would ultimately rise to become head of all car and truck operations in summer 1957.

With a struggle under way for control of the T-bird program in the upper echelons of the company, a different struggle was shaping up for the design. As the paper program of analysts and engineers gave way to the charcoal pencils and airbrushes of styling, the design center was in upheaval. Frank Hershey had left toward the end of restyling the '57 car and truck lines, including the Thunderbird; lead stylist Rhys Miller would be promoted to advanced design (to be replaced by Elwood Engel in October 1955 when Miller would leave Ford), and designer Bill Boyer would become head of the Thunderbird studio. In addition, the design/styling operation was in the process of being spun off from the control of engineering, which had held precedence since the days of Henry Ford Sr. This transition, wherein styling would gain a greater control over its destiny, would bog down the development of the T-bird's advance program for the 1958 model year from August 1955 through the beginning of February 1956.

The evolution of the 195H program was also intertwined with the schizophrenia of the two-/four-seater battle. With designers not knowing what the final result would be, there was fear that the T-bird program could possibly die.

Development of two- and four-seat proposals were under way during the summer of 1955 as 195X and 195H models. One of the two-seat proposals, photographed from the rear on July 21, 1955, gives a hint of the oblong rear pontoons and taillight insertion, though vertical on this example. This proposal is often pointed to as a possible starting point for the 1962–63 Sports Roadster, with the twin bumps rising from behind the passenger compartment. *Ford Motor Company*

Designer Bill Boyer frequently noted that during the mid-1950s, the T-bird was regarded more as a stepchild of Ford, and the T-bird design staff was relegated to a basement studio to carry out their facelift work on the 1956–57 models. Two-seat proposals under development during mid-1955 for the '57 facelift were also being used to probe ideas, including motifs for the rear end with a "tuning-fork" look, for both the proposed two-seat and four-seat plans.

Preliminary Design Development

Since the preliminary design process carried on from March through November, many different ideas were tried out. And, with the absence of engineering input (due to the restructuring mentioned earlier), those ideas were free from the constraints of the slide-rule-toting, left-brain types. During the initial showing of clay models on September 1, 1955, several examples were put on view with large body-side scallops, similar to the '57 Cadillac Eldorado Brougham's side trim (one side of a mock-up also had lines cut in for a four-door), but following the presentation, scallops disappeared. The idea, according to Boyer and others, was not seriously considered to go with a four-door at the time.

Another clay developed for the early September '55 showing was a two-seat model that featured what would

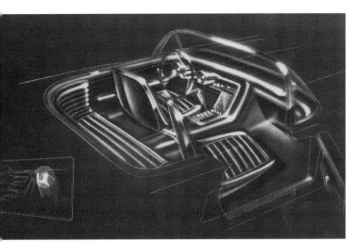

This airbrushed rendering dated October 6, 1955, illustrates many interior themes that would be used in the 1964–66 T-bird, including the wrapover console and wraparound rear seats. While the swivel bucket seat and console-mounted shifter were abandoned, the high driveshaft tunnel would be retained for the next nine years of production. *Henry Ford Museum & Greenfield Village*

become the front end for the final submission. Despite this, all two-seaters were pushed aside for the four-seat program.

From this point, the best of the proposals were brought together. By October 20, hard-line renderings by Maurice "Mauri" King showed the car pretty much in its final form. While the body was pretty much under control, additional thought had to be given to details such as ornamentation and to subassemblies such as headlights and taillights, bumpers, and so on. Parallel development by others in the studio would work out ideas such as trim textures, instrument panel and control layouts, seat design, and so on.

The major challenge with the package was the high tunnel for the driveshaft and transmission. The car's development as a unibody structure and the desire to keep height under 53in dictated that the drivetrain be placed higher in the body. The taller tunnel that resulted also provided a bonus of additional structural rigidity for the center of the car, both in convertible and hardtop versions. The challenge of the tall "hump" was also an opportunity for designers, and came to yield a trademark for the Vintage Thunderbirds that were built through 1966: front bucket seats and a full-length floor console.

Credit for the solution would be given to Boyer who was now in charge of the T-bird studio following the transfer of Rhys Miller in March 1955. Because the passenger compartment was in effect divided into four sections, it was reasoned, why not exploit the division and emphasize it. To do so, a vinyl-covered structure was devised to square off the top of the tunnel and provide a location for ash trays fore and aft, power window switches and a radio speaker. The console at the front swept up to the bottom

of the instrument panel, and a molded pad created "coves" for the instrument panel and the glove-box. The move created "personal" space for the occupants, and in a pinch a fifth person could use the middle of the rear seat (though leg placement would be a challenge). Boyer had originally intended for radio, power window, heater, and air-conditioning controls to be in the console between the seats, but fears of dirt entrapment and spilled drinks led designers to place them in more conventional positions. Even a floor shifter was considered, but various states at the time had regulations that required passengers to be able to exit a vehicle from the opposite side, and the high tunnel/console and a shift lever would preclude an easy transition from one side to the other, so it was dropped. An early proposal for the interior, rendered on October 5, 1955, would show the shifter/control layout, as well as wraparound seats and a dashboard arrangement that would serve as the basis for the 1964–66 Thunderbird's interior. A pair of swivel bucket seats were also included, but these would not be considered for production due to cost.

A rapid-fire progression would lead to the development of a "see-through" model with a fiberglass body and plexiglass windows by the end of November that would be very close to the final product, although continual work on refining the design would continue through the beginning of April 1956 on such items as trim, fabrics, colors, and ornamentation.

Engineering and Production Influences

As the 1958 program began to take shape, consideration on where it was to be built would affect the car's design in a major way. Ford's experience with the T-bird program at the Dearborn Assembly Plant led the company to consider an alternative assembly site. Lincoln Division had begun design work on a new assembly plant in Novi, about 20mi from central operations in Dearborn. The plant would feature state-of-the-art assembly techniques and pioneer for Ford the use of unibody construction. It had been decided that the '58 Lincoln would use the body-without-a-frame concept to take advantage of weight reduction and lower body height. But, because of the relatively low volume of Lincoln production, it would be desirous to build another car in the facility. With the Thunderbird being an all-new platform coming on-line around the same time, it only made sense to structure it for assembly at what would become known as the Wixom Plant, and piggyback on the production capacity of the new complex, sharing costs between Ford and Lincoln. This idea appealed to McNamara's penchant for conservative expenditures, and it made good business sense. Industry sages were aware that, sometime in the near future, a unibody car would be built. *Motor Trend's* column "The Rumor Mill" went so far as to note in its December 1955 issue that "general use of unit body construction" may be

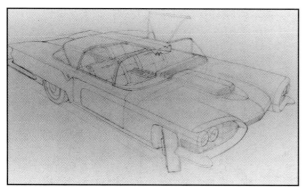

A hard-lined body drawing prepared by Maurice King during mid-1955 for an early 195H T-bird proposal. Influenced by the Mercury XM-800 and Turnpike Cruiser show cars, it contains such novelties as removable plexiglass roof panels and an overhead console. *Bradley King collection*

Another King rendering, dated November 11, 1955, shows the car's lines in near-final form. Exhaust outlets in the end of the rear bumper, "bullets" in the taillights, and a door panel that flows into the dash would not make it into final production. *Bradley King collection*

under development, with journalists being refused access to plants that make automotive frames.

Body engineering had prepared drawings by February '56 for the Budd Co., the builder of the little T-bird shells, for its own engineering and development of tools and dies. Before the drawings would go out, though, it was discovered that the car was an inch too narrow, resulting in the rear tires rubbing against the outer wheelhouses in leaning turns. Drafters simply cut the drawings in half and spliced in the missing inch with no obvious effects on the design, and in the styling studio, modifications were made to the clay model to match the change.

The Aborted Retractable T-bird

The final styling clay was presented to upper management on April 9, 1956—thirteen months after its beginning. Engineering was well under way, including preliminary design for a retractable hardtop version of the car. The attractiveness of a retractable-style T-bird was quickly lost when designers realized that the rear deck lid would have to be revamped to accommodate the roof in its down position, and the complicated mechanism would be cost-prohibitive on a car that was expected to sell fewer than 5,000 units per year. Similar reasons were given for dropping the idea on the 1956–57 Mark II, and after the '57 Ford Skyliner had been on the market several months, warranty problems and customer complaints of tops stopping in midcycle or not working at all would kill the thought of using it on the T-bird. Before the plug was pulled, though, Bob Hennessy, one of the Mark II/Skyliner's primary engineers, had worked out at least four possible versions for the T-bird, along with John Widman and Ben King. Of the four versions, three were tried and abandoned: (1) a traditional convertible-style arrangement that would have the top simply fold into sections and flop back into the trunk behind the rear seat; (2) a shortened roof with its forward portion fixed to the wind-

shield frame (similar to the early '50s Hudson convertibles), allowing a solid unit to fall back into the rear; and (3) a revision of (1) in which the roof fell back as a solid unit.

The final version that would have come closest to approval was called a "clamshell" by Boyer. Split in half at the middle (roughly above the back of the bucket seats), the roof would fold in on itself, then flip back into the trunk, with the C-pillar tumbling back behind the rear seat. A working "buck" was built to test it, but again, as in the other proposals, clearance with the rear deck lid was too tight.

T-Tops

With the retractable hardtop option now ruled out, another alternative was desired by product planners for an open car. Taking a cue from Mercury's XM-800 show car, developed in Elwood Engel's Advanced Styling Studios during late 1954 and early 1955, an idea for removable roof panels was developed. The panels, an innovation brought to the XM-800 through Gordon Buehrig, were seriously considered for the '58 T-bird as a standard item. Buehrig, who was already a major name in the design business (having operated his own studio before hiring on with Ford in 1948 to work on the 1952–54 program and the Continental Mark II), had developed a T-top for a proposed sports car of his design in the late '40s, the Talgo, and brought this to reality by modifying a hardtop for his personal '55 T-bird, with both solid and transparent panels. He had even tried to sell the idea to Ford for the two-seater, only to be turned down (magazines reported that he was rebuffed over the asking price for the rights to the design, rumored to be $5,000); promotion in *Motor Trend* and even *Ford Times* failed to generate enough interest for bringing it into production as an aftermarket offering.

The T-top idea would eventually be shelved, but not before it was considered by planners as a possible option for the 1960 model. As late as March 1957, it was still being considered as the standard (and only) roof, but engi-

The upper front three-quarter view of the same proposal from mid-November 1955. The 1956–57-style T-bird nose emblem can be seen. *Bradley King collection*

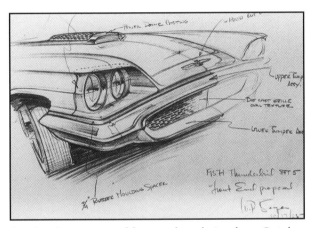

Another Boyer-penned front end rendering from October 17, 1955, illustrating the die-cast headlight housing and an oval-textured die-cast grille. *Bradley King collection*

neering and tooling expenses were considered prohibitive (by this time, most of the engineering and tooling budget for even the '59 and '60 facelifts had been spent). This meant that once again, the '58 T-bird line might not include an open model, but work had already been authorized on a soft top version.

Tumbling Routine

On November 19, 1956, Ford's Administration Committee would finally commit to the development of a convertible model either for the '59 model year or midway into '58 production, possibly as early as April '58, or three months after the projected start of hardtop assembly. Because of the workload on Ford's engineering staff, the project was turned over to Wettlaufer Engineering with assistance from Hennessy. This arrangement would create challenges for the Ford engineers who were attempting to coordinate design, tooling, and prototype development between Budd (bodies), Wettlaufer (convertible-specific items), and Ford's in-house team.

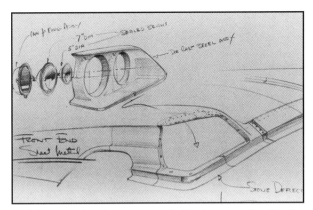

Problems in developing a single fender stamping for the front fenders led to this proposal for a multipiece assembly (as evidenced by the lines above the wheel arch and below the headlight opening) with a cast housing for the headlights. It was drawn by Bill Boyer in October 1955. *Bradley King collection*

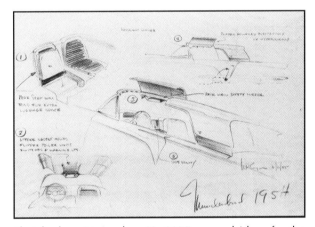

Sketched on November 11, 1955, several ideas for the 195H T-bird are proposed by Boyer, including storage compartments beneath the rear seats, an overhead console and flipper roof panels. The roof panels would become almost a running gag on design proposals and would be submitted on every model well into the 1964 series, only to be rejected due to cost and engineering considerations. *Bradley King collection*

The convertible's operating mechanics were developed from the aborted retractable hardtop. The top bows were linked to a panel behind the rear seat, which was bolted to a hinge/bracket assembly that was pinned to the front portion of the trunk floor. After the rear deck lid was unlocked by depressing a key-accessed button under the dash, which activated a pair of electric solenoid latches, a person would have to finish opening the deck lid to a vertical position. A switch on the driver's side of the trunk allowed the top to be raised or lowered once two header clamps had been released. Once the assembly had been raised up and rolled

"Bodies in white" are shown on a special trailer. Assembled in the same plant as the1955–57 T-birds, Squarebird shells were trucked to Wixom and inserted into the assembly line for final finishing. *Ford Motor Company*

back into the trunk cavity, the operator could pull on a knob that would release a filler panel hinged at the front end of the deck lid and flip it into position and close the trunk. The result was a car that had a smooth rear deck. It also meant that if you wanted to tour with the top down, that you didn't have room in the back for a picnic basket or anything else save for very small bags, as the convertible top and framework literally ate up the available space.

Engineering Prototypes

A preliminary hardtop body was patched together by March-April 1957, using a combination of prototype sheet metal components for the roof and inner structures and exterior sheet metal left over from '56 T-bird production stock for evaluation of the unibody concept. Concerns were that the spot-welded structure might not hold up as well as a body-on-frame model, based on past experience with competitors' attempts such as the Hudson of the period. The key to the new T-bird's strength would lie in its spine: a high transmission/driveshaft tunnel. The depth of the tunnel acted like a deep-section framing member, creating a stiffer center-line axis that limited body flexing.

Engineers James Hollowell, Donald N. Frey, and James L. Martin produced a paper for the Society of Automotive Engineers that was presented at its summer meeting in Atlantic City, New Jersey, from June 8 to 13,

1958, which gave design and development details for the car. The high-tunnel concept would be proven at Ford's Kingman, Arizona, proving grounds during May '57, when it was driven over 1,500mi on a "torture track" composed of alternating sections of potholes (2.8mi), sunken railroad ties (1.8mi) to simulate washboard conditions, and a flat stretch (3.1mi) to provide a "cool-down" period for suspension components (shock absorbers would only be good for 120mi, or about sixteen times around the 7.7mi circuit). Compared with a '56 Hudson (which only went 800mi before being pulled off the course) and a '57 T-bird, the prototype did amazingly well—some failures of spot welds occurred early on around the front suspension crossmember, front side rails, rear-suspension support brackets, and floor pan, these were repaired and reinforced. At the end, while neither the '57 nor '58 showed evidence of exterior sheet metal failure (i.e., buckling), comparative measurements showed a sag of 0.6in at the rear for the body-on-frame '57. The prototype '58 only deformed 0.3in, which was deemed within tolerances. Even tests with the final design prototype, with final production-type components, yielded the same results.

Engines and Drivetrains

Powertrains were being contemplated as well to continue the performance image. On April 17, 1957, the

A 352ci motor with an automatic transmission and belt-driven windshield washer pump (mounted between the power steering pump and the radiator coolant expansion tank) is guided into position in one of the first 1958 T-birds assembled on December 20, 1957. *Ford Motor Company*

Product Planning Committee approved three versions of the all-new FE-series big-block motor, all sized at 352ci. The standard motor would be the 300hp version with a single four-barrel carburetor, while power options for '58 and '59 would differ: For the first year, a supercharged version rated at 352hp was proposed, and a fuel-injected assembly for '59 was slated to pump out 335hp. The kibosh on power packages would come as a result of the AMA ban and Ford's subsequent cancellation of performance options two months later, but the surviving 300hp motor was still a hot little number with "EDC" cylinder heads producing 10.2:1 compression, and mechanical valve lifters. These heads were so hot, in fact, that their use was discontinued in midproduction and replaced with lower-compression versions to "detune" the motor.

There was also consideration of using the Lincoln's 430ci motor in the '58 as well, with one of the prototype units being fitted with what was the largest production-car motor at the time, and several test "mules" during 1958 to test the installation for '59 production. Hopes were high enough for introduction of the larger mill that

by May 1958, advertising for the new convertible was also touting a 350hp optional motor. But, engineering problems and production scheduling would delay its introduction until early in '59-model-year assembly during October-November 1958.

The transmission of choice would be a new dual-range automatic known as Cruise-O-Matic. The oil-cooled unit would provide a choice of starting gears to match driving conditions in either low or second. Although manual-shift three-speed and overdrive transmissions were available, the vast majority opted for the convenience of the automatic.

An odd combination, which was not advertised in domestic sales literature but promoted in the export market, was the smaller version of the 352, the 332ci motor (used in the Fairlane 500 and other full-size Fords) and the two-speed Ford-O-Matic transmission. The smaller motor and lesser transmission were offered to allow the car to be used in areas where high-octane gasoline was not available, and to lessen the cost penalty due to road-use taxes, where cars were assessed based on their axle weight

Comparison between the 1958 Fairlane 500 (left), 1958 T-bird (middle), and 1957 T-bird (right) shows how the latter two are lower than their full-size brother. This photo was taken as part of a February 1958 session for *Motor Trend* magazine, which would proclaim the 1958 T-bird as its "Car of the Year." *Ford Motor Company*

and motor's cubic displacement. While no production figures were published on the number of '58 T-birds exported, an extremely small number of examples have been accounted for in Europe through the Vintage Thunderbird Club International (VTCI). These cars were also available with speedometers that registered in kilometers per hour, and all heavy-duty components (larger-capacity battery plus higher-rated front and rear coil springs) were fitted to cars designated for overseas sale.

Options That Did (and Didn't) Make It

Availability of options for the '58 T-bird was tremendous. All typical power assists were offered—steering, brakes, and windows—but only the driver's seat could be had with the four-way mechanism worked by a lever switch along the outboard side of the lower seat assembly and a pair of electric motors and servos. Along with the power assists, convenience and comfort options abounded—spotlights, integral air conditioning and heater, semi-transistorized AM radio with a choice of either a front-

fender-mounted or rear-deck antenna, and a unique windshield washer system that also operated the vacuum-powered windshield wipers at the push of a switch on the driver's side "dogleg." And, to make for more trunk room (especially in the convertible), a Sports Spare Wheel Carrier was also available as a dealer-installed item.

The option for many that equaled performance, the tachometer, was abandoned during planning in May 1957. In its place would be the electric clock, which could be deleted by special order. The dropping of the tachometer would be justified as reinforcement of the personal-luxury concept and the move away from a performance emphasis. At the same time, problems with the '57's Dial-O-Matic memory seat led to the dropping of it for consideration.

Another controversial add-on that was supposed to come of age for the 1958 model year, an air-spring suspension using rubber bags connected to a compressor and air tank in the engine bay, was also dropped, but not before the T-bird would be designed to use them, potentially as standard equipment. The front shock absorbers were

A public relations photograph of Styling Vice President George Walker and his granddaughter in a 1957 T-bird Junior, taken in early 1958. The 1958 T-bird would be the first all-new car to be developed during Walker's tenure as head executive of Styling. *Ford Motor Company*

mounted outside and to the rear of the coil spring to allow the "air domes" to occupy the space, and the rear was engineered to use trailing arms and coil springs, abandoning the semi-elliptic leaf springs of the past. As development of prototype and early production full-size '58 Fords with Ford-Aire suspension revealed problems with air leaks and bladder bleed-down after prolonged idleness (it was reported that it took twenty minutes to air-up the bags satisfactorily in a worst-case scenario), product planner Tom Case issued a memo just after official start of T-bird production in January 1958 stating that the package was being shelved, probably to the relief of dealers who were putting up with complaints from the 200 or so Ford owners with the air springs already on the road.

Production and Promotion

Although the popular press was confirming by early fall 1957 that the new T-bird would be a four-person, unibody car that would in essence be a "baby Continental," public introduction would coincide with New Year's Eve at the Thunderbird Golf Club in Palm Springs, California.

Following this, during the first full week of January, the Chicago Auto Show would be the primary access point for the automotive enthusiasts to view it. Prototype cars were test-driven by automotive writers during late 1957 to meet long lead times for February publication, which would be when the major advertising push would begin under the direction of JWT, including television commercials featuring actor Dick Powell touting the ease of entry into the rear seat through the 4ft-long doors (longest in the industry). The ad agency also secured spots on the "Lucy and Desi Comedy Hour" featuring Lucille Ball and soon-to-be ex-husband Desi Arnaz, coinciding with dealers' introductions in mid-February. Images of people at marinas, polo pony fields, and airports reinforced the upper-level image of a new luxury Ford for couples on the go. A hard-sell to affluent people in the middle of a mild recession, the car was also linked with the lower-priced Ford lines in promoting "Thunderbird GO" with use of the "Thunderbird Interceptor" motors in Fairlanes and Customs.

To get further mileage out of the new car, executives selected the T-bird to represent the fifty-millionth Ford car to be

The prototype 1958 convertible in the Engineering Garage in late April 1958. Production would begin on the drop-top version by the beginning of May. *Ford Motor Company*

produced. The car selected would be built around St. Patrick's Day, photographed with the fifteen-millionth car, a '23 Model T Phaeton, and two models in respective period dress. It's new owner, a Mr. O'Reilly, would be photographed at the end of the final inspection line taking delivery of a Cascade Green hardtop, which was called Irish Green in press releases.

The crowning bit of press response would be penned by Sam Hanks during February for the May issue of *Motor Trend*, in which editors would proclaim the '58 T-bird as its Car of the Year, based on its packaging and engineering advances in construction and styling. Some critics have claimed that the honor was really nothing more than an orchestrated PR ploy between *MT* and Ford, but it would remain that the car was perhaps the most revolutionary vehicle on the road at the time, and deserving of the honor.

Other magazines were less-flattering, though. All would attempt to draw comparisons with the first-generation T-bird and be disappointed in the addition of the very things the public cried for. Some would also attempt to compare it with the '58 Corvette, when actual comparison could be better made with cars like the Chrysler 300 or Pontiac Bonneville, which were full-size cars with a performance and personal-luxury bent. The closest comparable,

Studebaker's Golden Hawk, was by now a not-so-serious contender, as it became more apparent that the company was going downhill and that its days were numbered.

Getting the Convertible on the Road

Sales of the new hardtop were much better than expected in a soft market. Reports of first quarter sales of over 6,500 and orders for more were good news in a climate where the Edsel was giving Ford a black eye from customer dissatisfaction. The push to get the convertible into production became a lesson in frustration for planners, as delays in completion of prototypes and in supplying necessary parts pushed the first build dates past the projected April 15 target date. Only one convertible prototype could be spared for use in Wixom's training area to instruct workers on how to assemble and inspect the car. Finally, on the first week of May, the first drop-tops began to join the flow of hardtop T-birds and Lincolns. To fulfill orders already backlogged, the Wixom plant went into a heavy overtime mode before delivery of convertible bodies in mid-April. Saturday work and nine-hour shifts along with a speed-up of the lines would bolster production from about 200 units per day to almost 250, and

A prototype of the 430ci motor installation in a 1958 T-bird is shown in this photo. Though promoted in magazine articles during the car's introduction in early 1958, and advertised as early as June 1958, it would not appear until after the beginning of 1959 assembly in September 1958. Unlike production cars, the prototype was provided with a Holley four-barrel carburetor. *Ford Motor Company*

would continue virtually until plant shutdown for changeover to '59 production at the middle of September. By the end of production, 2,134 ragtops were assembled.

Problems with the '58

As production of the new Thunderbird was accelerated during the early part of 1958, complaints by owners were beginning to roll in about poor braking, handling, and the various problems associated with a new car. On the up side, rattles and squeaks were virtually nonexistent, thanks to its all-welded unibody construction.

The rear suspension, with its novel trailing arms, allowed the car to "wallow" down the road; the ultimate correction for this would be the return of leaf springs for 1959. Noise complaints were solved by the end of December through replacement rubber bushings and mounting brackets that reduced road and axle noise trans-

mission. Many Ford dealer mechanics, though, would resort to a low-tech fix for the bad bushings: stiffening them by driving nails into the rubber.

Braking was a sore point with the '58 for several reasons. First, a new composite brake shoe lining was being introduced with the car. The linings, containing a ceramic section in the center of a metal-imbedded asbestos ribbon, were supposed to be an improvement, but problems with pulling and noise would force Ford to drop them from production by early April, and create a "campaign" (another word for "recall") to replace the Cermetallic shoes with asbestos ones. To compound the dilemma, original plans to use a 3.5in-wide front shoe on the front were dropped in favor of a 2.5in assembly. Engineer James Hollowell related to Richard Langworth in his book, *The Thunderbird Story: Personal Luxury*, that the decrease in brake size was "to accommodate steering."

Operation of the convertible top was similar to that of the Ford Skyliner retractable hardtop. Though not fully automatic, it relied on hydraulics to work the top bows, while the operator opened or closed the rear deck lid and positioned the flipper panel. This example of a 1958 convertible was restored by Michael Ogletree. *Alan Tast photo*

In addition, placement of front brake lines, both the rubber flex and metal piping, was under constant revision. The original positioning of the lines was related to the planned Ford-Aire suspension system, which was abandoned. Technical bulletins and service letters to dealers advised them on repositioning of brackets and lines to avoid interference with the passenger-side upper control arm, as well as with the automatic transmission dipstick tube (which was creating a buzzing noise).

When the model year came to a close in mid-September 1958, Ford's executives were very pleased with the success of the car. In less than ten months, it had sold almost double the amount of '57 production, although convertible sales were below projections. McNamara's gut instincts were proven right, and the roll would continue upward for the next two years.

Pontiac's Bonneville hardtop represents the closest competition T-bird had aside from Studebaker's Hawk series. Though a full-size car, its upscale trimming and powertrain would be one of GM's challengers in the midpriced personal luxury field. *Pontiac Historical Services*

Chapter 6

THE CAR EVERYONE WOULD LIKE TO OWN

The success of the new four-seat Thunderbird for the 1958 model year was welcome news for the Ford Division, and the '59 T-bird would be more of the same. Planning for the '59 and '60 models began as soon as the 1958 program was well underway during 1956, as part of a strategy to use the same basic body shell for three years with minor changes for identity and introduction of engineering improvements. A full-blown attempt at restyling the interim model would not begin in earnest until the spring of 1957, allowing time for "bugs" to be worked out of the '58 during engineering development.

On May 14, 1957, the Product Planning Committee gave approval for the '59 program as well as advance direction on the '60, which would be a facelift of the previous two years. A timetable for development of the program would fast-track the styling and engineering aspects, since primary changes would only be in trim detailing for the hardtop, but development of the open model (which would also be covered in part by the '58's budget) would also incorporate a running change to make the top mechanism fully automatic. As the plan was laid out, styling would be given until July 9, 1957, for approval of trim changes, with their portion of the work to be completed by Labor Day, giving them less than four months to arrive at a solution. Engineering, on the other hand, would have until March 3, 1958, (about ten months) to have their last service evaluation and production review ready.

Since changes wouldn't need to be major, attention focused on ornamentation and how to tie in '59 full-size styling into the T-bird (in actuality, it would end up the opposite, since the '59 would take cues from the '58 T-bird program, such as the headlight eyebrows and lower rear quarter "spear," which would move to the top of the full-size car's quarter panel and serve as a place to position the optional back-up light assembly). With clay models of '58s already developed, it was simply a matter of trying out different ornamentation layouts, grille themes, and color/upholstery modifications.

Changes in the interior would not be many: The dial faces for instruments, plastic knobs on the dash and window-crank handles, and power window switches were changed from black to white. For the first time, leather upholstery was offered as an option (the only material choices for 1958 were an all-vinyl or vinyl-cloth combination). Additional colors would also be available, as well.

Ornamentation for the body would finally settle on the use of a chrome-plated pot-metal casting shaped like a spear tip at the leading edge of the lower "bomb" sculpting, after weeks of consideration of a variety of darts and spears on either the quarter panels or front of the bomb. Unlike the lower-side treatment, the V-winged emblem used on the nose and rear deck lid was copied and reduced in size to fit on the C-pillar where the round, plastic-lensed 'Bird appeared in '57 and '58.

Placement of the nameplate would also be a long-debated item, with it moving from the area behind the front wheel cutout to the door to the rear quarter. After much wrangling, it finally ended up behind the spear by the end of September '57, at final approval.

To further emphasize changes, grille and rear taillight background panels were provided with new texturing. Instead of a rather delicate mesh of circles and lines that formed a geometric pattern, the '59 used a unique horizontal-bar motif. This simple layout had a period influence from custom cars with grilles made from chrome-plated tubing—and was easy to model and bring into production. Thus, restyling kept the car looking fresh, and retooling costs were minimal.

Adding the Lincoln 430 Motor

With the decision of June 21, 1957, to cancel high-performance development for the Ford line, hopes for a fuel-injected 352ci motor evaporated. But a review of package sizes for the FE-series and the monster 430ci M-E-L motors was quickly undertaken by engineers and planners. The 430, which was rated at 350bhp at 4800rpm, was a natural

A rendering from mid-1957, during the development of facelift proposals for the 1959 T-bird, reveals one of the options planners were considering for the grille and side trim. Portholes in the C-pillar and a targa-style roof were thoughts on paper for product planners examining different roofs for either 1959 or 1960. *Ford Motor Company*

This styling sketch of the front end with horizontal grille bars is close to the production version, but the single-piece bumper guard would be held back until 1961 model. *Ford Motor Company*

As it had done with the 1955–57 T-bird, the PowerCar Company of Mystic, Connecticut, produced pint-sized electric- or gas-powered versions of the Squarebird in fiberglass to be used for dealer promotions and sold to the public. Bodies were also supplied to builders of carnival rides. The 1959 version, shown in front of Ford's World Headquarters building, was photographed in July 1959. *Ford Motor Company*

choice for the 'Bird. Availability was guaranteed as it was also being supplied to Wixom for the leviathan Lincoln. It was only slightly larger than the 352, and only a few modifications for motor mounts and transmission would be required. With a choice of motors, a way was found to appeal to power-hungry customers, but the option could only be had with an automatic transmission, and most 430-equipped cars were given a high-ratio 2.91:1 differential, limiting the amount of torque available for acceleration.

The 430 was not a powerhouse in the same way that the supercharged 312 was; though both would produce comparable brake horsepower, torque curves were very different. While the 312 would hit a peak around

4800rpm, the big Lincoln motor was a low-revving cruiser—it hit its peak before 2800rpm (although its maximum torque of 490ft-lb was achieved at 3100rpm). Following the surprise performance of race-modified T-birds at the Daytona 500 in February, enthusiast magazines, excited about the large motor from a conceptual standpoint, were let down by the low-revving characteristics of the 430, lack of steeper rear-axle ratios, no manual and overdrive transmissions, and lack of better braking. A *Hot Rod* article in May 1959 reviewed a 430-equipped hardtop and went so far as to suggest fitting a triple–2bbl carburetion package marketed by Bill Stroppe (who was carrying on Ford's performance work on the side until it became clear that Chevrolet and others were providing covert support to others for racing applications). Though some thought it an obvious match, a Mercury-offered three-deuce option, the Super Marauder rated at 400bhp with a unique cast-aluminum air-cleaner housing, would not find its way onto T-birds in production, but could be fitted with some modifications by speed junkies.

Turning a "New" Leaf

Perhaps the biggest disappointment in the suspension department for the '58 T-bird had been its use of coil-spring rear suspension. The tried-and-proven semi-elliptical parallel leaf-spring arrangement was quickly reintroduced for '59, meaning that engineering and tooling would have to revise or start from scratch all of the suspension mounting points and brackets. The "new" suspension would provide a more familiar feel for drivers, and lower installation costs for the car.

Family Influence

The formal roof-line of the T-bird was a prime identifier for the car. At the time, most cars were using a sloped rear windshield (with exception of the Fairlane 500 Skyliner retractable hardtop). The desire by McNamara to kill the Edsel as a step between Ford and Mercury would play into a directive to styling for an upscale Fairlane 500, and the squared-off rear C-pillar of the T-bird would provide some rub-off value for the upscale Ford. Designated to be a midyear introduction, work on the new Galaxie series commenced during the spring of 1958; by June 27, a Fairlane 500 two-door hardtop was photographed with a T-bird roof fitted to it as a prototype for the new line.

Introduced in December 1958, advertising proclaimed "A Marriage of Two Styles," playing up the T-bird's progeny for the Galaxie. The theme would continue into sales catalogs, where association with the 'Bird would also filter down into engine names, though most were never intended for the four-seater.

Public Reaction

The 1959 T-bird was unveiled at the end of the World's Fair in Brussels, Belgium, in early September in conjunction with a promotion surrounding the new '59 full-size Ford (publicists ordered stories about the event withheld from publication until mid-October). It was launched formally during the week of October 20, 1958, with offering of the long-anticipated 430 option capturing most of the attention. Production would begin slowly, with approximately 3,800 by the end of October. Before the end of production in August 1959, that rate would climb to an estimated high of 7,800 in June and July. Though highly hyped, sales of the 430 package would only account for just over 5 percent of '59 T-birds, which must have been disappointing for planners.

A late-winter dusting of snow covers the grass outside the Ford Rotunda while a 1959 T-bird poses outside the entry canopy. The Rotunda was a popular tourist attraction for visitors to the Detroit area until it burned to the ground in 1962. *Ford Motor Company*

Not helping the new T-bird or the case for the large motor was an article developed in March 1959 for the June issue of *Road & Track*, in which a road test of a 430-equipped car pointed out that the car had some major minuses. Because of the car's sheer weight, its suspension was weak, steering was considered poor, and even the 8.50x14in four-ply tires were considered insufficient to carry the car through demanding driving. In the same breath, the writers praised the use of the Lincoln 430 by comparing the use of larger motors in passenger cars, such as the V-16 Cadillacs, V-12 Packards, and others. And, of course, there was the cursory slam of Ford for dropping the

A Marriage of Styles. Placing the squarish T-bird roof on the full-size Ford was proposed by Ford Division VP Robert Mc-Namara during early 1958, and the result was the formal-roofed Galaxie series. This photo shows a Town Victoria with the new roof, but with "Fairlane 500" script in this circa October 1958 pose. *Ford Motor Company*

two-seater. But, as with the '55 T-bird, Ford wasn't out to impress performance magazines, but was going after the Walter Mittys who wanted bragging rights about who had the biggest, baddest car in the country-club parking lot.

Convertible sales would rise substantially, with supply problems worked out from the '58 run allowing for the manufacture of 10,261 examples, or 15.21 percent of model-year production. Introduction of a fully-automatic operating system for the top and deck lid/filler panel, which was advertised in sales literature by late-February '59, would not reach production until the 1960 model year.

Production Problems

Few production/service problems were reported on the '59 T-bird, with exception of the 430ci motor. Owner complaints of oil leaks led to a replacement valve cover and gasket being offered by the end of January 1959. Just over a week later, a revised set of exhaust manifolds was placed into production with thicker outlet flanges and depressions cast into the areas around the lower surfaces of the inlet flanges. A generator mounting bracket misalignment, solved by placing washers or spacers between the block and

bracket, would be a minor inconvenience, but noises coming from the stamped steel valley cover would lead to an entry in an August 4, 1959, product service letter for a field fix that placed a 1in-diameter rubber hose between the cover and the bottom of the intake manifold.

Among the first changes following the beginning of production would be to the steering gearbox, which was due to a modification in the splining on the steering shaft and coupler. Other running changes would include a change in the dash wiring harness in mid-December for hardtops (with the same change for convertibles in late February), deletion of a stop-light relay after New Year's Day (which was replaced by a hydraulically operated switch in-line with the outlet of the master cylinder), and a change in the convertible top's main-pivot support bracket from a welded stamped-steel assembly to a metal casting on February 12, 1959. The power-window gearboxes were revised by the middle of March to allow for faster operation, and by mid-June a revised dual-advance distributor reached production. To make service technicians even happier, cars without air conditioning received a new power-brake booster assembly that bolted to the

The rear view of the prototype 1959 T-bird convertible, photographed at the Dearborn Test Track during summer 1958, reveals the horizontal-ribbed background for the taillight panel. *Ford Motor Company*

Another view of the prototype 1959 convertible with Greenfield Village in the background. Close observation reveals the use of 1958 "Gold Ball" fender ornaments. *Ford Motor Company*

engine side of the firewall, instead of under the dash between the firewall and brake pedal lever.

Complaints would also arise from placement of horns: Two service bulletins were released covering '58 and '59 T-birds that gave instructions on how to remount the high- and low-tone units from between the grille and body to inside the engine bay to cure problems with road-splash shorting out the noisemakers.

Another onus for service departments was noted for automatic transmissions used with the 430 motor: It was discovered by late April that governors for the gearbox could be installed incorrectly, with the effect of either delayed upshifts or a lack of shifting altogether. Service managers were notified in early May of the problem, and modifications were made in production to eliminate the possibility of misplacement.

While the '59 would be a relatively unchanged car, it did pump up enough sales to end production on August 22, 1959, with 67,456 units coming out of Wixom and being distributed across the United States, Canada, and the rest of the Free World.

Back-Door Competition

Even though Ford Motor Co. was officially out of the racing business effective with McNamara's decision to honor the AMA ban of June 1957, it did not mean that competitors in organizations such as NASCAR would sit back and do without their benevolent benefactors; they would just have to get more creative in obtaining parts and assistance from factory sources.

The fabled stock-car building team of John Holman and Ralph Moody of Holman-Moody (H-M) of Charlotte, North Carolina, had been left out in the cold by the AMA ban. Technical support and direct access to new components from Ford had sustained their business of preparing stripped-down two-door sedans and convertibles for the oval dirt tracks and super speedways of the South. Continuing with the '57 Fords already in the hands of drivers such as Curtis Turner for the '58 season was not an appealing thought, since other builders had somehow worked out deals to get support (access to new '58 bodies and larger motors), either covertly or outright from renegade automotive divisions. With their fortunes pinned on using Fords, the prospects of obtaining similar help were nil.

A loophole of sorts opened up for H-M around the fall of 1958, when established contacts within Ford revealed that instead of trying to buy new cars and strip them for racing, the necessary components needed to assemble a stock car could be obtained from parts that were rejected for scrap or in need of repair. With this information in hand, Holman approached managers at the Wixom plant and made an offer to purchase parts that were otherwise deemed unusable for production '59 T-birds. According to Leo Levine, author of *Ford: The Dust and the Glory,* plant managers were under the assumption that the people wanting to buy what they considered scrap bodies, chassis components, and for some strange reason, Lincoln 430ci motors were going to dispose of them in the same manner that other salvage contractors did. Stated Levine, "All they knew was he had money, knew exactly what he wanted, and was willing to pay several times as much as they could have gotten from their usual sources." Little did the managers know, but the people offering them cash for otherwise useless "junk" would load their haul of goodies into trucks and speed off toward the southeast until they reached Charlotte and H-M's Power Products Division shop.

Holman managed to acquire enough reject parts to build eight hardtop T-birds (according to others, though, twelve cars were completed). The cars were prepared for use in either Grand National or Convertible divisions by cutting off their roofs and reattaching them with nine bolts in the windshield header and C-pillars. With the build-up came necessary safety modifications—pinned doors, roll cages, and repositioning of the gas tanks. Using suspension arms and brakes along with the large motors from Lincolns would yield most of the suspension/driveline package, but a little more guts were needed for transmission of power to the track: The lowest-geared rear end available for the T-bird and a heavy-duty three-speed manual transmission were adapted for use with the 430, which otherwise was only mated to an automatic transmission and a highway-geared 2.91:1 rear axle. One major hurdle to clear, though, was the size of the motor: NASCAR had set limits on maximum displacement, which the Lincoln motor exceeded. Since there were virtually no Ford products in competition, a waiver was granted "only to lend some extra interest to the race" according to Levine.

By February 1959, the cars were ready and available for sale to racing teams in time for the annual Daytona SpeedWeek finale, the NASCAR Grand National race on February 22. The new tri-oval, hard-surface "super speedway," on which construction had begun in 1957, was now ready for its first major event, the Daytona International Sweepstakes (later renamed the "Daytona 500") Grand National race. But first, qualification races would have to be run. On February 20, T-birds driven by Fritz Wilson, Tom Pistone, Eduardo Diobos, and Johnny Beauchamp would capture second, third, fifth, and eleventh places, while two other cars driven by Tim Flock and Curtis Turner would drop out due to engine and transmission problems.

On the big day, the same six cars would be ready to run, and in the end, two of the cars would again drop out of a race that would average 135.561mph. As the race reached the 500mi mark and the finish, Beauchamp ran nose-to-nose with NASCAR legend Lee Petty, driving a new Oldsmobile, across the finish line in a virtual dead heat. The apparent winner was Beauchamp, and he was ushered into the winner's circle. However, with the finish too close to call, an inquiry was convened, and almost two and one half days later, studies of motion-picture footage and still pictures revealed that Petty had actually crossed the line first.

To this day, the race remains a dark spot on NASCAR history, with claims that Beauchamp was one lap ahead of Petty. It was alleged by Beauchamp supporters (and, they claim, confirmed by an investigation) that the Petty family had been allowed to keep their own score and that in reality good ol' boy Lee was one lap down from the Harlan, Iowa, firebrand. The official record to this day remains in Petty's favor much to the aggravation of people close to the Beauchamp team. As a side-effect of the loss, according to Dale Swanson, Sr. (Beauchamp's chief mechanic during most of his NASCAR career), Beauchamp's sponsor Roy Burdick of Omaha, Nebraska, later had the car repossessed by H-M. Burdick continued to run T-birds through 1960.

The controversy did not stop in Daytona. Upon learning that new T-birds had been run in the race and had generated large amounts of publicity, McNamara became furious—not because the T-bird had lost, but because they were in the race at all! By the Wednesday after the race, though, it became apparent from all the media attention that interest was up in the Lincoln-powered hardtops and convertibles. Requests were coming in from magazines such as *Hot Rod, Road & Track,* and *Speed Age* for drive tests using 430-equipped T-birds, and Ford was reaping a PR bonanza from the weekend's events.

During meetings to begin determining how Holman-Moody obtained new cars and motors and what should be done in the aftermath, it was pointed out by product planner Bob Graham, who attended Speed-Week with George Merwin from sales as Ford's only official representatives, that GM had maintained an overt presence in Daytona during runs on the beach and at the new speedway. (In fact, Graham was seated during the 500 next to the president of Chevrolet, Ed Cole. Levine noted that "[Graham] was given one of the box lunches prepared by a catering firm for the large group of Chevy and Pontiac executives and engineers who attended. At one stage of the race, when a Thunderbird was momentarily leading the field, Cole kiddingly told Merwin that if the T-bird won, Cole would make him pay for the meal!") Not only were they in the stands, but they were also in the pits and on the track, from Pontiacs as pace cars to Zora Arkus-Duntov's experimental Super Sport Corvette, along with other show/go cars from Oldsmobile and Cadillac tearing up the asphalt in demonstration laps. To make matters worse, the only other Ford in the race, a '59 Fairlane two-door sedan, was forced to drop out before a Studebaker Lark!

As the review progressed, Graham had informed McNamara, Vice President of Engineering Hans Matthias, and Executive Engineer of Product Planning Don Frey that one of the reasons for GM's dominance was the Chevrolet 340hp 348ci motor, which could develop peak horsepower at 6500rpm, while the Lincoln motors could barely break 5000rpm and not even come close to the advertised 350hp or Chevy's 340hp. Graham made it clear that Ford was being outgunned, and that the AMA ban was virtually dead. If the Company was to remain competitive, it needed to get serious again about supporting racing.

Several actions were taken at the end of the pow-wow. McNamara approved the re-entry of Ford into development of high-performance components, resulting in development of the 360hp 352ci high-performance motor for 1960. Negotiations began with GM to either have them return to compliance, or Ford would get back into the fray; by April 27, no response had been received to letters, so the company got back into the business to develop racing equipment. And, an investigation was started to find out how H-M got the T-birds and parts. By the beginning of March 1959, internal sleuthing began to reveal how Holman obtained the "scrap" from Wixom. To end such practices, new procedures and policies were put into place that in effect killed the acquiring of reject components from the factory unless the parts were rendered useless beforehand.

The H-M T-birds would continue racing around the nation's network of dirt short tracks and paved speedways, earning victories and not-so-near ones. By 1960, 360hp Ford sedans and convertibles were blowing the 430-engined T-birds off the tracks. Following the '61 season, the H-M T-birds that had not been rendered useless due to crashes were relegated to local dirt tracks. But perhaps the biggest victors were the thousands of Ford enthusiasts who benefited from the T-bird forcing the company back into competitive events. By June 1962, Henry Ford II declared the AMA ban dead, and no holds were barred in the return of Ford to racing.

Several 1959 T-birds were used as test-beds for option development. This example, photographed in the summer of 1959, illustrates the perennial flipper-roof proposal, designed to make entry and exit easier for taller people, and an experimental swing-away steering column, which would be adopted for use in the 1961–66 T-birds. *Ford Motor Company*

An easy way to spot a 430ci-equipped T-bird is to look for an extension that attaches to the air cleaner inlet. The extension snorkle also had a tube which connects to a shroud over the driver's side exhaust manifold. Other 430 visual clues are the fuel pump mounted high and to the front of the motor, rearward-facing spark plugs, and the stamped steel cover over the center of the motor under the intake manifold. *Alan Tast photo*

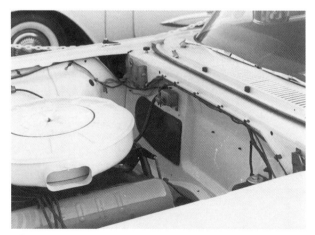

T-birds through 1962 could be obtained without a heater on a special-order basis. One such example is owned by Bill and Hazel Kurrasch of New York, seen here at the 1988 VTCA International Convention in Toronto, Ontario, Canada. Equipped with an equally rare three-speed transmission, it was originally sold in Southern California and was reported to have been originally ordered for use as a stock car at Daytona. *Alan Tast photo*

Chapter 7

OPENING UP A WHOLE NEW WORLD

At the dawn of the 1960s, hopes were high for a better and brighter tomorrow: Dialogue between Washington, D.C., and Moscow was polite but not chilling, rocket scientists were gaining in their quest to put man in space, and the American standard of living was growing ever higher. With such an increase, more people were buying new automobiles, and Ford would provide an even wider choice of models to capture sales from GM, Chrysler, and the remaining independents. But when would the other manufacturers meet the challenge of the Thunderbird?

With the tooling budget for the 1960 facelift being very limited, several suggestions for restyling the front and rear of the car were rendered in late January to early February 1958. The lower two renderings may be suggestions for the 1961 T-bird, which was in the beginnings of design around the period. *Ford Motor Company*

Low Budget, High Visibility

The 1960 model year would be a watershed for the Ford Division; it would take advantage of public demand for a smaller, economy-based car and churn out the Falcon. Nothing fancy, the Falcon was steeped in Ford's conservative approach to engineering and design, as opposed to Chevrolet's Volkswagen-like Corvair and the visual garishness of Virgil Exner's Valiant/Lancer for Plymouth and Dodge. In the full-size line, the restyled Ford/Fairlane/Galaxie succumbed to the excesses of the previous year's fin-fetish in a tasteful manner. Sales would drop so significantly that the proponent of the restyled Ford's shape, noted designer Alex Tremulis, would be chastised by upper management for creating a Ford that "didn't look like a Ford." Only the Thunderbird would be alone against competing manufacturers in the personal-luxury market, and in the last year of its second triennial, would rack up sales that would send production managers scrambling for overtime and extra capacity!

Timing Is Everything

Like the preceding year's Thunderbird, the 1960 T-bird's evolution began in 1957 with finalization of the '58 program. Having decided that the same body shell would be used for three years to gain the most use from tooling and amortize costs over a longer period, the Product Planning Committee decided that the 1960 T-bird's changes would be limited to a new grille and taillight assemblies, exterior ornamentation, interior patterns, and the addition of an optional roof treatment for the hardtop to call attention to the line. The restyling program would begin in the fall of '57, on the heels of approval for the '59 facelift, and progress through late August 1958.

Facelift

Advanced designs for the '60 T-bird ranged from mild to wild. With development of an all-new full-size Ford, stylists played around with a cross between the already established "Squarebird" design and exploring new territory for the upcoming '61 T-bird. Inspiration for some sketches of the '60 T-bird would come from work on the '60 Ford, which was influenced by Ford Advanced Design examples such as the two-wheeled Gyron exercise, or from the LaGalaxie show car being prepared in the studio for the 1958–59 show season. Bits and pieces from other design studies would also drop in and out, with some resurfacing in later production models such as the 1967–69 T-bird. With most whimsical ideas, a jet or turbine-like influence could clearly be seen.

One proposal that made it to the clay-modeling stage was actually intended to be for a turbine-powered '59 or '60 T-bird. Ford had been experimenting on a turbine-powered vehicle that could run on virtually any fuel. An early '55 T-bird had been modified to use a Boeing gas turbine, but by 1957 Ford had developed its own 701-se-

During late 1957 thought was given to developing a gas-turbine-powered T-bird. Chrysler and GM were also working with prototype cars using the unconventional powerplant at the time. This clay, utilizing the door trim of a 1959, was an exercise in rethinking the car's design for use with turbine motors. It was never produced in metal. *Ford Motor Company*

ries turbines, and would put some in modified production cars of the period—four '59 T-birds were reportedly equipped with the experimental powerplants, according to Richard Langworth in his book. The turbine T-bird design exercise would have a radically restyled front end since it didn't need a radiator, just air inlets for the turbine. The rear would also be subjected to a major transformation, with a large opening in the center and twin exhaust pods at the outboard ends. While production of a turbine-powered T-bird never got past the experimental stage, ideas from the styling exercise would provide an advance look at roof development for 1960–61 Fords.

People in the T-bird design section would settle down by mid-January 1958 and "render up" several proposals for grilles, taillight treatments, and side ornamentation. As directed by the planners in May 1957, different roof proposals were explored. One idea gaining early attention was a brushed stainless steel roof panel between the windshield header and the C-pillar. Pioneered on the '57 Cadillac Eldorado Brougham hardtop, use of the material was being considered for the side spear as well. This would lend a "formal" flair to the car, looking like a town car but with a fixed roof. The C-pillar was proposed to be either vinyl-covered or painted, but by the beginning of March 1958 another proposal with a two-tone roof—possibly suggesting a vinyl half cover—was also being shown. A variety of grille textures, trim packages, and scripts would be explored, but eventually the final configuration settled on a defining pattern that relied on added ornamentation.

Defining the '60 T-bird's exterior would be a new, simplified emblem with thin, widespread wings; a square-mesh grille with a heavy center bar and three vertical teeth; a stylized script for the door; three sets of three vertical bars on the rear quarter; and, to carry the triple concept to the rear, three-lens taillights. The inboard taillight

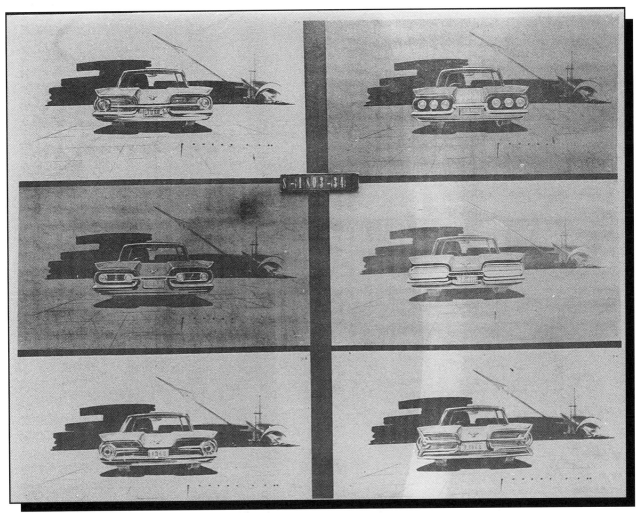

Renderings from the late January to early February 1958 period. The upper right sketch with six taillights was ultimately chosen. *Ford Motor Company*

would be the location for an optional backup light with a white center lens, while the outer two would serve for the brake lamps and turn indicators. Another change, which would only last for the first few months of production, would be a shorter, simplified molding for the base of the C-pillar—a smooth, chrome-plated casting in opposition to the taller ribbed one used for the two previous versions. This would be replaced in production on December 14, 1959, when a slightly taller, ribbed trim would appear.

Grand Opening

As discussed in Chapter 5, several roof proposals were investigated for the second-generation T-bird. First of these was a T-top, which was proposed for the '58 during mid-1956 and abandoned during the planning stages in 1957. The Targa roof or stainless-topped proposals of early 1958 were also dropped as not being, in the eyes of Vice President of Styling and Product Planning William Clay Ford, "sporty" enough. As work continued on the '60 update, a

variety of events would bring about another more palatable option for production: the sliding panel sunroof.

Sunroofs in closed cars were not new; they were popular in Europe in either folding fabric/vinyl or solid-steel-panel versions. They were also used on some prewar American automobiles such as the 1940 LaSalle, but abandoned due to poor sales. William Clay Ford wanted something that suggested a convertible-type feel without actually having a convertible, and this would be as close as he could get.

During the early months of 1957, Golde and Co., a manufacturer of components for a power-assisted sliding sunroof panel system in Frankfurt-am-Main, West Germany, established an office in Detroit to work with manufacturers and custom fabricators, with a goal of getting their patented sunroof into American production for the 1958 model year. While they would do business with individual customers wanting a sunroof for their own cars, no contracts with any major companies for a production installation were forthcoming.

From the rendering stage, full-size "see-through" models were built up from fiberglass covered with DiNoc and aluminum foil, along with plexiglass windows and windshields. This example illustrates a proposed stainless steel roof panel over the forward two-thirds of the roof as part of the exploration for a different roof treatment to set the 1960 apart from its two earlier model years. *Ford Motor Company*

Around the end of April and beginning of May 1958, designers were still playing around with side trim and grille texture. The simulated vents in the front fender were also showing up on clays for the 1961 proposal under development at the time. The roof has lost its stainless cover in favor of a two-tone paint scheme. *Ford Motor Company*

During mid-1957, when it was decided to go ahead with a third roof style for the 1960 T-bird, much attention was placed on developing removable roof panels. This fiberglass studio model of a 1958, photographed during summer 1957, has a T-roof. The idea was killed due to cost, but not before it was considered as the sole 1958 model in lieu of the convertible. *Ford Motor Company*

By late 1958, the concept of a sliding sunroof panel utilizing patented components from the Golde Company of Frankfurt-am-Main, West Germany, was seriously being evaluated. This photo, taken in early 1959, shows one of the prototype units installed on a 1959 T-bird "mule" for evaluation. Note that the windbreaker bar is in place. *Ford Motor Company*

Golde had placed feelers in the marketplace with designers, engineers, and the like in the industry, including Budd, which during the period of early to mid-1957 was working on body engineering for the new '58 T-bird. When Ford decided that it wanted to return outsourced work to its own staff, an engineer for Budd, Milton Kaltz, would help in the transfer of work-in-progress, and be offered a position on Ford's engineering team for the Thunderbird project. Kaltz, familiar with the Golde system, would suggest its use to designers, and by mid-1958, work had begun on adapting the hardware for use with the Thunderbird roof structure.

Development work progressed from mockups to prototype form through the fall and early winter of 1958. Approval of the package would come on a cold January day in 1959 at the Dearborn Test Track. T-bird Stylist Bill Boyer, Product Planner (and future president of Ford) Donald Petersen, and William Clay Ford took a test-drive in a '59

hardtop fitted with one of the prototype sunroofs, and Kaltz was asked to ride along to answer technical questions from the trio.

The primary concern of Ford was wind and its resulting turbulence getting into the car. Kaltz and his staff devised a deflector (what would become known by insiders as "towel bar") to lift the oncoming stream of air up and over the open area of the panel. Held aloft by cast-metal stanchions, a cupped strip of stainless steel would serve as the actual deflecting device. The height and angle of the bar would be arrived at through a period of trial-and-error testing to eliminate annoyances such as whistling.

With the sunroof open at a speed of 60mph and temperatures just above 0deg F, approval would hinge on a simple test: Ford, sitting in the rear seat with Kaltz, held

A detail photo of a restored Sunroof owned by Howie and Marian Cammack of Denver, Colorado, reveals the windbreaker bar and some of the hardware around the edge of the opening. Drain troughs fed water into four rubber hoses which channeled the water away from the opening and to the ground. Cammack found the car as a shell missing many of the Sunroof-specific parts in the mid-1980s and restored it. *Alan Tast photo*

up a lit match to test for turbulence. According to Kaltz, who related the story to Larry Seyfarth for the January 1975 *Thunderbird Scoop*, the match flickered, but did not go out. The sunroof passed the test, and approval for production was granted.

Details of the sunroof installation were tricky, since Golde held patents on the design. It would supply the hardware necessary for installation to Budd, which would modify hardtop bodies by cutting out the roof hatch, welding in the necessary channels, stiffeners, and bracketry, and add a stamped metal drain pan for the panel when it would be in the open position. When the bodies were ready, they were shipped out with the other nonhardtop ones. At Wixom, the sunroof-equipped units would have their own trim line for installation of headliners, weatherstripping, and other unique pieces of hardware.

The sunroof gave the '60 T-bird the gimmick that was desired back in mid-'57, but not too many buyers in 1960 thought it was worth the extra money. In the end, only 2,536 would be modified for the panel, making production levels too low to justify its continuance.

As an aside, it must be noted here that because of confusion stemming from the sunroof component supplier's

This Ford Motor Company press photo was taken in 1976 of the Raven Black Sunroof restored by VTCA president Larry J. Seyfarth. A series of articles in the club's *Thunderbird Scoop* magazine chronicled its rejuvenation from rusted-out hulk to prize-winning restoration. Note that the Kelsey-Hayes wire wheels and white-band sidewalls were not authentic for the car, since the ones shown were from a 1963. *Ford Motor Company*

A prototype 1960 hardtop photographed in the studio during mid-May 1959. At this time it was undecided whether or not to continue the tradition of using wheel covers from the model year's full-size Ford line. This car wears such covers, but before final approval was given it was decided to retain the 1959-style "Sun Ray" covers with black-painted struts. *Ford Motor Company*

name, stories have appeared over the years suggesting the production of a "Gold Roof" Thunderbird in addition to the sunroof, with various writers claiming that 2,500 '60 T-birds had received a gold-colored roof as a special trim option. No such version was ever offered, advertised, or promoted, but some have been conned over the years by unscrupulous or unknowing individuals attempting to two-tone '60 hardtops with gold paint. Obviously, the people who penned these stories had failed to see the connection between supplier and statistics, resulting in another myth being propagated over the passage of time.

Stainless Steel Hardtops

A unique pair of T-birds were special-ordered from Ford for production toward the end of the model year by one of the major suppliers of stainless steel in the United States, Allegheny-Ludlum Steel Corp. of Brackenridge, Pennsylvania. A-L, as the name was abbreviated, had worked with Ford during 1931 to produce a few Model A sedans to test the nonrusting alloy for use in production of automotive bodies. In 1936, it supplied material for six Tudor sedans that were sent on a nationwide promotional campaign, with some ending up in private hands a decade later. The two '60 hardtops, though, would be a modern equivalent of the '36 promotion, and remain in the hands of the company (although requested by Ford).

Both of the cars were meant to illustrate the use of stainless steel in as many areas as possible. Exterior body components were stamped out of T306 alloy. Bumpers and grille were T430 polished to match the reflectance of chrome-plated steel, while the body panels were given a satin-like brushed finish. Exhaust pipes were formed from T304, and mufflers were constructed using T409 stainless, which A-L claimed was the first production use of the material in a muffler. Except for the windshield wiper bezels (which were chrome-plated pot-metal), the Exterior Dress-Up Kit components of headlight doors, rear fender extensions, and hood scoop were all crafted from highly polished stainless steel as well. Oddly, though, rear fender skirts were never supplied.

Body-shell assembly would be done in Budd's body plant in Detroit, separate from the conventional T-bird line, and then fed into the Wixom assembly line in June or July for completion. The first car, serial number 0Y71Y-170331, would be tagged with a build date of June 20, 1960, while the second car carried a much-higher serial number and a July 11, 1960, date. The data plates, interestingly, carried neither a paint code nor a special production code. The reason for late production, it was stated, stemmed from the stamping operation at Budd. The stainless steel chosen for body panels was much harder to form than the carbon steel used in normal production, and fears were high that the

A front bumper is in the process of installation on this 1960 hardtop during this March 1960 photo. A Lincoln can be seen behind the T-bird with its bumper just coming out from between the parts racks in the background and above the T-bird's fender. *Ford Motor Company*

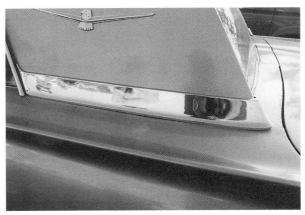

Hardtops built before December 12, 1959, used a smooth, chrome-plated base molding for the C-pillar, as evidenced by this car built in early-December 1959 and owned by longtime VTCA/VTCI North Central Regional Director Daniel J. Likar of Springfield, Illinois. Following that date, a ribbed version was substituted. *Alan Tast photo*

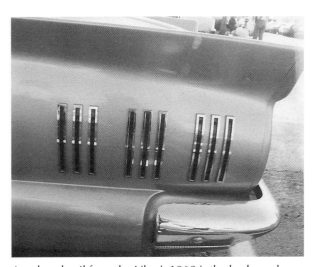

Another detail from the Likar's 1960 is the hash marks on the rear quarters. Early production versions used a type which were fastened from the outside with screws. Cleaner-looking castings were used for most of the production run and were retained by spring clips from inside the trunk. In mid-April 1960, even these were redone to reduce the number of different individual pieces being used. *Alan Tast photo*

T306 alloy would ruin over 1,000 dies, which were nearing the end of their useful life after pounding out almost 200,000 Squarebirds and replacement parts. Once enough stocks were set aside to complete remaining orders, the go-ahead was given to bring in the special metal. One problem would be the roof skin, which under normal conditions was made from a single stamping. The stainless panels available were too narrow to allow for this, and a compromise had to be made by stamping the roof in two pieces and welding them together down the centerline of the car. As predicted, the dies were rendered unusable after the two cars' panels were stamped out, and they were scrapped.

The inner body structure, though, retained the carbon steel sheet metal components of regular production cars, presenting engineers with the challenge of providing fasten-

Interiors for leather-trimmed T-birds differed from the vinyl or cloth-and-vinyl ones for 1960. One of the differences is the vertical pleats used in the seat inserts and on the upper door panels, as shown on the 1960 Sunroof owned by Howie and Marian Cammack. The standard trim panel used a series of large pleated squares in the upper panel and seat inserts. *Alan Tast photo*

An accessory that is more popular today than when it was first introduced is the Sports Spare Wheel Carrier (aka, Continental Kit). A stylish appendage to the rear of the 1958–60 T-bird, it extended the car's length by 11in and created more luggage room by freeing up the existing spare tire well, but created problems if parallel parking spaces or garages were too short in length. This example is a 1960 hardtop owned by Rainer and Ellen Brehl of Frankfurt, Germany. The car was imported from the United States during the mid-1980s and given a cosmetic restoration. The lower license plate is a temporary one used by Germans, which is obtained for short durations such as weekends to allow collector cars to be driven to events such as the All-American Car Show in Lindau, Germany. *Alan Tast photo*

ers and other protection from the deleterious effects of di-electric corrosion, which results from placing two dissimilar metals in contact with each other. Copper spacers were used between the stainless and conventional steel stampings, while bolts, nuts, screws, and other fasteners were conventional off-the-shelf items (originally they were stainless steel).

Although the cars were touted as being able to look as good as new in the year 2000, some restoration has occurred over the years. The pair had each logged over 130,000mi on the road in the United States and in Europe by the mid-1980s. By that time, their 352ci motors were in need of overhaul, front floor carpets and trunk mats were worn, and the red leather interior trim needed attention, including dash pads, which were notorious for decomposing from the inside and sagging. Carl Davis, one of the early proponents of the Vintage Thunderbird Club of America (VTCA, which was renamed Vintage Thunderbird Club International in the late 1980s) and its long-time vice president, agreed to help with the restoration of both over a period of a few years beginning in the early '80s, preparing one for the VTCA's North East Regional Convention in Williamsburg, Virginia, and then the other in the middle of the decade. They had been altered from stock condition with finned aluminum valve covers, early and mid-'60s-style Ford wire wheel covers (which were fancier than the stock Sun Ray covers; these were quickly dolled up by A-L with red instead of black-painted "struts" by 1961), and a smaller variety of maintenance-induced modifications. Though these items would not be returned to 1960 specifications, the mechanics and interior components were refurbished, and the cars returned to A-L's plants in Brackenridge and Wallingford, Connecticut.

Public Acceptance

Even though the T-bird was by 1960 a dated design in light of the new offerings from Ford, demand for it was stronger than ever. In the end, 92,843 units would be invoiced from Wixom in the longest production run for the era (one year and one week, as opposed to an average of eleven to eleven and a half months), and several trends were emerging from orders. More cars were ordered with power assists than not, especially power steering (97 percent), power brakes (89 percent), and automatic transmission (98 percent), indicating that the typical car was being optioned for ease of operation. Power windows would be chosen for slightly better than half of the cars (54 percent), as was tinted glass (53 percent). The result was that more items would be considered as standard equipment for 1961 and beyond, with items such as manual-shift transmissions becoming history. The fully automatic convertible would be hailed as an improvement, along with higher-rate springs and the reskinned interior.

Running Changes

Problems with the car were few, as is typical with a car in its third year of manufacture. Production changes would include a revised cylinder head for the 430 in early December 1959 (and other minor changes through the end of production), trim piece changes for the rear quar-

The speedometer of an exported 1960 convertible photographed in Lindau during 1988 reveals the 240km/h graduated markings. Other features of exported cars included heavier suspension components, such as springs and brakes, and a higher-capacity battery. *Alan Tast photo*

One of the two stainless-steel 1960 hardtops built for Allegheny-Ludlum Steel Corporation, displayed at the VTCI's 1991 International Convention in Falls Church, Virginia. Outer panels and trim are made of stainless steel, while the underbody is conventional steel. Wheelcovers over the years have been replaced with mid-1960s Ford simulated wire covers. *Alan Tast photo*

ters and C-pillar in mid-December (of which the hash marks would again be revised in mid-April), and a revised stanchion for the sunroof's windbreaker bar to cure complaints of whistling noise and turbulence in the passenger compartment. An adapter kit would be offered late in the year to allow the Bendix power-brake booster to be mounted in cars with air conditioning, thus abandoning the original underdash brake booster unit.

The biggest problem for convertible owners was batteries losing their charge following top operation. Originally, the automatic system relied on ten relays on a panel behind the rear seat to control the sequence of functions. It was discovered that this arrangement was creating a drain on the battery if the car's motor was not running and was pulling a higher voltage than desired for it to work. By October 19, 1959, production cars were being fitted with a twelve-relay panel that would allow the electro-hydraulic system to function at a lower voltage. Strangely, the correction never made it into the shop manual or wiring diagrams, with the exception of a Product Service Letter dated September 15, 1960—almost a year after the change was made! This has proven very frustrating for people working on the '60 convertible who are not familiar with this running change.

Comparisons with cars such as the Chrysler 300, which was now boasting a similar seating arrangement of front bucket seats and a console for its floor-shifted automatic or four-speed transmission, were inevitable due to the presence of the 430 engine, but performance would not be in the same league. Writers would look upon the T-bird as a cross-breed between compacts such as the Falcon and Comet platform (due to the close-coupled arrangement of seating and its 113in wheelbase) and a full-size luxury car because of its appointments. The *Motor Life* article of June 1960 would pan the T-bird's cross-

Though the T-bird did very well for the year, the big news at Ford was the Falcon. Forecasting styling for Ford in the early 1960s, it was developed as an American compact car to compete with Volkswagen's Beetle as well as domestic offerings such as the Chevrolet Corvair and Plymouth Valiant. Falcon's front suspension would be a test bed for a similar setup which would be used in the 1961 T-bird. *Ford Motor Company*

dressing by stating in its last paragraph: "The Thunderbird is sometimes regarded as a blend of luxury car and compact, but it really lacks the refinement of the one and the convenience of the other. Still, it does combine performance, comfort and prestige with reasonable size and price. In that respect it is unique. Despite the increasing variety of cars available, there is still nothing quite like it." This would not last for much longer.

Chapter 8

PROJECTILE ON THE ROAD

The change brought about by the revised 1960 Ford and introduction of the new Falcon and Comet created quite a stir in the automotive industry. While the little sedans were to McNamara what the '49 Ford had been for Ernest Breech and Lewis Crusoe in raising the stature of Ford with the public (especially with over 700,000 Falcons and Comets being produced in the first year, setting a record that would be broken in 1965 with the Mustang), the full-size car was a bomb in the unkindest of terms. Mercury, Lincoln, and T-bird would be due for a major overhaul for the next series of restyling in the 1961 cycle, and the results would prove to be exemplary.

Banana Nose

Influences of the Space Age and the excesses of contemporary automotive design were beginning to make their impact on the futuristic Advanced Design Center by the end of 1957, when planning for the 1961 Thunderbird program began. Designers had grown weary, and

perhaps somewhat aghast, at what was being put on the road. What once were clean, straightforward, and streamlined monuments to design restraint were now being slathered in brightwork, ever-rising fins, and becoming garish metaphors for American prosperity. The intrusion of upper management in the design process of such cars as the Edsel would also sour their attitudes toward design-by-committee, but there wasn't much that could be done about that. A rejection of the status quo was on the way.

Stylists had plenty of sources for inspiration: Speedy jet fighters and high-flying rockets with their payloads of scientific satellites and menacing nuclear warheads were perhaps the logical choices for interpretation into a sporty car. They were slippery, devoid of ornamentation, and functional, but influenced by their high-speed environment. Americans were on the forefront of technological change, and Ford planners were determined that the Thunderbird was to be the division's test bed for new ideas that eventually would or would not filter down to

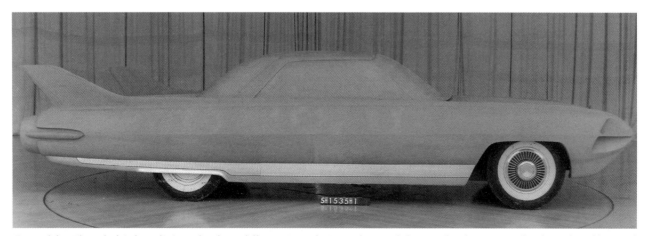

One of the Thunderbird studio's early clays (fall 1957) exploring advanced themes for the 1961 T-bird. High tailfins and pointed prow suggest blending of Oros' favoring of the Cutlass fighter and what Boyer calls a "fleet submarine" front end. The roof form with a thin C-pillar can also been seen in the turbine car proposal (see Chapter 8), also from around the same period. *Ford Motor Company*

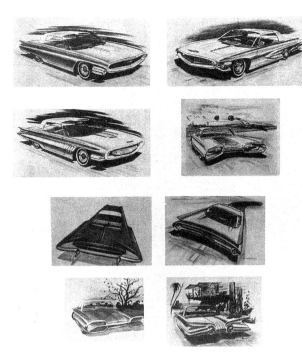

Early renderings from late 1957 to early 1958 show conceptual sketches for the third-generation Thunderbird. *Ford Motor Company*

the lesser lines. Therefore, the trend-setting T-bird would no longer be tied to a full-size Ford, but a would-be progenitor for the rest of the line.

Tom Case, who was on hand for the birth of the two-seater back in 1953 and took keen interest in the line, decided to move on to a more challenging assignment in the development of the Falcon and Econoline during February 1958, leaving product planning to Donald Petersen. A fresh outlook for the new T-bird was also to develop based on an economic directive: The T-bird and the new Lincoln both would use the same cowl and firewall structure to write-down tooling and engineering costs.

Split Personalities

In the grand tradition of inspiring creativity through competition, Styling Vice President George Walker asked the Ford Studio, under Joe Oros, and the Advanced Design Studio, under Elwood Engel to develop proposals for the '61 T-bird. The T-bird studio was already under way on a proposal that borrowed heavily from aircraft motifs with a pointed front end and high tail fins that mocked rudders, as well as a roof form similar to the '60 Turbine T-bird exercise, which was being developed at the same time in late 1957. The development of this design track would

A clay model from early spring 1958 reveals some of the themes carried on in sketches such as the wide front grille and turn-indicator pods. The bumper/grille combination would be abandoned for the 1961–66 series, but be resurrected for the 1967–69 models. The renderings on the studio wall show the rear end of another turbine proposal (possibly with a rear-mounted engine), integration of the scoop at the upper center of the windshield with the C-pillars, a profile drawing of a Squarebird, design sketches of rear ends influenced by the la Galaxie show car, and ideas for new T-bird emblems. A 1958 T-bird and a clay for either the 1960 or 1961 full-size Ford can be seen in the background . *Ford Motor Company*

More sketches from early to mid-1958 reveal the influence of la Galaxie with its oblong rear bumper pods, the developing 1960 Ford's flattened rear fins, and hints of turbine car design as well as the triangular Gyron and air-propelled Levacar, which were also coming through Ford's Advanced Studio during this period. *Ford Motor Company*

be refined by March 1958 into a more subtle silhouette, but another study also was underway that tied in emerging themes found on the '60 Ford: wide, low-profile hood and grille, along with a full-length body fin. This early-1958 study would provide a hint of the full-length fin to be found on the '61 T-bird, and its grille and bumper combination would serve as a basis for the fifth generation 1967–69 Thunderbird's "sucker mouth" form.

As spring came and went, the projectile '60 T-bird clay underwent several changes. The March design's hidden headlights gave way to a quad system set into a more conventional grille, a rebound "hump" was flattened out over the rear wheelhouse, and a full rear-wheel cutout appeared, along with the then-standard wraparound wind-

shield. Still not quite there approval-wise, work continued through the summer and fall for approval in late November or early December.

As the projectile-like study was developed further, consternation over its progress led Walker to order Engel to develop a more formal Thunderbird in June 1958 (though designer John Najjar recalls this as June 1959). This inter-studio rivalry was an attempt to explore other options for the car, which Walker and others recognized was moving into more of a luxury market than a sporty one. Engel, who played a major part in the development of the Lincoln-Mercury studios, had free reign to roam all Ford studios as chief studio stylist in charge of the Corporate Studio, which was housed in the basement of the

A few weeks later, in early-August 1958, the Engel 'Bird again was taken upstairs from the "Submarine Service" studio and photographed in the Styling Rotunda showroom. The ornamentation has changed somewhat, and the car has lost its fender kick-up. This is the model that McNamara would request be made longer to accommodate two rear doors and turned into the 1961 Continental. *Ford Motor Company*

The first "Continental T-bird" was this clay, prepared by Engel's staff and displayed during late June 1958 in the Styling Rotunda showroom. Return to a rearward-slanting windshield post, slab-sided styling and hints of the Mark II-inspired fender kick-up are evident, as well as a more-conventional front end, which Engel would not forget when he moved to Chrysler in 1962. While not modeling an interior, the beginning of curved side glass can be seen in the foil-covered verticals simulating window frames. *Ford Motor Company*

By late July 1958, the Advanced Design Studio's T-bird had progressed to see-through status, with a restyled front end featuring the high-override bumper and "meat cleaver" fender blades. *Ford Motor Company*

Photographed during a Product Planning Show for executives during November 1958, a near-final T-bird convertible emerges with "flower-pot" taillights and subtle fin. The plated lower top trim, slender door handles, trunk-mounted gas-filler door, block letters, and ribbed lower rear bumper would be abandoned for the next phase of development which would lead to the final product. Hash marks from the 1960 T-bird were considered well into early to mid-1960, and even showed up on drawings prepared by the Technical Service Labs for early service bulletins and other such publications. *Ford Motor Company*

A preproduction photo of the 1961 Lincoln Continental four-door convertible. Sharing the same cowl as the T-bird for a starting point, the remainder of the car would be a powerful testament to clean, balanced design. *Ford Motor Company*

The major influence on rear end design for the 1961–63 T-bird was the 1952 Continental-X (later renamed X-100) show car. Large round taillight housings, rounded body-side sculpturing, and the stubby ventral fin were carried over. Today the show car resides at the Henry Ford Museum in Dearborn, Michigan. *Alan Tast photo*

Design Center. Corporate Studio was actually a combination of responsibilities for work on tractors, international projects, and the Special Products Team. It was Special Products that would take on the T-bird challenge.

One of the members of the team, veteran designer Robert "Bob" Thomas, went upstairs to the Ford studios and obtained package sizes for the T-bird project, focusing on cowl dimensions and plan dimensions. With Najjar (who previously had been the chief stylist in the Lincoln studio) as lead stylist, along with Colin Neale (who had come to Dearborn from Ford's Dagenham, England, operation where he was chief stylist) and Joe Orfe, Engel would have some of his best talent available to take on the Thunderbird challenge.

The first design to make it to a full-size clay by late June was a slab-sided affair with high fender ridges, a Continental-like kick-up at the rear of the doors, and a

wraparound grille/bumper arrangement that would foreshadow Engel's work on the '60s Chrysler Imperials (the rear deck's squared-off Continental "hump" and up-turned bumper would almost appear on the '64 Imperial intact). And, in a move away from the then-popular wraparound windshield and its knee-knocking protrusion into the door opening, a slanted A-pillar was reintroduced, cleaning up this sore spot for the public. After it was reviewed by design staffers in the styling rotunda showroom, the clay went back downstairs and under the clay modelers' knives.

Almost a month later, the clay's front and rear were revamped, and a "see-through" fiberglass model was constructed, presenting a more pleasing and unified look to the whole. Wraparound grillework gave way to a high-

Although by mid-1959 the car had been finalized for engineering development leading up to production, ideas for refining the design were still being tested out in three dimensions. Here, an April 8, 1960, photo shows what would be the 1961 T-bird, except for a low-mounted hood 'Bird and parking lights mounted above the headlight eyebrows in the hood to provide better visibility. Windsplits were added to the 1961 hood late in development after complaints from dealers that the wide expanse of flat sheet metal between the power dome and the fender ridge needed to be broken up—this may be one of the proposals leading up to their implementation. *Ford Motor Company*

centered bumper/grille combination, pierced at the outboard ends with teardrop-like openings for the quad headlights. The rear featured a simple pair of round taillights that were recessed into the body (the rear bumpers dipped down to reveal the full area of the lenses).

During an executive design review for Henry Ford II and other high-level executives, the Engel and Oros studios' competing models were put on display for reaction and comments. Oros, related Katz in his book *Soaring Spirit: Thirty-Five Years of the Ford Thunderbird*, was asked which car he preferred for the Thunderbird: the more formal-looking Advanced Studio version or the projectile-like model his staff had revamped to look more like the finally

approved '61. He pointed out that the more aggressive-looking projectile car was the obvious choice for a sporty car as opposed to the more staid and squared-off version of his competition, and Ford in agreed.

Engel's T-bird design underwent one last push as a two-door concept when the side was modified to eliminate the kick-up and the rear was changed to move the taillights out of the rear deck and into the vertical area created by the body side and bumper. This time, however, it would not be Walker who rendered a final decision, but McNamara. As the two visited what was referred to as the "Stiletto Studio" (because of its 40ft-by-70ft dimensions) or "Submarine Service" (because of its basement location), McNamara is

Exploring a third body option for the 1961 T-bird was this proposal called the "Constellation," photographed in late 1958 or early 1959. Interior detailing had not progressed beyond blanking out everything below the belt line, but the wrapover rear window and "targa"-style roof insert were what was being examined. Though the car would not progress into development, the idea would be carried to Chrysler by Engel, who used it to turn the Valiant hardtop into the fabled 1964-1/2 Barracuda fastback in an attempt to compete with the new Mustang. *Ford Motor Company*

said to have suggested to Walker that the car be lengthened to accommodate front and rear doors, and to make it a Lincoln. This Engel did and he received production approval. Following this, the model and all related materials were transferred to Eugene Bordinat's Lincoln studio, where the '61 Lincoln had until that point been designated to be a facelift of the 1958–60 series, which was not doing well in sales against its competitor, Cadillac.

Engel, flush with victory with his T-bird gaining favor as a Lincoln and displacing Bordinat's facelift, wanted to retain the design for T-bird as well to exercise his influence on both car lines. This was rebuffed, and Oros' staff under Boyer would continue work on their T-bird proposal. With final approval time approaching, common traits between the Lincoln and T-bird would begin to form. The full-length fender ridge of the Engel car was adapted to the T-bird, and for good reason: The fin allowed for a pinch-weld seam that would be hidden by the snap-on stainless steel trim, resulting in lower stamping and assembly costs. Headlight and front bumper assemblies on both cars became more identical with their distinctive eyebrows and high impact bars.

By November 1958, the car had cleared the adolescent stage of development, and was firmly in the refinement phase. Rear bumpers now featured Q-like housings for the round taillights, a subtle fin defined the upper edge of the body's profile, and the front end had settled down to its distinctive taper. At this point, the design was released to engineering to develop drawings for tooling, and to begin

work on building a prototype for chassis research.

A last-minute change to the car occurred just about the time it was to be released for production. Dealers who saw the advance photos for the new T-bird complained to Ford executives that the "flat" hood might turn off buyers. According to Oros in *Soaring Spirit*, Walker ordered Engel to modify the hood just as Oros was leaving for a European vacation. The final change would see the addition of two windsplits in the space between the power dome and the fender edge.

Front-Wheel Drive

During midyear 1958, preliminary work had begun on a radical new drivetrain for Ford: front-wheel drive (FWD). The advantages of FWD in traction and power-distribution were very desirable, but attempts by American companies to build FWD vehicles during the prewar era (most notably the '36 Cord) were expensive and mechanical headaches.

Frederick J. Hooven, who was in charge of the Advanced Car and Engineering Section, would be given credit for the development of the program to build an FWD T-bird, along with engineers J. D. "Jack" Collins and Frank Theyleg. Eyeing the unibody Thunderbird being planned for 1961, Hooven and the Thunderbird engineering staff under Donald Frey designed a suspension layout that could be used for a conventional rear-wheel-drive T-bird, and with a change in spindles, could be adapted to FWD rather easily. The front structure of the car was used as an open spring pocket (called a spring "tower"), with a coil spring placed above the upper control arm, which was bolted to the inner fender apron and braced to the cowl by a pair of stamped steel braces. The lower suspension arm was held in place by a single bolt near the engine cross-member, and a drag link provided triangulation to the front of the substructure. Its layout was similar to the front suspension used in the Falcon/Comet then under development, which also used the high-spring-and-drag-link system.

The high-spring arrangement would allow driveshafts to have an unobstructed path to the front wheels, but a way had to be found to transfer power from the crankshaft to the axles. Several different drives were tried—gears, belts, and shafts—but the final arrangement that met with satisfactory results was a chain-driven transmission devised by Collins that was placed against the lower engine block. A short axle was used between the driver-side wheel and the gearbox, while another axle passed through the oil pan and over to the passenger side wheel. To handle power transmission, constant-velocity joints were used between the axles and wheels, and inboard disc brakes were developed to replace the traditional drum units.

Development of the FWD platform would be pushed back for possible '62 introduction.

Motor Life magazine got wind of the FWD work in late 1959, and by its July 1960 issue was relaying rumors of pending production of the idea (it also was noting that rumors were in the air for a retractable hardtop to appear in 1961, which may have been confused with the convertible program). The idea was kept alive for '63 introduction, and finally for 1964's scheduled change. Ultimately, FWD was not used on the T-bird because of not only the cost to bring it to production (which was ten times the $3 million research budget), but also because the T-bird's strong conceptual identification with the four-passenger compartment bisected by a high driveshaft tunnel would be lost to a flat floor.

The 'Bird Takes Flight

After all the preliminary wrangling and fussing throughout 1959 on engineering and manufacturing problems, final approval for production tooling would come at the end of December. Though exterior trim had not yet been finalized ('60 hash marks were used on the fiberglass mock-up), the remainder of the interior was

Also photographed during the same June 24, 1960, photo session, this convertible illustrates the front end which some have called their least-favorite part of the car. A full-size Ford rear-view mirror without the day/night provision can be seen through the windshield. All 1961 T-birds came standard with the polarized day/night assembly. *Ford Motor Company*

Photographed on June 24, 1960, a preproduction 1961 Thunderbird exhibits the now-familiar spear-like rear quarter ornaments. Gray rubber gaskets between the bumpers and the body were available as well as the more-common black ones for early cars, though the gray ones were eventually dropped. Note that the radio antenna is mounted on the driver's side, which also happened on some early production variants. *Ford Motor Company*

finalized. Art Querfeld and Bill Boyer had sculpted an updated version of the 1958–60 interior that used a coved instrument panel/dual cockpit theme and modified it to move the glovebox into the console. Ribbed aluminum panels extended from the console to fill in the middle section of the cove and continued onto the door panels toward the rear of the interior. The bucket seats became boxier, but both could be ordered with four-way power assists, and the rear seats again would mimic the bucket-seat theme. A new feature that would have automotive pundits scribbling was a floating rear-view mirror, held in place by a cast metal bracket that was glued to the windshield with a two-part epoxy.

Another innovation that really grabbed attention and served a useful purpose was the Swing-Away steering wheel. Deemed "gimmick engineering" by some, the ability to move the column over 10.5in did help to make getting in and out of the driver's seat easier, especially for larger people. The wheel and column could be moved over (only when the transmission was in park) by raising the gearshift lever slightly past the park position and pulling the assembly toward the center of the car. This option would become very popular: 77 percent of all '61 T-birds were equipped

with the column. Acceptance led product planners to make it standard equipment and a Thunderbird identifier from 1962 through the end of the vintage era in 1966.

Larger Motor, Same Horsepower

Engine choices for the 1961 program were purposely curtailed to use an upgraded version of the FE-series block that had been bored and stroked from 352ci to 390ci. This motor, destined for the full-size Ford as well as the T-bird, would be the largest offering for the model year because disappointing sales of the Lincoln 430 motor during 1959 and 1960 assured planners that carrying the option over for 1961 was not viable, especially since its width would make it a difficult installation between the new spring towers. Rated at 300hp (the same as the previous year's 352ci motor), the 390 offered the torque needed to move the two-plus-ton car down the road, and a stronger power curve than the loafing 430 or the smaller 352. As in 1960, the high-performance motor (in this case the 375hp 390-4v) would not be available for the luxo-cruiser.

Providing the only link between crankshaft and differential was a refined Cruise-O-Matic dual-range transmission. Gone were the "three-on-the-tree" and overdrive;

The teardrop-like styling of the T-bird and Lincoln headlights and other styling cues also influenced the Advanced Studio's work on cars destined for overseas assembly, such as the German-built Taunus 12-M, photographed at the All-American Car Show in Lindau, Germany in the summer of 1988. The Taunus was a direct beneficiary of research work done for the front-wheel drive T-bird program. *Alan Tast photo*

marginal sales of 2 percent for the pair combined were taken as a signal that the T-bird buyer preferred to plop the lever in "D" and go, so engineering was spared development time and dollars by limiting powertrain choices to the single automatic gearbox. A choice of conventional and limited-slip Equa-Lock rear axles were offered.

Taking Flight

Following shutdown of '60 production in mid-September, the Wixom plant would be down for another half month as fixtures and assembly equipment were put in place for the '61 T-birds and Lincolns. For the first time, T-bird bodies would be assembled in the Wixom plant, as opposed to being brought in from Budd. The body assembly area was expanded, and the assembly lines began to move slowly the first week of October. By the end of the month, an accelerated build-up program would lift monthly production to nearly 900 units as adjustments were made to the assembly process. Production climbed to 5,500 cars per month before the July slow-down period.

Introduction of the 1961 Thunderbird in dealerships was delayed until November 10, 1960. Prior to this, teaser ads were run in magazines such as *Time* and *Sports Illustrated* calling attention to the Swing-Away steering wheel and other new features. Photographs of prototypes and advance test drives for writers were provided during September for long-lead deadlines to coincide with the November release. A rash of articles on the new car appeared in the November *Motor Trend* and *Motor Life*, with

Toward the end of 1961 production, wide whitewall tires were phased out in favor of a narrower 1in band. This 1961 hardtop was built on June 7, 1961, and purchased new a week later in Alexandria, Virginia. After two months on the road, it was stored with less than 1,850mi rolled up by its owner, who became obsessed with preserving the car. Following his death in 1994, it was sold to Auto Krafters of Broadway, Virginia, and has yielded much information on production details for VTCI members. *Alan Tast photo*

An interior view of the 1,850mi 1961 hardtop reveals a standard dash with a fixed steering column. Most people opted for the swing-away column, which slid 10in toward the center of the car when the car was placed in Park. The swing-away column would become standard in 1962 production. *Alan Tast photo*

comprehensive road tests following in *CARS* and *Motor Trend* in December 1960. Two-page advertising in magazines such as *National Geographic* and *Newsweek* would play up "The New Adventure in Elegance," and its luxury-car target audience was bombarded with metaphors usually allocated for larger sedans, with a smattering of performance jingles.

Hail to the Chief: The Kennedy Inaugural Parade Cars

November 1960 would usher in a wave of changes in Ford and the nation. In the presidential election of November 8 (two days before introduction of the '61 T-bird) Vice President Richard Nixon had narrowly been defeated by Senator John Fitzgerald Kennedy of Massachussetts, who began the process of assembling his advisory committee, the cabinet, almost immediately. The day fol-

A view of the engine bay of the 1,850mi 1961 T-bird, revealing a need for cleaning but otherwise original (except for the battery cables and reproduction battery). *Alan Tast photo*

The 1961 T-bird was chosen for use as pace car for the 1961 Indianapolis 500. Pictured here is the primary pace car with Beige leather interior; its back-up car had a black interior and the same graphics. Another thirty-three cars received different lettering emphasizing their use during events leading up to the Memorial Day classic. The car, per tradition, was given to winning driver A.J. Foyt after the race. *Ford Motor Company*

lowing the election, the presidency of Ford Motor Co. was awarded to Robert McNamara. McNamara, though, quickly earned a place on the Kennedy administration's short list of cabinet officers, and by the end of the month was being wooed to join as secretary of the treasury. McNamara did not feel comfortable enough to accept the position, but agreed to become secretary of defense. Though Robert Lacey noted in his history of Ford that McNamara was regarded as a moderate Republican, the call to duty and the chance to manage the largest military force in the Free World weighed heavier than kissing good-bye large corporate bonuses and stock options.

Kennedy was said to have been in love with the styling of the new Thunderbird, and with this in mind, McNamara expedited arrangements to provide the inaugural festivities with new Ford products. New Lincoln Continental four-door convertibles had been chosen as limousines for the president, replacing an early-'50s Lincoln used by President Eisenhower, but a high-profile Ford was wanted for the drive down Pennsylvania Avenue. The Ford Division agreed to provide fifty new Thunderbird convertibles for the use of dignitaries and in the ceremonial parade from Capitol Hill to the White House. On December 30, the batch designated for parade duty was given a simple tag-line on their routing sheets: ORANGE BALL/INAUGURAL PARADE. The ragtops, some painted in Lincoln's Presidential Mahogany, were shipped to Washington, used during the weekend of the inauguration, and then auctioned off by the Washington Sales District to Ford dealers across the nation.

A Golden Opportunity:
The Indianapolis Pace/Festival Cars

The shift in power allowed an ambitious Lido A. Iaccoca to finally gain the vice-presidency he had set his sights on (though a year later than his goal of achieving it

on his thirty-fifth birthday) and gave him the chance to show everyone how he thought Fords should be built and sold. Unlike McNamara, Iaccoca was in tune with public demand for exciting, sporty cars, and immediately he directed the division to increase Ford's exposure in competition and to develop option packages to turn mundane two-doors into lively performers.

The '61 Thunderbird was no exception. Though the extent of Iaccoca's involvement is unknown, the car was picked to become the first T-bird to serve as a pace car for the prestigious Indianapolis 500 race on Memorial Day. Ford dealers from the Indianapolis area offered to supply two gold-painted pace-car convertibles and thirty-three additional ragtop festival cars to serve the needs of track officials and dignitaries during the period leading up to the race. By mid-March approval was given, and their production was scheduled for the first day of spring on March 21, under Pre-Approved Order Number 8479.

The two pace cars differed from festival cars in that they received unique graphics and were provided with brackets to hold flags. The primary pace car was fitted with a beige leather interior, while the back-up car was given black leather. As for performance modifications, the dealers approached Ford's engineering staff to help with upgrading the two. On April 25, 1961, during an engineering planning meeting between Advanced Car Engineering head Frederick Hooven and Dave Evans, who was in charge of the division's performance and technical evaluation section, it was decided that the two pace cars would be modified by Bill Stroppe Engineering. Don Frey, vice-president of engineering, dictated that involvement in the modification of the pace cars should not be direct, but that funding could be found to assist the Indianapolis consor-

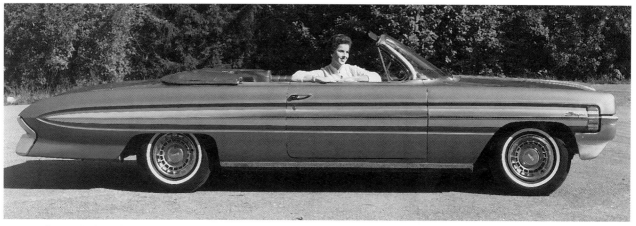

More in line with the T-bird was the 1961 Oldsmobile Starfire convertible. Offered only in a convertible form, it provided bucket seats and a floor console for people who preferred a more traditional, sedan-sized, midprice car. *Oldsmobile Historical Services*

tium in hopping up the T-birds. Just fourteen days before the race, on May 16, Evans announced to Hooven that he had met with Ken Holloway and Jerry Alderman, who were representatives for the dealer group, and agreed to assist in providing technical assistance, while Stroppe would handle the actual work in preparing the cars.

Actual modification work was never spelled out in Ford records, but speculation is that one of the high-performance 390 packages was fitted to the cars, most probably the 375hp Police Interceptor version with an aluminum four-barrel manifold and a Holley carburetor.

Festival cars, on the other hand, did not receive performance modifications. The thirty three were painted in a specially mixed gold metallic paint that was not carried in the Ford catalog and were given graphics that identified the supporting Indianapolis-area dealer and the fact that they were festival units. The significance of the gold color was that 1961 would be the fiftieth anniversary of the In-

Providing competition for the T-bird was another personal luxury heavyweight, the 1961 Chrysler 300. Offered in both hardtop and convertible versions, it would not sell as well as the T-bird, but did offer more-impressive performance, especially in letter-series form (G model shown). *John Lee photo*

dianapolis Motor Speedway (though the actual race was only in its forty-fifth running).

At the end of the race, winner A. J. Foyt was presented with the primary pace car as per Indy 500 tradition. The remaining back-up pace car and festival cars were then sold through the participating dealers, sans markings. The disposition of Foyt's pace car is unknown—speculation is that it was either wrecked or sold. Several of the black-interiored festival cars have turned up over the years, with most of them being repainted to resemble the back-up pace car and not reflecting their actual status as festival/parade cars.

Teething Pains

The '61 T-bird was radically new—so much so that it would have lots of little glitches to be corrected. Water leaks because of undersized antenna base gaskets, various buzzing noises, poor-fitting interior trim, lack of rear-bumper adjustments, and other quality-control problems occurred throughout the first few months of production. A delay in the supply of the trademark "THUNDERBIRD"-stamped valve covers (which would be corrected on November 10, 1960) created the need to paint "FORD"-stamped ones silver-gray to match the 390's identifying color. Substitution of a redesigned brake booster provided by Midland Ross during early December would eliminate the need for an auxiliary vacuum reserve tank. With the redesigned booster, it was discovered that the bore of the master cylinder could be reduced from 1in to 7/8in, which was done in production on June 9. And, to really create a concern in the engineering department, it became known in February that gas tanks were developing cracks and leaking; by July 1, a revised tank and filler neck were introduced in production to cure the problem, which was due to flexing of the inlet pipe from the

As part of its sponsorship of National Hot Rod Association (NHRA) events during 1961, Hurst-Campbell, Inc. of Glenside, Pennsylvania, famous for its aftermarket floor shifters, presented Jack Chrisman, the competition car driver who scored the highest number of points during the 1961 season, this T-bird hardtop at the end of the NHRA Nationals in Indianapolis, Indiana, during Labor Day weekend, where the car is pictured making a pass down the Indianapolis drag strip. Hurst also gave away a Pontiac Catalina two-door hardtop (which was a duplicate of the car sponsored by Hurst and prepared by Royal Pontiac of Royal Oak, Michigan) which was fitted with its famous four-on-the-floor to the driver scoring the most points in NHRA's stock division, in this case, Bruce Morgan. No indication was made as to changes in the T-bird, which was fitted with a standard 300hp, 390ci, four-barrel engine and Cruise-O-Matic transmission. *Courtesy Petersen Publishing Company/PPC Photographic*

tank and resultant cracking of the mounting flange. The redesigned tank would use a solid filler pipe that was allowed to flex inside the opening of the tank.

Another new idea being pioneered on the T-bird, the integral power-steering box, did away with a hydraulic piston assembly attached to the steering linkage and moved it into the steering gearbox. By February 1961, dealers were receiving complaints related to the steering, especially with regard to failure to return to center and front-end wander. A change in the size of the idler-arm bushing on April 4, 1961, it was hoped, would take care of the problem, but problems still persisted (and would get worse during 1962).

As more convertibles entered service, complaints of tops failing to operate were traced back to loose or improperly adjusted limit switches and the flipper lid gearbox assembly. The number one complaint about the convertible was not how it worked, but again would be the lack of stowage space in the trunk with the top down.

Less Than Anticipated

By the time the '61 model year was winding down, sales were behind the pace set in 1960. In the end, 73,051 of the "Bullet 'Birds" were produced. Like the '60 Ford, the '61 T-bird was perhaps too aggressive for some people. Quality problems inherent in the first-year model may have scared off buyers as well. What was also occurring in the marketplace was that the competition was finally starting to arrive, albeit via made-over full-size cars. The bucket-seat/console personal-luxury niche discovered by Ford was now facing a limited onslaught from GM, which was fielding similar interior packages, larger engines, and flashier trim in cars such as the Oldsmobile Starfire convertible, and Chrysler still was pumping out the 300 in letter and nonletter form. And this was only the beginning of the first wave.

The '61 T-bird's emphasis on innovation made it an object of attention in the showrooms, but changes in the works for 1962 would really make people stand up and take notice.

Chapter 9

FOUR THOUSAND POUNDS OF FIREWORKS

A period of five years had passed since the last two-seat Thunderbird was available as a new car, and along with it had passed the man to whom its death was attributed. A new "king of the hill" was on the verge of shaking up the industry in a way that would take everyone by surprise and leave in its wake an exciting time to be an automobile enthusiast.

Intuition

The departure of Robert McNamara on January 3, 1961, was to "car guys" in Ford a day of rejoicing. The no-nonsense approach of the chief "whiz kid" may have played well with fellow bean-counters and stockholders, but it left Ford's product offering looking as bland as a vanilla wafer. The Falcon, the Model T of the new era, was

The front end of the 1962 prototype photographed on April 18, 1961. A heavy stainless steel molding spanning between the eyebrows was proposed for the hood lip, and a T-bird with longer wings was also considered. The idea was dropped due to cost considerations. Some early cars were also built without the hood 'Bird. The 1961 hood and wide white sidewall tires would be supplanted as well. *Ford Motor Company*

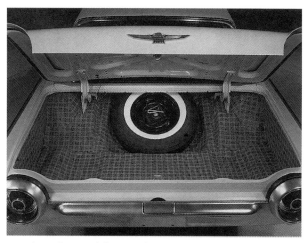

Another photo of the April 18, 1961, prototype hardtop shows the shallow trunk. Holes toward the front of the deck lid between the hinge brackets were punched out for the convertible hardware. Sheet metal interchangeability was maximized in the T-bird, including windshield header structure and inner panels. The primary difference between hardtop and convertible lids lay between the inner frame and outer skin where heavy steel bars and bracketry were placed to hold up the flipper panel and its related parts, as well as mounting points for the rear hinges and hard points for the hydraulic rams which opened and closed the structure. The trunk mat pattern shown, used in 1961, would be changed to a speckled design by the time it reached production. *Ford Motor Company*

a solid, economical little car that struck a chord with the working man. The full-size Ford, restyled in the wake of the '60 faux pas in trying to go Chevrolet's '59 Impala one better when even Chevrolet decided that it wasn't worth the effort, was rebounding in sales but not at a meteoric rate. Even the star of the division's line-up, the Thunderbird, didn't have anything spectacular to offer.

Lido "Lee" Iaccoca knew he could get the public excited about Ford; all he needed was the opportunity and

Another photo from the mid-April prototype session this time showing the convertible. The wide molding and 'Bird can be seen. *Ford Motor Company*

A passenger-side, rear three-quarter view of the prototype convertible. Stamped aluminum rings were placed inside the dished taillights, which replaced the cast-metal housings and smaller lenses of 1961. *Ford Motor Company*

A quick way to create a new model: Glue to the roof a textured vinyl cover over padding, place chrome-plated S-bars on the C-pillars, and, *voila*, the Landau is created. This example is of an original Sahara Rose car owned by Tim and Laura Pundt of Kansas City, Missouri. *Alan Tast photo*

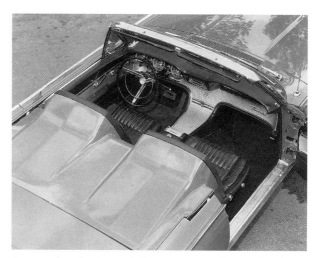

A service technician illustrates how a prototype tonneau is removed from the car. A steel tab on the back edge of the cover slides between the top of the rear seat cushion and the painted steel panel between the seats and the deck lid. Production cars would later be equipped with a pair of thumbscrews and threaded sockets in the outboard area of the rear seat header panel to cure problems of the outer rear corners pulling up from the body. The headrests on the prototype cover were fitted with a sewn vinyl cover, as opposed to the molded vinyl-over-foam version of the production cars, and are shorter to allow greater clearance over the top of the front seats. *Ford Motor Company*

An overhead view of the prototype Sports Roadster, photographed in mid-July 1962. The grab bar can barely be seen under the passenger-side dash cove. *Ford Motor Company*

the product. What got Iaccoca hot was speed, styling, and image. The '62 Fords had already been approved under McNamara during spring 1960, and they were more of the same conservative, boring themes that were fast becoming a corporate trademark. It was time for a change!

If It Ain't Broke, Don't Fix It

The facelift that was locked in for 1962 would not be radical by any means. As with the 1958–59 change, only a few trim details and some mechanical improvements would be needed to establish a recognizable identity for the new model. Early proposals prepared in April 1960 for a possible facelift suggested moving turn signals into the hood above the headlights were rejected. Front-wheel drive was also rejected. The only radical change was in the grille pattern, which consisted of aluminum squares suspended between horizontal bars, and three elongated, ribbed rectangles that replaced the four spears used for 1961. Up until the last minute in spring 1961, a revised hood ornamentation was considered that used a wide molding that spanned the area between the hood "eyebrows," only to be broken up in the center by a restyled 'Bird emblem with a wingspan almost double of the original. This change was canceled for cost reasons, so the original hood emblem and molding were retained for the remainder of the series. An

improvement was removal of the two windsplits placed between the "power dome" and fenders.

Packaging and the Landau

Iaccoca was a believer in the rub-off benefits of specialty packaging. He was turned on by exciting and stylish automobiles, and in his gut he knew that there were millions more who were, too.

With McNamara out of the way, Iaccoca's penchant for spicing up the existing line-up with trim packages and midyear introductions could be tested. Midyear introductions were not new—after all, the '58 T-bird was really a half-year car (even more so the convertible). As the Ford Division's marketing manager before his advancement, he attended design-review shows and was aware of work to dress up the '60 T-bird with different roof treatments before the sunroof would finally push this idea aside. This kind of a dress-up option could add substantially to the car's looks without a lot of expense and generate a real profit at the retail level. What could be better than spending $50 and getting $300 back? And how come McNamara couldn't see it?

Lessons of the '60 T-bird were not lost on Iaccoca or the product-planning staff. Like it or not, it wasn't speed lines that were moving the T-bird off dealer's lots, it was the air of luxury and formality. The time to dust off those roof-covering proposals came in spring 1961, and within a matter of weeks a vinyl-roof option would be developed in studio for Iaccoca to approve. A handsome fake Landau bar was created to emulate the classic styling of the '20s and '30s for the C-pillar, with the center pivot-point being occupied by a pair of raised concentric rings and a plastic T-bird emblem. To simulate a Landau roof, a long-

A public relations photo taken in late-July 1962. Wire wheels, tonneau cover, and fender emblems are revealed. Fender skirts were deleted with the wire wheel option due to interference with die-cast spinners, especially in hard cornering situations. *Ford Motor Company*

grain vinyl was selected to give the roof a heavy texture, and the vinyl was placed over a heavy felt pad. With only the roof being affected, designers were content to leave the interior alone so late in the game.

The Sports Roadster

Recognizing the cries of two-seat enthusiasts, Iaccoca was also keen to the sporty image of Thunderbird. Resale value of 1955–57 T-birds by 1961 was astounding, but used-car sales did not help new-car manufacturers. How was Ford to take advantage of the demand? Much energy was expended to learn more about sporty-type cars and potential buyers prior to and during 1961, and design studies were ordered for concept cars from the Advanced Design Studios. Designers were given a chance to come up with exciting packages such as the Mustang I, Allegro, and Avventura during the latter part of 1961 and 1962, but a stop-gap measure had to be available for fall 1961 release.

Quick-thinking designers and engineers recognized that the Thunderbird's convertible-top arrangement gave it some unique advantages. The completely hidden top assembly, once it was folded back into the trunk, left a very pleasing look similar to that of the two-seat T-bird. A cover to hide the rear seats could be fashioned and set in place to create the illusion of a two-seat car, albeit with a very long rear deck. The problems with a cover were stowage (should it be collapsible to store in the trunk when the rear seats were needed?) and how could it work within the confines of front-seat adjustment, especially the four-way power seats? The final answers would be (1) like the first-generation hardtop, you'll simply have to leave it in the garage, and (2) mold the cover around the seats and disconnect the vertical adjustment for the power ones. The new T-bird trim package with the tonneau cover was dubbed the Sports Roadster.

The tonneau, which was also referred to early on as a "coaming," was a nifty shaping of fiberglass. After production had commenced, it was found that the outer corners of the tonneau would warp and pull away from the car, so a chrome-plated T-screw and threaded receptors were installed as a running change. Customers who complained about the warping were provided under warranty a retrofit of the retainers.

John Najjar, who was in good graces with styling head George Walker following his involvement with the prestigious 1961 Lincoln Continental, had been handed the responsibility of running Ford's interior-design studio during the spring of 1961, taking over for Art Querfeld, who was credited with development of the '61 T-bird's wraparound cockpit. In an interview with Michael Lamm for *Special Interest Auto*'s April 1978 issue on the '62 Sports Roadster, Najjar recalled that among his first duties as interior executive would be directing the development of the T-bird's fiberglass tonneau cover. Said Najjar, ". . . [studio

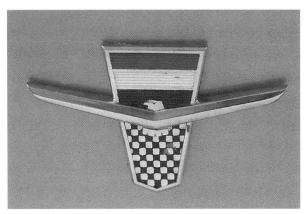

Badge of honor. The emblem used for the new Sports Roadster melded a stylized, thin-wing T-bird with a checkered lower section and tri-color upper shield. It was placed on the forward portion of the front fenders and on the tonneau cover upright between the seats. *Ford Motor Company*

designer] Bud Kaufmann had a devil of a time giving the finished, tailored look to the tonneau where it joined the doors and central console. I remember there was a terrific push to get it completed and put into production." The push was because of the last-minute decision by planners—spurred on by Iaccoca—to develop the option in time for 1962 production, just a handful of months away. Once the final engineering prototype had been made by mid-July, it was rushed across the Detroit River into the shop of a fiberglass fabricator in Windsor, Ontario. Cracking of the first covers would delay production of the first Sports Roadsters for almost one month, from August 21 until September 13.

Najjar's staff had to come up with some additional details for the Sports Roadster package. An abstracted T-bird emblem placed on a shield of red, white, and blue and a checkered flag pattern was developed, and a chrome-plated grab bar with a vinyl-covered pad was

The prototype Sports Roadster's engine bay is examined by a technician. The standard 390ci V-8 would again provide yeoman service, but an optional triple two-barrel carburetor package would give a little extra thunder for the 'Bird. *Ford Motor Company*

placed into the cove of the passenger-side dash. To emphasize the package, the first few Roadsters (and some convertibles) had no hood emblems in deference to the fender-mounted castings.

To add a final bit of sparkle for what would really be a dealership show car, the Kelsey-Hayes Co. of Romulus, Michigan, was contracted to build a chrome-plated wire wheel with a revised center hub (to fit the Thunderbird's wheel-bolt pattern) and a new center cap and pan to be designed by Ford. All that was left to arrange was obtaining tube-type 8.00x14in tires (the spoked wheels could not be made air-tight) when virtually all passenger cars then built were fitted with tubeless tires. In the end, tubeless tires were modified by pricking the inner sidewall with thousands of tiny holes to allow heated air to escape between the tube and inner wall of the tire, and designations for "tubeless" on the tire were ground off. The package was completed, and the process could begin to build a faux two-seat T-bird.

Problems with the wire wheels, however, would put a damper on their popularity. One of the first Sports Roadsters was provided to Elvis Presley during the fall of 1961. Presley, who at the time was heavily into cranking out movies in California, was not a passive driver; while out for a drive, one of the wire wheels collapsed, apparently during hard cornering. The incident made national headlines, created an embarrassment for Ford, and sent engineers at Kelsey-Hayes rushing to recalculate loading on the forty-eight adjustable spokes. It was discovered that they were undersized, and an immediate recall was ordered by Ford to remove the inadequate wheels from use. The size of the spokes was increased to 5/16in in diameter from approximately 1/4in, and the revised wheels were released for production and retrofitting. Negative press over the failure of Presley's and other owners' wheels dampened spirits for the plated beauties, which could also be ordered for any Thunderbird: flat tires due to slow leaks were also a major source of complaints.

Introduction and Public Reaction

Introduction of the Thunderbird was timed to coincide with the rest of the Ford line, including the all-new midsize Fairlane, on October 12, 1961. At the direction of Iaccoca, each dealership in a major metropolitan area was to be supplied with a Rangoon Red Sports Roadster with a black interior for their showroom to draw in customers. Between September 13 and October 2, the first 466 (about one-third of total '62 Roadster production) were completed and within the week were poised for their debut. Dealers not lucky enough to get the real thing had to settle for red plastic promotional models produced by Aluminum Model Toys (AMT) of Troy, Michigan, to display along with photographs and a special six-page brochure featuring a red-and-black example.

To counter vibration problems, Ford engineers took a page from the 1961 Lincoln convertible's handbook and added suspended weights, called "tuned mass dampers" in each corner of early convertibles and Sports Roadsters; this cast-iron brick in the trunk is an example. Before the end of December 1961, such dampers would be deemed unnecessary. Vibration problems would persist, though, until a redesign of the steering gearbox late in the model year would cure the problem. *Alan Tast photo*

Before the end of the year, Ford would keep potential buyers second-guessing color availability by offering Castillian Gold Metallic on the Thunderbird; though offered on other cars, it was a last-minute addition that didn't make it to press for supplemental material such as shop manuals. It would also spring on knowledgeable buyers real claws for the T-bird—a unique version of the triple-carburetor big-block V-8.

Talons for the Thunderbird

Even though McNamara relented in 1959 by allowing Donald Frey's engineers to proceed with a high-performance version of the 352ci motor in response to Chevrolet's hot 348ci motor, the fire-breathing 360hp motor would not be available in the T-bird. Officially, it was because it would not be adapted to work with automatic transmissions so prevalent in T-bird orders and because the 430ci motor was looked upon as *the* performance option for the car. Development of higher-output motors would really take off when Iaccoca took the helm in October 1960. By February 1961, the 401hp tri-powered 390 was ready for release, and four-speed transmissions were rapidly gaining favor. The full-size Ford took to the adaptations quite well, but what would happen if they were put in a T-bird?

Engineering had its hands full in preparing a new line of motors for 1962, including the high-output 406ci in four-barrel and tri-power versions. Demand for a high-performance motor for the Thunderbird looked like a simple bill to complete at first—take a 406 and drop it into the engine bay. But, inadequate clearances for the cast-iron exhaust headers, adaptation problems for use with automatic transmissions, and the mounting angle of the engine (in the Galaxie, the motor tilted back, while in the T-bird it sat level) created problems. The solution would be to create a hybrid motor using parts of the 390 and 406.

Distant Thunder: The M-Series Option

Development of the new T-bird optional engine, a 390ci with triple 2bbl carbs, coded "M" for identification purposes in the serial number, would delay the option's introduction until January 1962. Prior to that time, public knowledge was limited to brief paragraphs buried within new-model announcement issues, such as *Motor Trend's* statement in its November 1961 write-up on the new Thunderbird: "A higher-powered engine, appropriate for the new Roadster, is said to be in the works but no details had been released as this issue of *Motor Trend* went to press," which was in September. Even as late as *Car Life's* July 1962 review of the Sports Roadster, it would remark that the M option had not been promoted much. Strangely, no major publications bothered to conduct a road test of a tri-powered T-bird, perhaps regarding the added 40hp as a joke for such a heavyweight car.

Ford's prestige catalog for the Thunderbird, printed during August 1961, did not list the yet-to-be-released optional motor, and neither would the special brochure printed for the Sports Roadster. First official mention of the 340hp Thunderbird Sports V-8 in sales literature would be in a full-line brochure dated February 1962, and advertising touting the higher-output motor would be limited to simple tag-lines within the ad's copy. Thunderbird advertising during the period was deliberately low-key, with exception of a limited series of advertising promoting the Sports Roadster in magazines such as *Sports Illustrated*. It wasn't the options as much as it was the car that was being promoted. The M-series motor was never pushed as forcefully as was Ford's high-performance options for the Galaxie, and so it was lost to obscurity and doomed to extremely low sales.

In simplistic terms, the M-series was a 390ci motor with a modified aluminum intake manifold that held three 2bbl carbs. The manifold differed from full-size versions to allow for vacuum fittings, pollution control valve (PCV) hardware, a pair of mounting bosses for the throttle/kickdown linkage, and a flat profile to allow the three Holley 2bbl carburetors to sit level, which was important to allow for hood clearance in the rear, and to provide the proper attitude for the operation of the carbs. The progressive throttle linkage was revised to provide for an anti-stall dashpot and received a bright finish. Topping off the carburetors, an oval cast aluminum open-element assembly was carried over from the Galaxie, with a cutout provided to mount a T-bird emblem. The upper casting received a satin-like polished finish, as opposed to unpolished castings used in the standard nonemblemed Galaxie version.

Inside the motor, a higher-lift, longer-duration camshaft was fitted to allow more of the air-fuel mixture to be brought into larger-capacity cylinder heads, which had been adapted from the 406. The dual-pipe exhaust was enhanced with 2in-diameter tubing (as opposed to 1-3/4in used for the four-barrel version), but the stock box-style exhaust manifolds were retained to clear the spring towers. Other changes would include a higher-volume oil pump, dual-point distributor, and a recalibrated valve body for the automatic transmission to handle added torque.

To impress friends and service station attendants, a package of chrome-plated parts was provided as standard equipment on the Sports V-8. The primary items that received the bright finish included valve covers and retaining bolts, oil filler cap and dipstick handle, radiator expansion tank and cap, master cylinder cap, and power steering reservoir cover (both the standard pump with a reservoir bolted to the top of the pump, and the remote-style canister used with air conditioning). To make matters confusing for people restoring M-series T-birds in later years, shortages of various parts would sometimes result in an M-series car leaving the factory without a plated master cylinder cover, dipstick, or any of the other items (except for the valve covers, which served as the identifying item for dealers that the car was fitted with the hi-po motor).

Mid-Life Crisis

The '62 Thunderbird was a better automobile all-around than previous versions. Writers were elated about the Sports Roadster as the long-awaited answer for the displaced two-seater.

The drawback, however, was that the competition was catching up to the T-bird. The Oldsmobile Starfire's model choices were expanded to include a two-door hardtop, matching the T-bird body-style-to-body-style. By February 1962, Buick would unveil an interim challenger at the Chicago Auto Show in the Wildcat, a big-engined two-door hardtop with bucket seats and a console, along with a floor-shifted automatic. Pontiac would also go for personal luxury and performance with its Grand Prix, a dechromed version of the Catalina and Bonneville two-door hardtop. And Studebaker would revamp its aging Hawk into the Gran Turismo, even mocking the T-bird's formal roof line and wide C-pillars. Along with these upstarts, word on the street was that a true contender for the Thunderbird's crown was being developed in GM's studios by William "Bill" Mitchell for introduction as a 1963 model.

Wanderer

As early as the mid-February 1962, complaints from T-bird owners of vibrations, brake noise, brake pulling,

The move toward the personal luxury concept gained a performance edge in Pontiac's Grand Prix, a bucket-seated version of the Catalina. With a hardtop roof restyled to more closely resemble a convertible, the GP would, along with cars such as the Chevrolet Impala SS, dig into the T-bird's sales territory in greater numbers as GM caught on to the concept. *Pontiac Historical Services*

and other similar woes were being addressed in technical service bulletins. Sources of the problems were not readily identified, but by late summer, these problems expanded to include what was called "on-center rattle" and "sloppy" steering. Band-aid fixes would again change the size of the idler-arm bushing and expand to changing the lower steering column bushing and "rag joint" coupler in mid-March production, but the problem still would continue. Investigation of steering gearboxes returned to engineers in Dearborn revealed nicked seals that let fluid past the hydraulic piston of the integral steering gear, voiding the effectiveness of the steering mechanism. A "campaign" was launched to replace gearboxes by late summer with improved units and to isolate gearboxes from the subframe with rubber-bushed spacers to cut down on vibration transmitted from the substructure.

Running Changes

There were other running changes as the model year progressed that weren't so critical, especially during the month of October. The steering wheel would be changed from a hard rubber rim to a semitranslucent plastic called "Tenite" on October 2, 1961; the engine oil dipstick would be lengthened on October 8 to allow easier use when an air conditioner was installed, and on October 20 the convertible top's circuit breaker was relocated from the inner passenger fender to underneath the front radiator support. Various other minor changes were made to items such as the turn-signal switch/lever assembly and the heater control valve.

Convertible and Sports Roadster owners were also subjected to a short-term experiment in tuned-mass dampening. The '61 Lincoln convertible had been equipped with a set of cast-iron weights suspended in each corner of the car to absorb vibrations in the unibody, and the idea was carried over to the '62 T-bird program to counter similar problems. Up front, between the front wheels and bumper, 50lb "pucks" were hung off steel brackets, and in the trunk, two "bricks" were placed above the floor between the inner quarter panel and the hydraulic cylinder mounting. Before the end of 1961, the excess weight was removed from production, deemed to be "overkill" and not effective for the car.

The biggest noticeable change came on April 16, 1962, when modified dash pads and door panels were first fitted. The change helped simplify assembly of the dash by eliminating a rubber welting that filled the gap between the dash's outside corner and where it met the door panel.

Other significant changes in production included revised power-window motors on May 5 (front windows) and May 8 (rear windows); a modified remote power-steering reservoir (for air conditioned cars) with a larger supply line to the power steering pump and a generator splash shield on June 1; and a major structural modification with the elimination of the bolt-on connection for the front subframe assembly on July 16 (probably to cure some of the vibration and rattle complaints).

Keeping the Numbers Straight

Addition of Sports Roadster and Landau models would bring complications to Ford's bookkeeping and ordering system. They were originally intended to be trim packages with no special designation, so keeping track of special problems for them (especially for warranty adjustments) meant that a method of identification would be needed. The coding for hardtops and convertibles was already established as 63A/83 for the hardtop and 76A/85 for the convertible; squeezing in two new models resulted in new codes of 63B/87 for the Landau and 76B/89 for the Sports Roadster. The changeover was officially was phased in by February 2, 1962, for the Sports Roadster, but deviations to this have surfaced to the point that the code change may have actually occurred almost two months earlier.

According to a review of gate release/invoice copies retained from Ford by T-bird enthusiast Lois Eminger and culled by Dean Macklem, along with Bill Bain of the short-lived Thunderbird Sports Roadster Society in 1974, the last 76A/85-invoiced Sports Roadster was 2Y85Z-114640. The changeover 76B/89 Sports Roadster, 2Y89Z-125032, was believed to have been built after the February 2, 1962, code change. Serial numbers on file with VTCI and as part of a published M-series reference manual prepared by VTCI 1961–63 Technical Editor William Wonder indicate that T-birds built at the same time as -114640 range were assembled on November 3, 1961, while cars built at the same time as -125032 would have appeared in early

Down but not out, Studebaker took direct aim at the T-bird with its Gran Turismo Hawk, a reskinned and contemporary-flavored version of the Golden Hawk. Featuring a new roof with squared-off, wide C-pillars and a bucket-seated interior, the Hawk would come the closest to capturing the essence of the T-bird. *John Lee photo*

December—most probably on December 4, 1961. Another reference to serial numbers in the March-April 1978 *Thunderbird Scoop* cited the change happening with 2Y89Z-127027. Again, numbers on file with VTCI indicate this would have been built on December 11, 1961.

The Landau changeover date is even less clear. One of the earliest recorded examples in VTCI's Owner's Survey files was built on October 24 (which was the only one on file with "A" as the third digit in the trim code, indicating that the car was fitted with a black vinyl top), with another following on October 25 (verification of early cars can be made by checking the bottom of their rotation/build sheets to find the word "Landau"). By late November 1961, the 63B/87 designation was appearing on Landau plates and in their serial numbers. Regretfully, Ford never kept separate production numbers for the Landau and hardtop, but if later production figures offer a valid comparison, it may be possible that up to 15 percent of hardtop production may have been with the Landau vinyl roof.

Significant Accomplishment

Production of the '62 T-bird would cease during the second week of August 1962. As the Wixom plant shut down for changeover to '63 production, a review of reports show that more '62s were sold than '61s, even with mediocre attempts by other manufacturers to cut into the T-bird market. (It must be remembered, though, that the total built for '62 was still over 14,000 units below 1960's record.) Addition of the Sports Roadster and Landau most certainly helped in the 5,000-unit gain over 1961, but sales of the tonneau-equipped convertible were not even enough to cover development costs.

The Thunderbird was now poised to make one last grab for the performance enthusiast, but it was painfully clear that even a fancy set of wheels and a cover for the rear seats could not hide the fact that the car was inexorably set on a course to become for Ford what the Continental was for Lincoln-Mercury.

Chapter 10

PRINCESS OF THE ROAD

Evolution of the Thunderbird and its scheduling pattern dictated that every three years the car was to be reborn into a more contemporary and technologically advanced masterpiece. With the 1963 model year being the last of the third generation, a dated-looking body shell was being forced to compete against the more angular examples that were being introduced to the public during the fall of 1962. For 1963, the Thunderbird would be a tough sell.

The Facelift

By 1961, tastes were changing away from heavily chromed road hogs, and consumer sophistication was rising: People wanted more creature comforts as well as value for their money. Design and engineering budgets were, as it was for the 1957 and 1960 models, very tight, and limited effort were allowed for restyling.

Exterior changes in the front end were considered during March 1961 that were radical, including a C-scallop that ran into the door from a more angular grille-bumper arrangement. On the other side of the body, a reveal line ran from the juncture between the bumper/fender back into the door where it curved downward. Another proposal took cues from the Oldsmobile Starfire (which was just hitting the market) for side-sculpturing, with a rather unappealing "pug" nose and single-headlight treatment that was more comparable to the Chrysler Turbine cars of 1963–64 in appearance. The body side crease that would eventually define the '63 was lifted from the first proposal, and by summer would be approved for

By late November 1961, sheet metal changes for 1963 were firmly in place, but exploration of trim choices was still being conducted. In this photo, a two-tone Landau roof with enlongated S-bars is explored: on the floor under the rocker panel, a portion of material which matches the missing roof cover section can be seen. The front wheel cover appears to be close to the final design, and a three-bladed spinner sitting on the floor under the front bumper is waiting its turn to be photographed in a mock-up of what would become the optional cover. While the door trim is in final form, a 1961–62-style nameplate was again on the forward portion of the front fender; the script would be moved to the rear fender and take on a new design by mid-1962. Examples of this trim placement can be found in the 1963 Shop Manual supplement, for which artwork production began during April/May 1962. *Ford Motor Company*

Photographed on June 25, 1962, the prototype 1963 hardtop reveals the new nameplate on the rear fender and standard full wheel covers with conical center. *Ford Motor Company*

The interior of the prototype 1963 hardtop features a different dash and console trim which, though proposed for the end of the three-year cycle, was rejected in favor of retaining the 1961–62 design. Closer study also reveals that the 1961–62-style emergency brake release was used on the prototype—this would be replaced with a more conventional lever release by the start of production within two months. Another item, the air conditioner register, would also be changed by late August (a 1962 unit is installed in the photo). Note the vacuum door latch switch and relocated emergency brake warning light. *Ford Motor Company*

tooling. To create an additional way to identify the '63, the triple emblem/"hash mark" motif was redone in a style that harked back to the check-mark casting used on the 1955–57 T-bird. The nameplate, originally to be a reuse of the 1957–59/1961–62 version, was to go on the front fender similar to 1961–62 orientation, but below the feature line. This was abandoned by May 1962 when a new, rounder script appeared on the rear quarters ahead of the rear bumper. A turbine theme was chosen for wheel

An interior view of the prototype Landau interior from late June 1962; a brushed stainless band can be seen separating the walnut woodgrain trim from the lower dash. This would not be carried over into production, but can be seen in the first printing of the 1963 full-line brochure. *Ford Motor Company*

covers and rear taillamp trim, while the grille would become a "waterfall" of vertical bars.

Other exterior changes considered were varying the trimming of the Landau top, even going with only a vinyl band across the C-pillars and leaving the front roof painted. An experimental car was built during late 1962 to try out the idea of a targa-style removable half-roof, called a Sunbonnet, on a '63 hardtop.

Interior trim was slated for a major overhaul, but proposals were rejected in favor of retaining the existing aluminum panels in the hardtop, convertible, and Sports Roadster models. The Landau, on the other hand, would be provided with a richer-looking walnut appliqué over smooth panels, giving the interior an identifier. Door panels were provided with a courtesy/warning light assembly in the bottom, same as on the 1962-1/2 Galaxie 500/XL, which had been adapted from the dome light assembly of the T-bird.

Seat upholstery patterns were finally changed for 1963. The new upholstery used two distinct grain patterns—a crinkle grain for the bolsters and a vachette grain (which looks similar to the "Cobra"-grained vinyl roof cover) for the inserts—and featured a narrow series of pleats toward the center of the seat in the all-vinyl and the leather covers; a nylon cloth insert with silver mylar threading was the third choice. Silver mylar tinsel welting was used between the bolsters and inserts, and a T-bird emblem color-coordinated with a vinyl insert was mounted in the upper seatbacks (a wood-grained version was used in Landau models).

Engineering Advances

The '63 T-bird featured several technological advances for Ford. The electrical charging system was changed from a direct-current generator to an alternator, improving charging rates at low speeds. Except for M-series cars, a large single-exhaust system was employed to cut costs—at a loss of performance—so the dual exhaust system was reintroduced late in the model year, on an optional basis. Front suspension components were beefed up, including upper A-frames, shock absorbers, and mounting brackets. The hood release was moved outside to the center of the new "waterfall" grille, and the emergency brake release was changed from a foot-operated lever alongside the pedal to a lever under the dash. Brakes, always a sore spot with automotive critics, were also improved with slightly finned drums to aid in cooling. Air conditioning and heater components were also mildly modified, including the in-dash register vane controls, which were now worked with a pair of levers (as opposed to thumb wheels). Power window switches reappeared in the console for the first time since 1960, and in the middle of the dash a choice of either an AM radio with front or front-and-rear speakers or an all-new AM-FM radio was offered. An offering unique to T-bird and Lincoln through the remainder of the unibody years was a hydraulically operated windshield wiper motor, which used power-steering fluid routed from the gearbox.

Death of the M-Series

As production of the '63 T-bird began almost as soon as the last '62 was designated to be completed, the fate of the M-series hanged in the balance. Even though it would be modified with revised cylinder heads, camshaft, and other internal changes, it still suffered from poor promotion by indifferent planners and frustrated (if not uninformed) advertising copywriters. Compounding a lack of knowledge by the buying public, the power option was also battling an image problem. Dealers who sold M-equipped T-birds received complaints from owners of poor gas mileage, and some would also suffer near-disaster when misadjusted carburetors would allow the motor to backfire and set fire to the engine bay.

Fed up with complaints and warranty work, some would elect to disconnect the outboard secondary Holley carburetors or replace the triple-carbed intake system with standard-issue four-barrel units. It was even related to William Wonder during research for his M-series manual that some dealers had inadvertently ordered the package due to the way order forms were laid out, and when upon delivery they found the sophisticated induction system, had their mechanics replace them with the easier-to-maintain four-barrel assemblies.

Eventually, Ford's marketing people came to realize that the M option was not being accepted well enough to justify its existence, and it was silently withdrawn from availability by the end of the year, with orders on-hand being completed as late as January 11. The only way a person could now get a higher-output T-bird would be over the parts counter: A tri-power kit was offered in Ford's catalogs for manual- and automatic-transmission applications, and the M's manifold, adapted for use on automatic-equipped cars, may have lived on in such a manner.

Command Performance

Marketing plans under Lee Iaccoca always had two seasons: the traditional fall introduction period, and another promotional blitz sometime in mid to late winter as the model year was approaching the half-way point. For the 1962 model year, the T-bird got the M-series engine as its new feature. Although the M was not talked about nearly as much as the highly visible changes to Ford's lower-priced car lines, the midyear promotion was a hit overall, leaving Ford with the question for 1963 of how to top "The Lively Ones" campaign of 1962.

The answer was in Ford's renewed involvement in racing. During June 1962, Henry Ford II declared that his company would no longer participate in the AMA ban on factory participation in racing, on participation in speed contests, and in advertising based on speed or horsepower claims, acknowledging the fact that competitors such as Plymouth, Pontiac, and Chevrolet were already flaunting the ban. The high-performance program would proceed full-bore in all areas of racing: stock car, drag-strip, off-road, and rallying. Ford was fielding what it felt would be a very strong contender in rally driving with a team of '63 Falcons provided with the new small-block 260ci V-8s. Ad-man Walter "Wally" Elton from JWT's New York office also recognized that a perfect promotional opportunity would appear in the Principality of Monaco, where the prestigious Monte Carlo Road Ralley would be held on January 19, 1963.

The choice of Monaco was intended to do two things: first, provide an elegant, exotic backdrop for the

The center of the Landau's roof ornament reveals the same emblem used on the 1962 version. The long-grained texture of the vinyl roof can also be seen in this detail. *Ford Motor Company*

introduction of the 1963-1/2 models, and second, take advantage of the popularity of America's fascination with Princess Grace (formerly Grace Kelly), the Academy Award-winning movie star of the early and mid-1950s who married Prince Rainier of Monaco in April 1956. People from JWT had learned during mid-1962 that she was considering reestablishing her acting career, and preliminary feelers were extended to determine the royal couple's willingness to participate in what would be a promotional opportunity for Ford that could be used by the former actress as well. Following various conversations and protracted negotiations with JWT's Paris operative, Gerald "Jerry" Souhami, the promotion, code-named "Project M" by JWT, was agreed upon, provided that Ford donated a new Falcon Squire wagon (to be outfitted as an ambulance) to the Monaco Red Cross, along with a financial contribution of $10,000.

People from Ford and JWT also wanted to produce a midyear trim option package for the T-bird and provide the princess with a specially trimmed Thunderbird Landau as a gift, but the royal couple rejected the idea of a "Royal Landau" as late as the beginning of December 1962. A compromise was reached when planners for the event, which was to include a fashion show tied in with the unveiling of the new Fords and presentation of the T-bird, agreed to an informal, private ceremony during which Benson Ford would present Prince Rainier with the car. Only 2,000 Limited Edition Landaus were to be assembled, and of those, Prince Rainier was presented with the first car, which

was shipped to Monte Carlo from New York on December 14 along with two Falcon Sprint convertibles, two white Falcon Sprint hardtops, one blue/black Fairlane Sport Coupe, one red/black Galaxie 500/XL Sports Hardtop, and the beige Falcon Squire wagon for the Monaco Red Cross. To distinguish the prince's car from other Limited Edition Landaus, a special silver dash plaque was designed with the crest of the Principality of Monaco (officials from Monaco would not allow the official emblem to be used on the 1,999 other Landaus) and identification that the car was a "Limited Edition Thunderbird Landau," along with a special serial number.

To reinforce the promotion's ties to the principality, the interior studio was commissioned in September 1962 to develop a trim package for the Landau. Originally, a beige exterior was planned (it was Her Serene Highness' favorite color), but after Souhami consulted with Princess Grace on September 19 and reviewed color samples, a white/beige combination was favored. By October 24, Souhami had been sent a sample of the dash plate, final swatches of beige and white leather, Mouton and beige carpet, and a rosewood panel for final approval. On November 2, Souhami relayed to Ford and JWT that "no special suggestions" had been made by the princess, and in a memo dated the same day, the Mouton color was considered for the carpeting.

In Dearborn, the prototype "Limited Edition" model would take form in a modified Corinthian White Landau T-bird trimmed in a unique combination of white leather seat covers; special white door panels with a carpeted lower section matching the dashpad and carpeting in Rose Beige; a white steering wheel with chrome mylar inserts; simulated rosewood appliques for the console, dash and door/quarter panels; and a reddish-brown-colored vinyl roof (though called Rose Beige in advertising, it would actually be darker than the interior components, which were also a slightly browner off-color from the more pinkish shade assigned the name; the roof color was also notorious for fading very badly, which results in some restorers recreating what actually is a sun-bleached hue).

By early November, the prototype Limited Edition Landau (with an incorrect mock-up for the dash plate), a white Hardtop, a convertible, a Sports Roadster, two white Falcon Sprint hardtops, two red Galaxie 500/XL fastbacks, and two blue Fairlane 500 Sport Coupes were forwarded to JWT to be photographed and filmed for the upcoming television commercials and Ford promotional films. The cars were held in storage during the period before the "International Premiere" for use during a rally planned for the visiting automotive press.

The JWT agency put together a package for 175 journalists and other invited guests to fly to Monte Carlo from Detroit on the evening of January 2 for a grand party to witness the unveiling, which cost Ford an estimated

Also from the late June photo sessions, this 1963 Sports Roadster is missing the front fender emblem and is wearing 1962-style solid center spinners. Early ads for the Roadster would continue to use the 1962-style caps until the plastic-centered 1963 versions could be obtained. Some of the early 1963s were delivered with solid centers. *Ford Motor Company*

Very late in the pre-approval schedule, a fiberglass mock-up of a 1963 Landau was studied with 1962-style solid center spinners on 1963 wheel covers, Sports Roadster emblems, and no door trim, along with a painted forward roof section. This may have been a preliminary study for the "Sunbonnet" removable roof panel. *Ford Motor Company*

$75,000. Robert Lacey notes in his book on Ford that this took on an all-night-party atmosphere for Iaccoca and his guests, with champagne flowing from the time two chartered airliners left the ground in Detroit to the time they touched down in southern France. Even as they attended a 10:00 a.m. audience with Princess Grace at the Grimaldi family palace, the drinking still continued. During the day, all the cars were on display on a terrace behind the Monte Carlo Casino, and Prince Rainier drove his new Landau from the palace to the show.

At the end of the trip, Car Marketing Manager Frank E. Zimmerman had 900,000 direct-mail pieces sent from Monaco to prospective customers in the United States to call attention to the "Monaco" Landau. Back in the United States, magazine advertising was reaching newsstands touting the car, and in the February 15 issue of *Vogue*, a special advertising layout showcased the Thunderbird hardtop, convertible, and Monaco Landau along with various female models wearing designer fashions. The climax of the promotional campaign would come on February 17, when Ford would cosponsor an hour-long special on CBS Television, *Tour of Monaco*, preempting Ed Sullivan with a presentation featuring Princess Grace giving a tour of the principality, along with a heavy dose of advertising for the new Fords. The first Monaco Landaus were officially made available in showrooms on February 22. To further pro-

Side profile of the Italien dated October 12, 1962. The car would be displayed on the custom car show circuit through mid-1963 and eventually sold in the Los Angeles area. *Ford Motor Company*

mote the cars, Limited Edition cars numbers 2 through 19 were sent to sales districts for displays at auto shows around the United States Some believe these cars were shipped to Monaco as part of the promotion, but their build dates fall after the January 3 show. No record can be found indicating a shipment of these cars to Monaco.

Bowing Out Gracefully

The tie-in from the Monaco Landau did not help boost sales of the Sports Roadster, so by spring 1963 planners were seriously considering dropping the option. Finally, the decision was made that the extremely low volume of sales for the model did not justify its continuance, and it was killed for 1964. Stories have been related to the author that dealers were informed during April that new orders were subject to availability of components; some dealers were forced to fill orders for Roadsters by using convertibles to which they added, piece by piece, the necessary parts to create Roadster "clones."

Thunderbird Killers

Meanwhile, the threat of direct competition had finally materialized, and ironically it would be named after the area adjoining Monaco, the Riviera. The Buick Riviera was conceived as a T-bird killer by GM's styling chief

Bill Mitchell. From day one, the Riviera was compared with the latest T-birds by the GM Styling Center. Each of GM's divisions, save for Chevrolet, wanted to lay claim to the car, but the eventual winner would be Buick, which would furnish the 325hp Wildcat 401ci motor and Turbine Drive automatic transmission.

Chevrolet was exploring its own T-bird killer at the same time by making Corvette a four-place car for 1963 with the fastback Sting Ray being designed by Larry Shinoda (who would also work briefly for Ford during the fifteen-month tenure of Semon E. "Bunkie" Knudsen in 1968–69, playing a hand in the Boss-series Mustangs). The four-place 'Vette was compared with a '62 T-bird hardtop for layout and packaging and almost made it to production. This idea would die just before final approval was given because Mitchell disliked the lack of headroom and rear legroom in the car, and getting into the rear seats was difficult for the tall gentleman. Vestiges of the four-seat proposal were left in the Sting-Ray, primarily in the center body structure.

General Motors was relying on exclusivity with the first edition of the Riviera. From the beginning, GM boasted that only 40,000 of the four-seaters would be constructed for 1963, but after that there would be no holding back. Undoubtedly, the T-bird suffered a loss of sales at the hands of the Riv, as well as GM's other full-size

Starting life as a 1963 convertible, the Italien fastback was styled by members of Ford's design studios to explore a fastback T-bird. It was built by a private contractor for the Ford Custom Caravan. The front reveals the custom-made egg crate grille and reuse of the 1962 prototype hood trim, while the body side trim contains fake fender air extractors and ribbed aluminum. *Ford Motor Company*

Rear view of the Italien. The roof and rear deck lid were made of fiberglass, and custom taillight lenses were made. Letters on the deck lid are the same as what would be used on the hood of the 1964 T-bird. *Ford Motor Company*

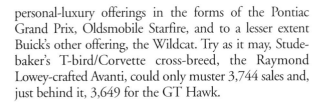

personal-luxury offerings in the forms of the Pontiac Grand Prix, Oldsmobile Starfire, and to a lesser extent Buick's other offering, the Wildcat. Try as it may, Studebaker's T-bird/Corvette cross-breed, the Raymond Lowey-crafted Avanti, could only muster 3,744 sales and, just behind it, 3,649 for the GT Hawk.

Flight of Fancy

The future of the Thunderbird was well in-hand for the next generation by the summer of 1962, but marketing and its promotional staff wanted to evaluate the feasibility of a third body style for the T-bird, a fastback. Development of the '63-1/2 models with their semi-fastback themes were nearing completion, and marketing hoped to field a group of customized Fords to tour the country during the winter and spring of 1962–63 at International Show Car Association (ISCA) events. The Ford Custom Car Caravan would allow designers to present potential styling themes for public reaction, from which they could develop modifications for the next-applicable models and promote the use of Ford products as the basis for customizing efforts. A Fairlane hardtop, a Galaxie 500 convertible, and a T-bird convertible were among the cars that had been selected for modification. The Fairlane received the Sunbonnet modification, while the Galaxie was

This interior view of the Italien shows a reuse of the center console trim from the prototype hardtop, custom-fabricated chromed floor rub strips, engine-turned door trim inserts, and a unique upholstery pattern on the dark red leather seats. The dash pad was also sheathed in a sewn leather cover. *Ford Motor Company*

Front end detail of the 1963 convertible owned by Donald J. Chase of Omaha, Nebraska. Purchased new by Chase during mid-1963, his original plans to buy a Roadster were thwarted by a Columbus, Ohio, dealer who advised him that the Roadster package could not be ordered late in the model year. Instead, all components except for the wire wheels (which came years later) were obtained and placed on the car. *Alan Tast photo*

out-sourced to created the Astro. The T-bird, to be named Italien, was also out-sourced, but its design was crafted by Ford stylists.

A production convertible was brought to the design center during September 1963 to serve as the basis for the fastback T-bird, and the car was subsequently stripped of all convertible components. Modelers constructed a wood form over which clay was applied and shaped to create the fastback, abbreviated rear deck lid, and inner quarter panels, from which plaster casts were made. Once the casts could be removed, they were laid up with fiberglass and plastic resin to create the roof, rear deck lid, and other parts for the car. The roof was held in place by sheet metal screws along the windshield header and at the rear.

The interior was trimmed in red leather. A new rear package shelf was also formed from fiberglass with built-in headrests, and door panels were fitted with engine-turned inserts. A unique ribbed console plate was fabricated that contained only two power window switches, since the rear windows were fixed, and chrome-plated "scuff strips" were used on the floor.

Outside, the Italien was painted Candy Apple Red and was fitted with '62-style wire wheels and spinners, a

A good view of the tonneau cover on Chase's car reveals the clearance between the top of the back seat and the bottom of the headrest. *Alan Tast photo*

118

Standing out within the Silver Mink engine bay, this authentic M-series Sports Roadster owned by C.T. and Carol Robertson of Newberry Park, California, shows off its oval, aluminum air cleaner and myriad plated parts. The car was owned by Carol's father who bought it new in 1962. It was passed down to C.T. and Carol and was restored during the mid-1990s. *Alan Tast photo*

The grab bar that came with the Sports Roadster package was a two-piece affair with a chrome-plated base which bolted to the underside of the passenger-side dash cove and a ribbed, vinyl-covered pad. *Alan Tast photo*

The engine bay of Chase's Roadster conversion. The chrome-plated components on four-barrel cars are a subject of controversy. While no engine dress-up kit including a plated four-barrel air cleaner for the T-bird is indicated in sales and parts literature, others claim that it was offered. Most probably, dealers may have had them plated and installed parts of the Galaxie's brightwork package. Another possible scenario is that cars with the M-series package, when replaced by dealers, were given a plated four-barrel air cleaner to match the Sports V-8's standard chromed valve covers, oil breather, and master cylinder caps, power steering fluid reservoir cover, etc. *Alan Tast photo*

Buick's 1963 Riviera would represent the first true Thunderbird competition from General Motors. To encourage exclusivity, Buick arbitrarily limited production to 40,000 cars in its first year. Undoubtedly, the Riviera ate into third generation T-bird sales, then at the end of its three-year body-style cycle. *Buick Division*

brushed-aluminum appliqué on the door, and a set of mock fender vents behind the front-wheel cutout. The radiator grille was made from dovetailed strips of aluminum, and the wide hood molding and long-wingspan 'Bird were salvaged from the '62 prototype. At the rear, individual letters spelling THUNDERBIRD were applied (they would be prototypes for the hood letters used for 1964), and a custom set of taillight lenses with a chromed T-bird in the center (similar to the emblem in the center of the steering wheel medallion) was installed.

The car was met with rave reviews from customizers and the industry press. Speculation that a fastback T-bird might go into production began to follow its display but that never happened. While the Italien was being built, a copy of the roof was made for a fiberglass study of the 1964–65 T-bird. The study was photographed, but the idea was not pursued any further. Following its retirement from the show circuit, unlike most Ford show/concept cars that are scrapped, the Italien was sold to Dale Robertson, son of actor Cliff Robertson. In the late 1980s, it was acquired by noted Ford collector Don Chambers of Los Angeles.

Finishing Touches

With a mix of old and new in the '63 T-bird, it would only be a matter of time before problems cropped up. The new alternator system made noise, and taillamps on cars built before October 15, 1962, were not properly ground-

ed, which resulted in a production change to incorporate a grounding wire. The engine was subjected to several changes during the model year, such as replacement of the camshaft thrust button used on earlier FE-series motors with a thrust plate at the beginning of '63 production. During November 1962, a variety of engine modifications were made to increase the durability of the assembly, including the use of heavier connecting rods and crankshafts, plus reinforcing ribs cast into the block's water jackets. On February 1, 1963, according to Technical Service Bulletin Number 6006-20 dated March 18, 1963, the standard Z-series 390ci motor was slated to be fitted with the higher compression and freer breathing C2SZ-6049-B cylinder head (used on the M-series and the P-code Police Interceptor engines). The high-compression heads were identified with the casting code C2SE-B or -C, omitting the 6090 reference number, as used on the lower-compression C1AE-6090-series heads.

The convertible top, which by 1963 was trouble-free, was changed with the replacement of various parts, such as the center side rails, for larger hinge pins. The main wiring harness from the firewall to the headlights, as well as the alternator to voltage regulator loom was changed on March 7, and eleven days later the door-lock and ignition-switch cylinders were changed as well. One of the last changes, on March 19, 1963, modified the door panels in the area of the finger cup used to pull the doors closed; the semi-elliptical form changed to a

The 1963 Pontiac Grand Prix retained its austere exterior and power-packed drivetrain and remained a challenge to cars such as the M-series T-bird. *Pontiac Historical Services*

narrow rectangular trough for the remainder of production.

The most common customer complaint was about the operation of the hydraulic wipers, which were prone to poor operation if dirt or other foreign matter got into the power steering fluid and up to the wiper motor. Another sore spot was still the power steering gear, but by now the problem was identified to be bad piston seals, which dealers could repair. Production-line problems such as a limited run of power-brake linkages that were too short, power window switches that were improperly wired, and the usual assortment of buzzes, squeaks, and groans were not unknown to '63 owners as well. Overall, though, Ford's desire for high quality control for both the Lincoln and T-bird would result in one of the best-built cars in the industry.

This unique Monaco Landau interior featured white leather seat skins, Rosewood-like dash panels, unique door panels with carpet on the bottom portion, and a host of other differences. It represented a premium option package that was overlooked by collectors for many years. Today, Monaco Landaus in like-new condition can be quite valuable. *Ford Motor Company*

Close of an Era

Cessation of '63 T-bird production on July 17, 1963, was the end of an era for the T-bird. With the halting of the assembly line, the Sports Roadster was dead, as was "Total Performance" and the M-series motors. Within a month, a reskinned platform would run down the same conveyor lines, to be called the 1964 Thunderbird.

Chapter 11

SYNTHESIS OF DESIGN

By 1964, at least one of the American marques, Studebaker, was in its death throes, having failed to gain the public's confidence that it could match the quality of the Big Three. American Motors was carving its niche in economy and specialty markets with the Rambler line. Chrysler was adapting, having retained the services of former Ford designer Elwood Engel, and was building a more acceptable (and more marketable) line of automobiles. General Motors was doing well, very much the top dog of the automotive community, but the company had its hands full with all the competition coming from Highland Park and Dearborn. Ford, on the other hand, was about ready to prove that evolution was one thing, but revolution was another!

Bringing the Fourth Generation to Life

The fourth generation Thunderbird would be the last to owe its parentage to Robert S. McNamara. When it was being designed, the whiz kid of Ford and vice president of car and truck operations was on the verge of becoming president of the company and, in a very short time, he would attempt to take on the Pentagon for the Kennedy administration. Two days before McNamara was named president, a meeting of the Product Planning Committee reviewed four specific proposals for the next generation T-bird. Three of the proposals were completely new, while the fourth was, in essence, an exterior facelift of the platform just placed in production.

Proposal A: An All-New Car with FWD

This car would have the same overall length as the '61 T-bird, but with a longer (38in versus 35in) and wider front end to accommodate a 62.5in front tread and maximum interchangeability with the Lincoln Continental. Engineering was proceeding with work on the package.

Proposal B: An All-New Car with Conventional Drive

This car's size would be similar to "the minimum compatible with 1960 Thunderbird seating and general level of styling complexity," with reduced length a possibility (down to 200in versus 205in) and a width reduction from 75.9in to 75in. It would have no significant interchangeability with the Continental, except for the engine and some suspension components.

Proposal C: New Body with Carryover Chassis and Underbody

A car with package dimensions essentially the same as those of the '61 T-bird, since it would use the same floor and underbody. Although it would be the least-costly of the schemes, it would not allow for new engine and suspension systems. Interchangeability with Lincoln would be very limited.

Proposal D: A Modification of Proposal B

This car was similar to Proposal B, with increased proportions to allow for interchangeability with the Continental's engine, front suspension, front end structure, dash and cowl top panel, and underbody components. Its wheelbase would increase from 113in to 126in. Engineering had begun preliminary design work on this example.

The proposals each had their plusses and minuses. Proposals B and D for an all-new car were ruled out due to the desire to keep costs down, but they could be exploited for development of the Lincoln. Proposal A with FWD could create an all-new concept for the T-bird, much as the '58 T-bird did in the change from two- to four-seater. The low-budget route, Proposal C, would require some thought on how to get more mileage out of what would be by that time a three-year-old design.

Proposal A was being considered due to the development work on the FWD project being explored by Fred Hooven's staff at that moment. A week after the November 7 meeting, McNamara, then second in command to Henry Ford II, would sit in on a presentation on the FWD to consider flat-floor proposals for the new car as a way to increase passenger capacity. One suggestion was to reposition the engine and transmission by moving them

An advanced proposal for the 1964 T-bird from March 27, 1961, reveals influences from the 1958–60 models with the headlight cove and body line running back through the door and the high-riding 1961-style grille. A Lincolnesque, slab-sided rear quarter, complete with kick-up around the door handle, provides a hint toward one of the directives from late-1960 for interchangeability between the two lines. *Ford Motor Company*

Almost eighteen months after the first proposals were reviewed, a portion of the 1964 door skin shows up on a 1961 T-bird mule in the Design Center, in this case to evaluate the use of fake air "waste gates" and the ever-present roof flipper panel. The door lacks a vent window, perhaps hinting at a move to do away with the assembly. *Ford Motor Company*

Even though shown on prototype cars, a handgrab in the door's arm rest was deleted from production, leaving people to use the pistol-grip-styled door handle to pull the door closed. To correct this oversight, an add-on pull strap was offered through dealers after midyear to those who asked for it. This example is on a late-production Landau. *Alan Tast photo*

forward 5.3in, tilting both downward to allow for a middle front seat passenger, or a combination of the two. Another proposal suggested that a turbocharged engine could be repositioned forward, and used in conjunction with a full bowed shaft transaxle. In each of these schemes, McNamara saw that a major expenditure of funds would be needed to test the concepts, and even more if it were to go into production.

A flat-floor T-bird was not the way to go, it was reasoned at the time because of the cost of developing the new platform and because the T-bird had become recognized for its high-tunnel four-passenger concept. Designers such as Joe Oros and Bill Boyer lobbied successfully against the flat-floor T-bird, and by the time McNamara was in Washington, D.C., Proposal C was far and away the front-runner. Four years later, their decision would come back to haunt them.

The Molting Process

Work on reskinning would consume most of the design staff's time through 1961 to prepare a final model for preliminary approval by November. One of the preliminary efforts focused on restyling the front end by mid-March 1961, but this would only serve to help with the facelift of the '63 T-bird. A second design development proposal would stretch into September as the '64 T-bird's shape became recognizable, with side sculpturing suggesting some of the developments in advanced design's work on two-seat concept cars. Aside from this, movement was being made toward an overall design with recognizable T-bird themes: the dual-pontooning of the rear end seen in the second and third generations and a pointed prow from 1961–63 with hints of 1958–60's hooded headlights. Updated in more angular form, this synthesis of the best of the past two generations came off very well. Concessions to more mainstream ideas also appeared: conventional door handles instead of the fin-integrated

Photographed on January 31, 1963, was a fiberglass-bodied, see-through proposal for the 1964 Sports Roadster with the Sports Tonneau cover and slightly modified Sports Roadster emblem on the forward portion of the front fender. The fake air extractors that appeared in the late-September 1962 photo are now refined, and 1963 components (script and wheel covers, which have been given a black accent color between the ribs instead of the 1963's Argent Silver) are present on the model. Because of poor sales, the Sports Roadster would not return for 1964, though the tonneau cover would be offered. *Ford Motor Company photo, William A. Wonder collection*

hand-grabs, flat instead of curved side glass, and for the first time, a nonfunctional hood scoop.

Exterior ornamentation was kept very simple, limited to the now-traditional C-pillar 'Bird (which was repeated in the oblong taillight lenses), reuse of the '63 T-bird's stylized script on the front fender behind the wheel cut-out, and block letters on the hood (previewed on the Italien show car). In the middle of the rear bumper, a metal-framed plastic insert carried the Thunderbird name, and below, a painted lower valence marked the T-bird's first departure from the traditional Ford edict of no sheet metal below the bumper. Back-up lights were housed in two metal-framed pods below the center of the turn signals. On the front fenders, a pair of chromed bullet-shaped housings contained rearward-facing lights that were wired into the turn signals. Instead of relying on indicators in the dash, the driver had to look at these assemblies to determine if his blinkers were working, and which side was on.

Body side vents were explored during the design phase. A paper profile photographed in late September 1961 included a scoop between the rear quarter "finlets" ahead of the rear wheelhouse (a similar treatment would later be found on the 1964-1/2 Mustang). By midsummer 1962, front-fender air extractors were regularly featured on clay models and renderings that resembled the

This press release photo of the 1964 convertible, probably shot during June 1963, shows the car in its final form with standard wheel covers; the long-base, exterior, remote-control rear-view mirror; and nameplate behind the front wheel opening. *Ford Motor Company*

'62 Falcon Futura's simulated ornamentation. By October 1962 they were abandoned, but the idea would be used in another form on the facelift for the '65 T-bird.

Inside, the car took on a whole new look. Drawing on elements of early proposals for the 1958 T-bird program, interior-studio head Art Querfeld spearheaded the drive for a mix between jet cockpit and cocktail lounge. Front seats were put on a bulk-reduction program, resulting in "thin-shell" construction, which added a little legroom for back passengers. A move into the world of multifunctionality was made with an optional passenger seat that had an adjustable back cushion. By lifting up a lever on the outboard side, the back could be reclined to a nearly flat position, and the upper portion could be pulled away and extended about 6in. This trick seat was not placed into production cars until November 1, 1963, according to an in-house memo, and the power passenger seat was also delayed until September 15 due to engineering changes.

The rear seats were a story in themselves. Envisioning an interior that wrapped passengers in comfort, Querfeld curved the back cushion from the quarter trim panel into the traditional cushion, and placed a fold-down armrest in the center. The desire was to gain legroom by encouraging passengers to sit "side-saddle," but the high driveshaft tunnel and return to a full-length console negated any significant improvement. According to comments from Querfeld and Boyer, the wraparound was a difficult

proposition to make work, but by going with vertical pleating, the back could be made in three separate panels, and the joint between the wraparound cushion and the back panel could be made virtually unnoticeable. To further integrate the interior, said Najjar, who took over final interior development as executive stylist of the interior studio in June 1962 when Querfeld was reassigned, "The door trim panels flowed from the instrument panel toward the rear of the vehicle and swept around the front seats into the cove rear seat."

Dash construction moved away from the dual-cowl theme by making the pad stretch across the width of the interior, serving as a hood for instruments and the passenger's side. Querfeld didn't want to interrupt the passenger's cove with a glovebox, so it again (as on the 1961–63 T-bird) was placed between the front seats in the console. Heeding complaints that the '61 T-bird's tray was too shallow, a storage bin was made by raising the height of the box. Like in the 1961–63, an ashtray and cigar lighter were placed forward of the compartment, hidden by a airfoil-like metal door with a satin finish. Moving up the console, power-window switches and a new seat-belt warning light occupied the flat area; a trim plate for the console face traversed up the dashboard and flowed toward the driver, containing the convertible top switch, heater/air-conditioner controls, a choice of an AM or AM-FM radio, the air-conditioner register (when

125

The Mustang, which was introduced to the public on April 17, 1964, owed much to the classic and vintage Thunderbirds for its birth. It rode on a 108in wheelbase (which was originally proposed for the 1958 T-bird), with standard front bucket seats (an optional bench was available). It was also a conceptual descendant from the aborted XT-bird program of 1961. Styled and engineered by people who had also worked on several of the previous T-bird programs, past influences from the early 195H models of nine years previous included the high-mouth grille opening and C-scallop in the body. This early pre-introduction version lacks the two horizontal bars that flanked the running horse emblem's "corral." The Mustang's range of options could put the best-equipped models in line with the T-birds of the time. *Ford Motor Company*

installed) and the headlight switch. A three-segment panel was devised to fill in the slot created for the Swing-Away column. For hardtop and convertible models, the inverted "L" would receive a brushed aluminum-like finish, while a woodgrain appliqué was used for the Landau.

Instrumentation took on a futuristic feel: Housed in four pods, analog gauges replaced "idiot lights" for the ammeter and oil-pressure indicators, and fuel-level and water-temperature units also occupied separate housings, which Najjar called "independent clear spheres." The speedometer was the most unconventional part of the package: Instead of a round dial face, designers and engineers created unique linear arrangement, with large numerals above a chrome-rimmed slit. Inside the speedometer head, a metal drum, painted with a tapered orange band, would be turned by the speedometer gearbox; as the car moved faster, the orange band appeared to lengthen.

Below the middle of the dash-pad overhang, a housing was placed for windshield wiper/washer and air-vent controls, map lights, and a clock—originally planned as a digital unit with numbers on reels, reverted to the more traditional sweep hands. As an added bonus for those who would specify its inclusion, a series of round lenses and toggle switches could be placed between the pod and the top of the dash/console trim. Called a Safety Convenience Panel, the option included a flashing light to warn that the fuel tank was one-eighth full or lower, that a door was ajar, and in conjunction with one of the switches, turn on a four-way emer-

gency flasher. A second toggle switch activated a vacuum-operated door-lock system, first used in the '63 T-bird on an optional basis. An additional safety-convenience feature, retractable front seat belts with a warning light in the console, reached production late on September 23, 1963. A memo dated August 30, 1963, noted that 635 early cars did not have the warning light, and about 2,000 cars would need to have the retractable seat belts added by selling dealers.

Interim Engineering

Under the skin, not much was new. Noticeable changes included adoption of low-profile tires on 15in wheels (with drum brakes carried over from '63), "bear-hug" door latches that gripped a stud protruding from the rear door jamb, an automatic parking brake release that was tripped by shifting the transmission out of park, and a redesigned integral power-steering gearbox to cure problems associated with the 1961–63 design. Transistorized ignition, first offered on '63 Galaxies with the 427ci motor, was made an option for the T-bird's only engine choice, the 390 with a four-barrel carb.

Big news copied in concept from the Mercedes-Benz 300SL was a feature called Silent-Flo ventilation, available for hardtops and Landaus. Under the rear window, a plenum with a vacuum-operated pair of doors was placed. With the car moving forward, the doors could be opened by flipping a lever on the console, and the negative air pressure in the area behind the window and grillework for the plenum would pull interior air out through the slotted package shelf.

Another big break was the redesign of the trunk area. Even though original plans were to reuse the 1961–63 platform, referral to owner surveys for the '61 T-bird revealed that owners wanted more trunk space. This was achieved by going to a deep-well design, which forced them to move the gas tank to behind the rear axle. The new trunk volume of 11.5cu-ft could hold more luggage, but getting items in and out would be tough because the rear bumper/taillight panel was at the same height as the top of the rear fenders. The well would also prove to be rust prone because hardtops and Landaus became notorious for having wet trunk floors. The deck lid was redesigned to control water condensing on the inside face, and several service bulletins pinpointing leak sources around the Silent-Flo assembly and its drain hoses (which would get plugged with debris) would help to stem the severity of the problem, but 1964–66 T-birds would all be plagued with this flaw.

Even though trunk capacity was increased, it would not be enough to help the convertible's chronic storage problem. In the convertible, the spare tire was mounted in the well and ate up what extra space was left (hardtops and Landaus had the tire placed under the package tray/Silent-Flo plenum and out of the way). The top's electrical nerve-center of relays would remain behind the rear seat on the floor above the rear axle.

The Buick Wildcat, introduced in 1962 as a midprice sporty coupe on par with the T-bird, was clearly a full-size car which lacked the compactness of the T-bird but gave passengers more room, not to mention a usable trunk if a convertible was ordered. *Buick Division*

Death of the Sports Roadster

Design work on a Sports Roadster for 1964 had pretty much been completed by spring 1963. Like the '62 and '63 versions, a fiberglass tonneau cover, wire wheels, grab bar, and special emblems were developed, but the decision by division at the end of May 1963 to kill the option was based on declining sales—only one-third as many had been ordered in 1963 as compared to the year before (sales of the '62 Sports Roadster also hadn't covered development costs, it must be remembered). The price premium for Roadster-specific items, research found, was scaring away buyers. People liked the tonneau cover, but if more than two people needed to ride along, the cover had to be removed and stored somewhere. Wire wheels, though they looked nice, had a history of problems (including collapsing) and required the use of inner tubes (which was a dying technology for passenger cars) and were hard to clean.

If people wanted the tonneau, marketers argued, let them buy it. Again, Najjar and "Bud" Kaufman developed a new version of the cover, and it was rather striking: Headrests were carried back into fairings by a padded vinyl segment, separated from painted surfaces by stainless steel moldings. Available as either a factory or dealer-installed option, the now renamed Sports Tonneau Cover reached final production—redesigned Sports Roadster emblems and the grab-bar never got beyond the prototype stage. Wire wheels were a simple carryover for any '64 T-bird, so a convertible owner could order just the tonneau, both the tonneau and the wheels, or just the wheels and forget the cover.

Various buyers would do just as was predicted: The tonneau was ordered both with and without the wheels. According to invoices collected by Eminger, at least forty-five cars were provided from the factory with the pair. But are they Sports Roadsters? Technically, no, for several reasons: the model designation 76B/89 had been dropped at the end of '63 production, factory literature made no mention of a Sports Roadster package for 1964, the tonneau could be ordered separately, and prerequisites for recognition as a Roadster—distinct emblems and dash-mounted "sissy" bar—were not provided. As the years wore on, confused would-be owners and fast-talking hucksters would promulgate the myth that a Sports Roadster was available for '64 and even later, and availability of reproduction tonneau covers and look-alike wire wheels would help to aggravate the problem.

Taking Wing

Development in design from beginning to final body-engineering models took place from February 1961 through July 1962, and engineering would continue with work on tooling and prototype development into the spring of 1963. By April 1963, running prototypes were photographed in studios to begin artwork for the owner's and shop manuals, and from May through mid July, a few were taken to California for location photography.

Production of the '64 T-bird began on August 12, 1963, almost three weeks after shut-down of '63 production. Public introduction for the car took place at dealerships on September 27, 1963. At the same time, competitor Buick would also introduce its Riviera, which was not much changed from the previous year's version. Unlike the T-bird, which was back to a single engine and drivetrain choice, the new Riv offered as standard the 340hp 425ci Wildcat 465 V-8, with a dual four-barrel carburetor option to raise output to 360hp.

To promote the '64 T-bird, television advertising was structured by JWT's Thunderbird staff to play off the interior's aircraft-like styling. Featuring a commercial airliner pilot complete with braided-cuff blazer, wings and hat, viewers were treated to jet-engine sound effects, with a background voice going through a preflight checklist of Thunderbird features. The link of flying and driving would be difficult to shake, but it created memorable images of T-birds "flying" in the clouds.

Another promotional move was the exhibition of a new customized T-bird show car, called the Golden Palomino. In essence a stock Landau, it was fitted with the often-proposed-but-never-adopted "flipper" panels, vinyl half-roof, a golden brown metallic paint scheme, Kelsey-Hayes wire wheels, fender skirts, and custom interior appointments. As in the previous year's Ford Custom Caravan showing at ISCA and other popular custom-car shows, the Palomino served to evaluate future design features and spur interest in the new T-bird.

The '64 T-bird's mostly new status would earn it a lot of exposure in enthusiast magazines in road tests and reviews. *Car and Driver* (formerly *Sports Car Illustrated* would get in their obligatory slam of the nonsports car, while *Motor Trend* would lump the T-bird together with the Falcon and Galaxie and proclaim the '64 Ford lineup as the Cars of the Year for their February 1964 issue. By April, another Ford product would make this statement very true.

Internal Competition: The Mustang

The midyear program for Ford in 1964 would only focus on one model, with no special edition T-birds. On April 17, 1964, Lee Iaccoca presided over debut of the four-place/2+2 Ford Mustang. It was instantly recognized as a breakthrough in the marketplace—an inexpensive, compact coupe or convertible with the ability to be optioned up into a "baby T-bird" or a hard-charging street racer. The car owed its roots to demand for a two-seater T-bird (the pink '57 T-bird owned by Wayne and Lois Eminger was even borrowed for comparison-making). Sharing Falcon's platform, Mustang captured the imagination of millions, and by the end of its first year had surpassed the 700,000-sales record for introductory models set by its mother, the '60 Falcon/Comet.

Planning for the new Mustang began during 1961 as part of Iaccoca's initial review of the direction of the Ford Division. Part of the process involved Iaccoca's belief that a sporty car was needed (shades of Crusoe in 1953). One quick way would be through a rework of the two-seat T-bird and mounting it on a Falcon floorpan. With Falcon and previous T-bird Product Planner Tom Case as liaison, a dialogue was established with the Budd Co. to determine if the T-bird dies were still usable, and if they could be altered for what would be called the XT-bird. By summer 1961, a '57 T-bird body was modified to take on a more contemporary look and mated to a Falcon chassis, but the look was still too dated. In the end, Ford decided that it

would be better to start fresh, and the idea was shelved.

The XT-bird project would begin a chain of events that eventually resulted in the Mustang I midengine sports car, the Allegro and Avventura four-seat cars (two facing forward, two facing back), and the Mustang II/Cougar. Designers of the Mustang would draw on various aspects of these cars, as well as the 1958 T-bird program for such things as the high-mouth grille, side scallops, and the high driveshaft-tunnel arrangement.

The Mustang's success would lead to a sales and PR boost for Ford, but would it hurt the T-bird? At the lower end of the sales spectrum, a fully optioned Mustang convertible with a power-assisted top could carry the same number of people, offer virtually the same options, and allow for trunk space that the T-bird didn't have with the top down! It would also be stingier on gas, easier to park, and just as eye-catching. Price-wise, a fully loaded Mustang could still beat the T-bird, but barely.

The Problems with Being New

The '64 T-bird had its share of new-model teething pains, but none were as serious as the all-new Speed Control. First proposed (and even advertised in sales literature) for the '63 T-bird, problems were to hold it back a year. Regretfully, problems remained with the option, and became highlighted in a freak accident that took the lives of two people. Investigation of the mishap, where the speed-control-equipped T-bird failed to stop after the driver applied the brake, pointed to a failure to disengage of the vacuum connection to the servo unit. Ford immediately ordered disconnection of Speed Controls already in the field, and by June 8, 1964, it had been revised with a new release switch, actuator, and cable assembly.

A variety of squeaks, creaks, and groans led engineers to also investigate and fix ill-fitting and improperly installed or designed components. Loose radiator fan clutches on cars built before October 21, 1963, created problems for warranty adjusters when water pump shafts began to fail. By February 1964, most service garages were notified, and the defect corrected. A modification of the standard exterior rear-view mirror used before January 31, 1964, would require a field fix by the use of electrician's tape to fix rattles. Thankfully for dealers and new owners, problems weren't as serious as they were in previous years.

Many updated and revised items were fed into the production line at Wixom, and as in any substitution process, these would deal fits to restorers long after dealers stopped stocking parts. On September 1, 1963, the convertible's main pivot support base was revised, along with the folding top's main pivot bracket. A month later, the main pivot support was again modified. By the end of September 1963, front-seat track shields with a beveled rear edge had superseded square-edged shields, the accelerator pedal rod had received a roller-tipped end, and the

Oldsmobile's Starfire for 1964 continued to emphasize the performance aspect of personal luxury, pumping out 45 more horsepower than the advertised 300hp of the T-bird's mill. Declining sales of this model would make it a near nonplayer by 1966. *Oldsmobile Historical Center*

console/radio access panel had been altered. Between October and the end of the year, the master-cylinder brake booster, turn-indicator switch and plate assembly, convertible windshield header-dowel striker, windshield-washer and fresh-air-duct control handles, back-window-housing drain nozzle for the hardtop, and lower instrument panel center molding were all changed in production.

In early 1964, the radiator was reduced 3/4in in width and 1/4in in height and thickness; the pulley fan spacer was also reduced in thickness. On January 6, 1964, the back-up light assembly was changed to allow for simplified installation in production (with a resultant change in the lamp body and lens door) and the air-conditioning condenser core was revised. A month later, the evaporator expansion valve was also modified. The door-lock control linkage was changed at the beginning of March, and by the beginning of May the main wiring loom under the dash had been altered, the front li-

cense-plate bracket had been eliminated, the metal line from the fuel pump to the carburetor had been lengthened almost 1/2in, and tubes from the exhaust manifold to the carburetor and air cleaner also had been stretched.

Last Hurrah?

By the time production was shut down briefly on July 24, 1964, for '65 changeover, 92,465 T-birds had been built at Wixom, making 1964 the second-best year ever. Convertible production was up sharply from 1963 with 9,198 being assembled, just under 10 percent of production (9.95 percent). Demand for the T-bird was not going to get much better. Buick's Riviera couldn't even manage the previous year's set moratorium of 40,000; only 37,658 would be built, in part because the new Thunderbird cost Buick sales. However, the pattern of previous generations were about to be repeated for 1965.

Chapter 12

THE MORE THINGS CHANGE, THE MORE THEY STAY THE SAME

The year 1965 marked a milestone for the Thunderbird: On October 22, 1964, Ford officially celebrated the car's tenth birthday in Las Vegas, Nevada, with a party, complete with a large cake. Frank E. Zimmerman, Jr., Ford Division's general marketing manager, hosted more than 150 dealers who were being honored for their performance in selling the car. In a quote from the *Las Vegas Review-Journal* (which was reprinted in the CTCI's November-December 1965 *Early Bird* magazine), Zimmerman stated in classic press-release fashion, "The Thunderbird has been the most imitated car in the industry during its first decade, from the distinctive roofline beginning with the original two-seater to the '65 model's sequential taillights."

As the '65 model year was beginning, the nation was in the middle of a philosophical tug-of-war between presidential candidate Senator Barry Goldwater of Arizona (a T-bird enthusiast with a modified '55) and President Lyndon Baines Johnson. The personal-luxury market was also being torn at the seams—not just by the T-bird, Riviera, and the competing middle-priced "bucket-bombs" such as Grand Prix, Mercury Marauder, and the Chrysler 300, but also from the lower-priced Chevrolet Caprice and Ford LTD. Studebaker's GT Hawk was gone, and imported cars were not quite in the same league. Market share for the T-bird would more than ever emphasize the word "share."

Mildly Warmed Over

As with every other generation of T-bird, the second year of a three-year cycle meant limited change to take the most advantage of tooling that was already in place. Minor changes in trim, ornamentation, and chassis design could be expected, but not much more. As the '65 T-bird

The prototype 1965 convertible, captured on film a few weeks earlier, has the optional three-bladed spinner wheel covers. Wire wheels would not be carried over as in 1964 because the 14in wire wheel's rims would not clear the new dual-piston front disc brakes. It was decided not to proceed with a 15in version due to cost and warranty concerns. *Ford Motor Company*

The prototype 1965 hardtop was brought into the photography studio on June 8, 1964, for its turn under the bright lights. Like the 1959 and 1962 T-birds, budgetary restrictions left little room for more than a few changes in trim and emblems, including placing a "corral" around the roof's 'Bird. The addition of a suggested fender vent moved the revised script back to the rear quarter. This car was shown with the standard wheel covers. *Ford Motor Company*

program was phased into the design schedule for 1962–63, car lines were being dramatically restructured. Since the T-bird had been the recipient of much of the styling and engineering departments' attention during 1961–62, little time would be budgeted for it.

Among the first options considered for the '65 T-bird was a restyled roof. The Italien was being developed during the same period, so a copy of its roof casting was placed on a fiberglass styling model of a '64 or '65 T-bird for evaluation. While it looked good to many with its rakish appearance, it would be rejected as being "too sporty" for the prestige image being cultivated for the car. Thus, stylists went back to the drawing board, and in between coming up with the new Fords and Mercurys, had a facelift ready for approval by mid-1963.

The air extractors that had been contemplated for the '64 T bird were worked into a fake front-fender reverse scoop on the '65, made by indenting the fender along the body feature line and trimming with a chrome-plated casting outlining the rim and a series of five "vanes" trailing rearward. The simulated extractors displaced the script, now with even more flourish, to the rear quarter panel. Enlarged T-birds graced the hood and the rear-bumper insert, and a revised version of the '64 hardtop roof emblem was given a body surround. Landaus received, when compared to the stylish '64 Landau bars and upswept C-pillar trim, a bland S-bar with simulated "Cobra"-grain vinyl inserts painted the same color as the material covering the roof. The grille's dental work was, in some individuals' opinions, done a disservice by taking the clean-looking horizontal bars and crossing them with a series of verticals.

One option that received little attention and creates confusion for restorers even today was the "letter-code" interior packages. Though they were not listed in the shop manual or sales literature other than showroom albums, white seats and door/quarter trim panels could be ordered in either vinyl or leather, with contrasting carpet, seat belt, console, and dash trim colors. The black-and-white interior shown is in a hardtop restored by Rocky Mountain Thunderbird Club newsletter editor Steve Ryder. The black-and-white interior differed from other letter-code trims in that the console was provided in white instead of the contrasting color. *Alan Tast photo*

Nineteen sixty-five was supposed to be the second year of T-birds with sequential taillights, but delays in getting states to change their regulations in time for 1964 delayed the introduction. The lens and grille trim would see use two years later on the Shelby GT-350/500 of 1967-1970, and on the 1968 Mustang California Special as well as the High Plains Special. *Alan Tast photo*

The sequential rear turn signals were one of the car's most-talked-about forays into "gimmick" engineering. A series of three light bulbs were placed in each of the signal "pods," and with a move of the turn-signal stalk, a motor and a series of relays in the front of the trunk would set in motion a repeating sequence whereby the inboard bulb would be illuminated, followed by the middle, and outboard in rapid progression, then cycle back to the beginning of the sequence. Sequential turn signals had been slated to appear for '64, but the laws of several states had to be rewritten before the sequential signals could be used across the United States; this had been accomplished by summer 1964.

Interior restyling was limited to a camera-case finish on the console and dash trim panels on non-Landau models and other minor changes such as finally providing a finger-grab in the door panel to close the doors. Landaus were given a different woodgrain panel on the doors and on console and dash trim. For the first time, power vent windows were available.

Seat upholstery and trim color choices were expanded by the introduction of two-tone interiors when a letter-series trim was selected. These white leather or vinyl trim options included white door panels without lower carpeting, white front and rear seats, and the console, carpets and other trim in a contrasting color (a black-and-white combination would have a white console to become an oddball scheme). These options were developed after the release of the shop manual and other early sales literature, so they are not listed therein. Upholstery patterns were carried over from 1964, but cloth seat inserts would differ. A new feature for the hardtops and Landaus was color-matched headliners. The added colors helped to distinguish the '65 interiors for the previous year's.

Much-Needed Improvement

Magazine writers had wailed and moaned ever since 1958 that the four-seat T-bird had weak brakes. Drum brakes were not providing satisfactory stopping power,

The Palomino was a styling exercise that hit the ISCA show circuit in 1965. Its primary exterior changes were the blind-quarter roof, heavily padded vinyl top, and 1964 T-bird Landau S-bars, forecasting the 1966 Town Hardtop/Landau. Cibie driving lights and a sheet metal lower front valence, ideas carried over from a 1964 T-bird customized for Ford dealer Bob Tasca, were also adapted, along with a vertical-bar grille. *Ford Motor Company*

Shown on the Styling Patio in mid-October 1964, the Palomino was provided with exhaust ports in the lower pan, displacing the back-up lights. The center of the bumper was removed, and the trunk lock was relocated inside the glove box. The Flow-Thru grille also carries the vertical-bar motif. *Ford Motor Company*

and in response to criticism, engineers from Ford and Kelsey-Hayes developed a dual-piston disc brake that outperformed the drums by a wide margin.

The T-bird's 15in wheels (new in 1964) allowed clearance for the disc-brake system's fixed caliper assembly, but placing an earlier 14in one in its place was out of the question because offset and interference with the calipers would not allow it to fit. This meant that the pretty forty-eight–spoke Kelsey-Hayes wire wheels offered since 1962 would not fit, so

the option was dropped. As early as 1965, aftermarket manufacturers attempted to make replacement wire wheels for the car, but they were not offered from the factory. During the late 1980s, aftermarket suppliers began building a lookalike Kelsey wire with fifty-six spokes on a 15in wheel and a proper offset to allow their use on the 1965–66 T-bird.

Along with brakes, another important engineering change was made for '65. This would be the first year for Ford's famous double-sided key, which allowed impatient operators the convenience of having to only stick the key in the lock or ignition switch cylinder once without worrying about whether or not it was in the correct way.

The Palomino's interior featured a unique handle-grip steering wheel, textured aluminum appliqués on the lower console and upper door trim panels, and a different upholstery insert as well as deeply padded bolsters. Note that the door panel's armrest carries straight forward instead of sweeping up toward the top of the door, and that the door handle is reversed. *Ford Motor Company*

The Palomino console bisected the center of the car and contained a separate radio for the two rear passengers. The wraparound rear seat was abandoned in favor of a larger trim panel/armrest. *Ford Motor Company*

The Special Landau was a trim option that originally was to carry its own body code, but like the 1963 Monaco Landau, it was ultimately identified by its interior code. Pictured here is the Emberglo-colored prototype, photographed on October 13, 1964. *Ford Motor Company*

A Private World

While the first full-line brochures and the Thunderbird's only catalog for the year were printed in late July 1964, promotion for the '65 T-bird began in late September. Production began on August 3, 1964, and by the time over 10,000 T-birds had been built, advertising featuring a Brittany Blue Landau with a blue interior began appearing in magazines. The introduction of the '65 was almost a month behind Buick's unveiling of their facelifted '65 Riviera.

Buick was very much pursuing a performance image by October when it began production of the Riviera Gran Sport (GS) with a dual-four-barrel 360hp 425ci motor, aluminum road wheels, larger dual exhaust, Positraction differential, optional heavy-duty suspension, and quicker steering. Again, the T-bird was left to eat the Riviera's dust. The 390ci motor was, once again, the only engine choice for the '65 T-bird, and other performance options were limited to a choice of rear-axle ratios: 2.80:1, 3.00:1 (standard), 3.25:1, or 3.50:1—and all were available with the Equa-Lock option.

Road-testing of early production or prototype '65s began in August 1964, and *Car Life* magazine prepared a story on the revised car for its November issue. Writers were happy the disc brakes were finally available, noting that the car now behaved the way it should have all along, but they judged the T-bird as "a luxury-class car for those who want to present a dashing sort of image, who worry about spreading girth and stiffening arteries, and who couldn't care less about taste." Harsh words, sure, but critics aren't exactly noted for their kindness.

Most of the press swooned again over the Mustang, which was now available as a fastback, and then became an asphalt-eater in Shelby GT-350 trim. The all-new Galaxie/LTD also captured the limelight for Ford, but few reporters or free-lance writers would ask Mr. Zimmerman for the chance to do a story on the T-bird.

The only engine available in 1965 was the 390ci, as evidenced by this restored 1965 Special Landau owned by Al and Marilyn Schulz of the Chicagoland Thunderbirds. *Alan Tast photo*

Palomino

For one more year, Ford's Special Vehicles Activity/Advanced Concepts Department would produce a show-car Thunderbird to be taken on tour, simply called Palomino. Unlike the previous year's Golden Palomino, it would reveal future T-bird styling with a blind quarter roof, which reached production for the '66 model year. Starting with a '65 hardtop, it was modified with a heavily padded Levant-grain vinyl top, '64-style Landau bars, wheel opening trim (another '66 feature), and rocker-panel molding. From the side it did not look much different than a '65 Landau. Up front, though, it had a body-colored sheet metal lower pan (also heralding the '66), Cibie rectangular headlights, and a grille with closely spaced vertical bars (the same grillwork would be copied in the Silent-Flo opening at the base of the rear window). The rear bumper was made into bumperettes with deletion of the center section, and the rear deck lid (which was opened by a remote-control switch inside the console) was allowed to dip down for easier access to the trunk. Back-up lights were replaced with oblong exhaust outlets.

The interior explored new territory with a handle-grip steering wheel and a true full-length console that included a radio for the rear-seat passengers. Seats were given deep bolsters and unique cloth inserts, which were also used on the C-pillars and headliner, and the rear buckets abandoned the wraparound concept.

The Special Vehicles Activity/Advanced Concepts Department completed the Palomino, assigned serial number 5Y83Z-101336, in early November 1964. By the end of January 1965 it was in the hands of the marketing office, which placed it on the show circuit during the winter and spring.

By mid-October 1965, it was decided to sell the Palomino, and on October 15 a man in Grand Rapids, Michigan, agreed to purchase the car under a sales contract that stipulated that the car would be used for display purposes. The car's whereabouts and disposition after that time are unknown.

A Special Request

The half-year sales promotion program returned to the T-bird for 1965 in a very tasteful way with the Special Landau. In conjunction with the celebration of the first decade of the Thunderbird, the Special Landau unofficially would be Ford's way of marking the occasion, but the buyer had to spend an extra $49.60 to join the celebration.

The Special Landau was an option much like the Limited Edition Landau had been in 1963, with a unique combination of colors and trims. The body could be ordered in either Corinthian White or, what was pushed in advertising and sales brochure photos, Emberglo Metallic (a reddish-copper color). Given the code V, Emberglo would only be available on the SL and the Mustang for '65, but for 1966 it would become a choice across the entire Ford line. Vinyl roofs for both were a light beige color named Parchment. At the base of the C-pillars, to distinguish the model from other Landaus, a two-part emblem with a gold-plated T-bird and a script panel denoting the model's name were placed toward the front of the belt molding. As an added touch, the optional three-bar spinner wheel cover vanes received Emberglo paint instead of the standard black trim.

The interior, likewise, was treated to the Emberglo-and-Parchment combination, with seats, headliner, door/quarter trim panels and dash-pad edge in Parchment vinyl, using trim codes of 7D for regular seats or XD if the reclining passenger seat was installed. Emberglo carpeting was fitted to the lower door panels, floor, console, and even the camera-finish dash background/cove. Instead of standard Landau woodgrain trim, a unique burled walnut finish was used, and door panels were given Special Landau plaques.

Production was advertised to be limited to 4,500 units to maintain exclusivity. Unlike the '63 Monaco Landau, in which a special plaque was affixed to the console panel with a number indicating which of the 2,000 copies it was, buyers of the SL were presented an envelope containing an engraved brass dash plaque with a self-adhesive backing, allowing them the option of either placing it somewhere in the car or omitting it altogether. The plaque had a cast T-bird emblem on it similar to the one on the exterior nameplate, the car's Special Landau number engraved in it, and at the dealer's, the option of having the new owner's name engraved on it as well. Not many of the cars were fitted with the plates, and today they are a desirable item to find with an original car.

A source of confusion for people attempting to identify the Special Landau would come from the 1965 shop manual. Printed during September 1964, it gave a serial number code of 81 and 63D for the body code on the data plate for the 2-Door Landau Special. These numbers would be used for the '66 Town Hardtop (81) and Town Landau (63D), with no connection to the SL. As they would finally be stamped, data plates would carry the same 87/63B designation that the regular Landau did. Since either the M (Corinthian White) or V (Emberglo) could be used in the color space of the plate, a sure way to verify SL authenticity would be to look for either 7D or XD in the trim-code section.

A detail of the burled walnut woodgrain panel on the door, with unique Special Landau ornamentation. *Alan Tast photo*

All original Special Landau owners were provided a personally engraved and numbered dash plaques, though not everyone bothered to install theirs. One exception was this car, originally sold in Lincoln, Nebraska. Only 4,500 Special Landaus were produced, of which this car was number 3,822. *Alan Tast photo*

The prototype Special Landau, painted in Emberglo, was photographed two days after the presidential election, on November 12–13, 1964, for artwork and advertising purposes. Full-line brochures began to feature the new addition starting in April 1965. Production of the Special Landau trim option began after the beginning of February 1965, and continued through most of the remainder of production. Ford did not keep track of how many were painted Emberglo or Corinthian White, but speculation among SL devotees and data compiled from the VTCI's owners' surveys point to a probability that 10 percent or even less may have been given the lighter color.

During the spring, advertising was placed in major magazines featuring an Emberglo-colored example, and a special six-page folding brochure was printed just for the option along with its addition in the April revision of the full-line

catalog. *Ford Times* even hyped the car in its July 1965 issue as part of wrapping up the anniversary celebration.

Little Setbacks

With introduction of disc brakes and sequential taillights, problems involving the new systems were bound to occur, but other minor glitches cropped up during production and the initial months of operation. For instance, on cars built before August 21, 1964, doors would mysteriously lock when shut. A missing spring in the lock mechanism was the culprit, and the assembly was replaced under warranty. Erratic and noisy speedometers on nonspeed-control cars were traced to a too-short cable, which was changed on November 2. Typical complaints of squeaks were attributed to excessive clearance in the nylon door-hinge bushings, improperly isolated joints in trim around the rear package tray, bucket seatback springs, a poor-

The 1965 Riviera Gran Sport was an attempt to create a performance version of Buick's three-year-old personal luxury car. Powered by a dual four-barrel 425ci motor and other heavy-duty components, it provided an upscale option to cars such as the muscle-bound Skylark GS. Ford would not have a T-bird model to directly compete with the GS in 1965. *Buick Division*

fitting reclining seat handle, and improperly adjusted lower window stops. A major rework problem announced in late March would involve the automatic transmission, as some were released with an improperly machined output shaft that would create a grinding or buzzing noise. Other components that were substituted during the production run were few, but included the convertible-top electrical solenoid, which was changed from the old-style round case to a block-style one on March 1, 1965.

Water leaks were still a problem, and most were theoretically "corrected in production" in such places as lock grommets, the cowl plenum, and vent windows. As for appearance, complaints of vinyl top "ballooning" led to the elimination of the top and side pads around November 9, 1964.

The Beginning of the End

As production ceased on July 9, 1965, to set up for 1966 production, it became apparent that the '65 model year was less successful than '64 had been. Orders were officially down to 74,972 of all models. The convertible's percentage was still holding above 9 percent, but not by much. Over half of all '65 T-birds built were hardtops, and when Special Landaus were factored in with standard ones, they accounted for one out of every three T-birds built in the year. Insiders were aware that the next run of T-birds would be a series of lasts, and thus the stage was set for the final act of a grand player.

Chapter 13

END OF THE ROAD

The 1966 Thunderbird, by default and tradition, was the most-improved T-bird of the fourth generation. Each generation before it relied on a modest mix of change to freshen up its appeal to potential buyers: The '57 got revamped rear sheet metal, a new dash, and some exciting engine choices; 1960 brought with it a collection of tacked-on chrome, restyled upholstery, and the sunroof; and 1963 got a similar interior makeover along with a mild bit of body sculpturing and a host of underhood improvements. This time, though, there was a bit of uncertainty about what to do. As the '66 T-bird was being prepared for its turn in the styling queue during the summer and fall of 1963, advanced thinkers were contemplating a new Thunderbird, more like a Lincoln than a Ford and one that shared more components. Long-range predictions stated that the days of the convertible as a viable T-bird offering were numbered, and its deletion from the line-up would probably make little difference if other cars such as Mustang and Galaxie were available with a drop top.

Going to Town

The move to go formal had become a target to aim for. Stylists examined the roof of the '64 T-bird and determined that by eliminating the quarter windows, which offered only a minimal view for rear-seat passengers, and filling the area with the C-pillar, the roof took on a very different appearance—one of privacy and exclusivity. Prewar convertibles such as the '40 Ford Deluxe and the '40 Lincoln Continental Cabriolet had carried off this concept quite well. Studies with fiberglass "see-through" models were ready by mid-October 1963 to check for blind spots behind the driver and overall appearance in three dimensions. Though the roof's profile took on a more radical swoop down and back (almost suggesting a fastback in its early development), it would be virtually unchanged except for early efforts to place a raised panel in the large open area to break up its massiveness.

The new roof style was used on two models, called Town Landau (with a vinyl roof and S-bars) and Town Hardtop (with a painted roof and T-bird emblem the same as on the conventional hardtop). To give them a unique in-

This photograph, taken on August 12, 1963, is reputed to being an early design for a facelifted 1966 T-bird. Hidden headlights would not appear until 1967, possibly meaning that this was an early exercise in exploring the feature. *Ford Motor Company*

terior package, designers developed an overhead console to contain the dash-mounted Safety Convenience Panel. Running the length of the ceiling, the overhead console divided the headliner in the same way that the floor console segregated the carpeting. A molded vinyl headliner was developed and fitted between the console and windows/C-pillar, and rectilinear lights were placed in the C-pillars.

As the design process continued through winter and spring 1964, side trims and ornamentation would be explored, but outside influences would play into the hands of L. David Ash and others on the Thunderbird's design team.

Outside Influence

During late 1963, East Providence, Rhode Island, Ford dealer Bob Tasca was approaching his zenith in the sponsorship of high-performance Ford products, earning a national reputation for the Super Stock Galaxies and Fairlanes his company was fielding at drag strips across the

Northeast and beyond. Tasca, head of the second-largest Ford agency in the world (according to Martyn L. Schorr in the October 1964 issue of *CARS* magazine), had a penchant for high-powered, exciting cars, and it was only natural for his staff to work with Ford engineering and marketing departments as a member of its National Drag Council. Desiring a personal car to handle daily duties, Tasca contacted his sources in Dearborn about acquiring a new '64 T-bird with a 427ci motor. After some behind-the-scenes maneuvering through Jacque Passino, who was assistant manager for competition at Ford, arrangements were made to honor his request for one of the mills to be fitted in a hardtop with an experimental version of a heavy-duty automatic transmission intended for drag-racing use. In addition, the car was assembled with an export suspension that consisted of heavier springs, shock absorbers, and front sway bar.

Tasca drove the car back east, then had the motor subjected to "blueprinting" along with additional suspension work. It was fitted with a single Holley four-barrel carburetor (a tapered spacer plate was milled to level out the carburetor), an M-series camshaft, and hydraulic lifters. The stock exhaust system was thrown away, replaced with Bellanger headers and exhaust pipes (intended for racing Fairlanes), and resonators replaced the stock mufflers. Rear springs were de-arched, and the front coils lost one full revolution to lower the car 3in. According to an article in *Musclecars* magazine by Tony Lyons, an electronic speedometer and a Rotunda "crossed flag" tachometer were fitted into the dash.

The modified 1964 hardtop ordered by Bob Tasca, the Providence, Rhode Island, Ford dealer. Restyled by the Alexander Brothers of Detroit at the direction of free-lance designer Harry Bentley Bradley (who was also working for GM at the time and would gain fame as the designer/creator of the Mattel Hot Wheels toy cars), it was taken to Ford's Design Center for review by stylists and engineers in late-April to early-May 1964. *Courtesy of Harry Bentley Bradley*

Tasca also wanted to have the car personalized before delivery, as he did not like the heavy front-bumper grille, and in conversations with Henry Ford II, asked for a source to handle modifications. According to Mike Alexander of the Alexander Brothers customizing firm (and now an executive with American Sunroof Corporation), a call from Ford's secretary would initiate their involvement in the project. Henry II had been familiar with Mike and brother Larry's work on the '63 Ford Custom Caravan and felt they could handle the job.

An early fiberglass see-through model of the 1966 T-bird with a Town roof. Fake fender vents were still an "in" thing, and the front bumper still resembles the 1964–65 version. *Ford Motor Company*

A sketch of a restyled front end for the T-bird, dated May 8, 1964, reveals the influence of Bradley's work. Note inset front license plate and Cibie headlights, elimination of bumper guards, and repositioned turn signals. *Ford Motor Company*

The Alexander Brothers turned to Harry Bentley Bradley, a Pratt Institute graduate and stylist at the GM Design Center, for help with the modifications. The car was shipped back to the Alexanders' shops in Detroit after it was mechanically modified by the Tasca dealership, and from Bradley's sketches and suggestions, the front was restyled by fabricating a rolled sheet metal pan and thin-bladed bumper that replaced the massive '64 assembly. An aluminum-barred grille occupied the area below the bumper, along with a set of rear back-up lights that were placed in line with the rectangular Cibie headlights to function as turn signals, and a recessed area for the license plate was developed. The front of the hood and fenders were reshaped, taking on a resemblance to the 1961–63

Two weeks later, a fiberglass mock-up of the 1966 T-bird contains the L. David Ash-designed grille and T-bird emblem above the blade-like front bumper, reducing the formerly massive amount of brightwork. Block letters on the hood would be rejected, as would be the turn signal assemblies on the lower valance and the plexiglass headlight covers with T-bird emblems. A raised panel was still being considered in the C-pillar. *Ford Motor Company*

Exploration of accessories for the 1966 model included this novel dual-cowl package, which consisted of plexiglass wind deflectors set into a cast-metal retainer that had an integral "sissy bar" reminiscent of the Sports Roadster. Sharp eyes will notice that this 1964 convertible has cloth seats, which were not offered in production on the soft-top. *Ford Motor Company*

T-bird's "eyebrow" treatment, and the fender-mounted turn indicators were "shaved" off. Body side modifications included a chrome-plated "rub rail" along the edge of the lower sculpture line, hand-crafted emblems calling attention to the owner and the motor between the front fender, and removal of the C-pillar 'Bird emblem. The center rear bumper insert was reworked for a single back-up light, since the original ones had been used up front, and the openings were filled in. The trunk lock assembly was pitched, with an electric solenoid operated from inside the car handling the duties. To finish the car off, it was painted a popular customizers' hue, Candy Apple Red.

Performance aspects of the Tasca 'Bird were astounding:

It was clocked going from a standing stop to 60mph in 6sec, and topped out at 135mph (the stock 390-equipped car would barely hit above 115mph, and acceleration was certainly not as impressive). Handling, thanks to the stiffer export package and lowering work, also was a marked improvement. But just as exciting was what was done to the body: It had been lightened by 150lb with the front end rework, and was considered one of the finest contemporary mild customs of the period.

Ford executives, impressed with the car, requested that it be taken to the design center at the beginning of May 1964, where stylists and engineers poured over it (Schorr remarked that "Ford Styling boys went wild when

A photograph of a prototype Town Landau, taken in spring 1965. The deluxe five-spoke wheel covers are accented by aluminum wheel-opening trim. The rear fender skirt was not fitted to this example. If it were, the wheel arch trim would be deleted, with a similar trim piece used on the bottom edge of the skirt. *Ford Motor Company*

Rear view of a Raven Black 1966 Town Landau owned by Donald J. Chase of Omaha, Nebraska, shows the fender skirt and lower trim, along with the wall-to-wall taillights and center-located back-up light, hidden by the T-bird's corral. *Alan Tast photo*

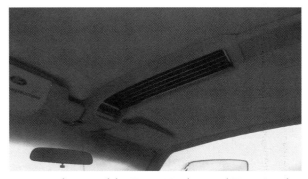

A unique feature of the Town Hardtop and Town Landau was the overhead console, which contained the Safety Convenience Panel of the two prior years. A molded vinyl headliner surrounded the sun visors and was split into two panels by the console and its extension. *Alan Tast photo*

The instrument panel of Chase's Town Landau reveals the instrument pods used in the fourth-generation T-birds. Turn signal indicators were located on the fenders, thus obviating their need in the dash. The speedometer's rotating drum can be seen through the slot directly beneath the large numbers on the board. *Alan Tast photo*

they saw the car" in his article). By the end of the week on May 8, sketches were appearing with the Cibie lights and a modified front bumper, revealing the influence of Bradley's free-lance work. Two weeks later, on May 22, a "see-through" model was prepared for display that revealed a close-to-final front end: Again, elements of Bradley's scheme showed up in the turn signals mounted low in a sheet metal valance, but the grille and bumper were refined. L. David Ash was given credit for developing a flat blade that wrapped around the front fenders (instead of a bar with a raised middle section to frame in the grille), a pair of bumperettes framed in the license plate area to create the illusion of a recessed panel, a thin chrome molding framed in an egg-crate grille that mimicked the 1964–65 T-bird's upper bumper bar, and a large T-bird ornament occupied the center of the stylish opening. While headlight covers and block lettering would be

rejected on the hood, its pointed prow and sharply angled fake hood-scoop casting would remain virtually as-is.

The revamp of the front end, with the previously forbidden sheet metal under the bumper, was controversial within Ford studios, as many stylists preferred the high prow of 1964–65. Public consciousness about safety, though, was questioning some of the wilder design concepts on the road: Some felt that the high-riding T-bird bumper offered no protection, and could allow it to run over small cars. Even Congress was getting into the act with hearings on vehicle safety, and executives feared that eventually it would mandate standard bumper heights and specifications. To stem potential moves by legislators and bureaucrats, Ford moved toward requiring cars be designed around a bumper "buck" that approximated the minimum and maximum desired heights for the assembly. While it may have restricted freedom for designers to

For 1966, Ford began painting its engines blue, as opposed to color-coding the air cleaner and valve covers for specific displacements. This is an example of a 428ci powerplant in a convertible owned by Randy Mattson of the Thunderbird Midwest chapter. *Alan Tast photo*

The 1966 T-bird was also the first T-bird to offer an AM radio with eight-track stereo tape player. Two speakers were mounted in each door panel, while the tape player was mounted just above the radio dial. *Alan Tast photo*

Chrysler's 300 lost its letter-series designations in 1966, but the Engel-styled beauty would continue to butt heads with the T-bird in convertible, four-door, and two-door hardtop (shown) versions. *John Lee photo*

The big news for auto enthusiasts was the reintroduction of front-wheel drive in the form of the Oldsmobile Toronado coupe. The Toro was only offered in a two-door hardtop with a 425ci motor and Turbo Hydra-Matic transmission. Despite its two-door configuration, it could carry six passengers. Ford could have beaten Oldsmobile by two years on a flat-floor, front-wheel drive platform with a proposed 1964 T-bird penned in late-1960 to early 1961, but the idea was dropped for cost reasons. *Courtesy Oldsmobile History Center*

come up with schemes such as that used on the 1961–65 T-birds, it also created opportunities.

Restyling of the rear became an exercise in integration. The center-mounted emblem was retained, but now the bumper stock was deleted between it and the taillight areas, creating "wall-to-wall" coverage. Lenses were changed, and the center emblem became, as with Tasca's 1964, a back-up light.

Interiors were not forgotten; they received new upholstery patterns. A new cloth was chosen for those who did not

like vinyl, and door panels on the new Town models received a different upper pattern along with a woodgrained insert.

Power to Spare

Ford had learned a lesson from Buick and others with their larger engine offerings: People would buy them! The experience with tri-powered 1962–63 T-birds and their low sales had made product planners gun-shy about exotic engine offerings, such as the 427ci motor. Customer complaints of engine fires, poor gas mileage, and general

Pontiac's Grand Prix received a facelift for 1966, and as the only Poncho to square off against the T-bird did reasonably well in the ever-splintering personal luxury market. In 1970, it would join with Chevrolet's new Monte Carlo in taking direct aim at the T-bird. *John Lee photo*

dissatisfaction were due more to the complexities of the M-series than performance when it was in tune. Dismal sales due to poor promotion of the M should be included as well, since it was not publicized to the same extent as 406- or 427-equipped Galaxies and Montereys/Marauders. The 427, much like the 360hp 352ci motor offered in 1960 Fords, was deemed too radical for the T-bird with its Cruise-O-Matic transmission and all the power assists, so no substitute short of using the Mercury 410ci was available that could meet the T-bird's finicky requirements.

The problem of a streetable mega-cube motor was solved during 1964–65 by development of the 428ci FE-block mill. Essentially an enlarged and stroked 390, the hydraulic lifter-equipped motor could produce a rated 345hp (a 30hp increase from the standard '66 390), equaling what Riviera and similar cars were offering. Dubbed "7-Litre" to reflect its metric-rated displacement, the move was made to place it in the full-size Ford and T-bird for 1966.

Although not externally identified by any special badges like the Galaxie 500/XL's 7-Litre model, a label on the air cleaner lid gave notice to people that a larger motor was nesting in the T-bird, and those familiar with serial number codes could pick out the Q designation for the motor. Nothing was different under the hood from a standard 390 installation, but mash the foot-feed to the floor and the Cruise-O-Matic would fling the 4,800lb car into action.

The 428/7-Litre was a high-output motor, but not quite on the same plane as the 427 because the 7-Litre was by no means an all-out racing engine, but simply a large-displacement, torque-producing bundle of dependability. You didn't have to lash the valves, change spark plugs every time you left the garage or rejet the Holley: Hydraulic lifters, a dual-advance distributor, and Ford's four-barrel carburetor were as reliable as Walter Cronkite reading the evening news on television.

In fact, the high-torque capabilities of the larger motor made it a shoe-in for trailer-towing, which Ford was constantly promoting. In its booklet, *1966 Ford Cars & Trucks for Recreation,* it recommended the installation of either the 315hp 390 or the 7-Litre if a Class III trailer weighing 3,500–5,000lb was to be pulled, along with the heavy-duty (i.e., export) suspension and battery, Extra-Cooling Package, and load-equalizing hitch. It may be hard to imagine a 428-equipped convertible pulling an Airstream trailer, but it certainly has been done over the years.

The 7-Litre was well-received by Thunderbird buyers. Given more prominence in Ford advertising since it was available from the beginning of the model year, it was even given a special advertising layout by JWT, with bolts of lightning behind a blue Town Landau and copy such as "428 cubic inches of V-8 authority" to stir the senses. Strangely, though, it was not reviewed by road-test gurus

Much like the change from 1957 to 1958, the replacement of the unibody T-bird with a body-on-frame version for 1967 was derided by fans of the pre-1967 cars. Sharing only the basic powertrain with the earlier cars, the Thunderbird became more obese as time went on until it became a victim of downsizing for 1977 in the wake of the 1973 OPEC oil embargo. Production began a downward spiral after models such as this one, a Landau owned by Bruce and Cindy Caswell of the Rocky Mountain Thunderbird Club in Denver, hit the streets. *Alan Tast photo*

in the popular magazines, who were knee-deep in the performance battles of "pony" and "muscle" cars.

The Best One Ever?

Few "bugs" were left to be worked out of the '66 T-bird, and several improvements were made. The speed control had been redone to move controls into the steering wheel, a new AM radio and eight-track tape player was offered, and for California drivers, a smog-reducing Thermactor system was developed to recirculate and more completely burn off exhaust gases.

Running changes included increasing the size of radiators in non-Thermactor-equipped cars built after December 1, 1965, which forced the redesign of the fiberglass fan shroud, battery tray/retainer, and shield. The master cylinder bore was enlarged from 7/8 to 15/16in on January 3, 1966, but the assembly would be superseded again on April 1.

Problems that required warranty work were substantially reduced, but as in 1965, transmissions created a stir when owners complained of harsh or severe reverse-gear engagement in units built before November 15, 1965. Another item, the seat-belt warning light, would fail to extinguish, prompting the addition of a time-delay relay to turn it off after between 30sec and 2min.

Full House and a Royal Flush

For the first time since 1963, four models of T-bird were offered: the conventional five-window hardtop, the convertible, and the upscale Town Hardtop and Town Landau models. Ford had hoped that the diverse line-up would appeal to a wider group of buyers, but in the end

passengers in roll-overs, which convertibles could not meet, and it would be those regulations and threats of increasingly hard-to-meet standards that made Ford decide to abandon the concept after 1966 for the luxury car. As early as 1963, when planning for the '67 model began, the convertible T-bird was factored out of the equation, replaced with the ultimate of horrors for enthusiasts, a four-door Landau.

It was also clear that the competition was not fielding convertible T-bird-killers. The Riviera was never brought to production as a ragtop, although one was considered for introduction in 1963; a new front-wheel drive Oldsmobile, the Toronado, was also a close-coupled four-place two-door hardtop, taking advantage of the flat floorpan that T-bird planners rejected back in 1961; and Cadillac was on the verge of bringing to market the '67 Eldorado as its front-wheel-drive upscaling of the Toronado. Chrysler's 300 was still offered in a convertible version in 1966, as was Pontiac's Bonneville/Grand Prix and intercompany competition Mercury in the Park Lane series, but they were by now simply full-size cars with nothing in common with the Rivieras, Toronados, and Thunderbirds, and more in common with big-block Galaxie XLs and Impala SS.

Lovers of drop-top T-birds scrambled to get their hands on the final edition before production ended. One story, which illustrates the heights of the T-bird's appeal, involves none other than President Lyndon Baines Johnson. By summer 1966, the world's most powerful Texan had decided to obtain a new T-bird convertible for his daughter, Linda. When informed that Ford had stopped production of the '66 in June, an immediate search was launched to locate a dealer with a new convertible still in inventory. Finally, a Candy Apple Red convertible was located and shipped to his ranch in the Lone Star state; it reportedly was one of the last convertibles to be sold new. Eventually, the car found its way into the hands of T-bird enthusiast Paul Nichols of Dearborn, Michigan, bringing the car back to its roots in the shadow of the Ford empire.

The '66 Thunderbird held up well against contenders, but it could not be taken much further. The platform it rode on, which was intended to handle front-wheel drive when first designed in the late 1950s, was dated. The massive unibody structure was heavy, and engineering advances had allowed for cars to sit just as low with a full-perimeter frame and weigh less. So, on June 10, 1966, the last of what would be considered vintage Thunderbirds received its final inspection, was driven to the holding yard, and waited for transport to some dealer, where it probably would be sold in a year-end clearance, overshadowed by a "sucker-mouth" '67. The car had its dedicated following, and in the years to follow it would become elevated to a position of honor along with all the other T-birds that preceded it out the doors of Wixom and the Rouge.

the Town Landau was far and away most-popular, claiming a fraction over half of all sales at 35,105 units. Convertible sales, on the other hand, slumped to 5,049, or 7.3 percent of all '66 T-birds built.

Production began for the '66 T-bird on the first Monday of August, with a two-month lag for build-up of inventory before they were released for public sale in October. Ford sponsored a contest in its *Ford Times* magazine for people who registered at their local dealers, with a Town Landau as first prize (and several follow-up calls from hungry salesmen as a bonus). Though receiving a very becoming facelift, the T-bird hardly caught any attention from the press, much like in '65. *Motor Trend* only gave it a one-page road test in its March 1966 issue, instead focusing on the Town Landau.

Discard

The heyday of convertible T-birds was at an end. The convertible's death was inevitable: Increasing sales of air conditioners, tinted glass, and growing vandalism concerns made top-down driving less appealing. Federal regulations were being developed to increase the safety of

PRODUCTION DATA

1955
Production by Month

Aug. '54	Sep.	Oct.	Nov.	Dec.	Jan. '55	Feb.	Mar.	Apr.	May	June	July	Aug.	Sept.
4	164	858	1,218	1,306	1,346	1,507	1,673	1,541	1,541	157	1,402	1,380	593

Note: Monthly production figures for August 1954 include ten early production vehicles, of which four were assembled during August 1954, and six during the first week of September 1954. A discrepancy of fifty units exists between the monthly production figures and the final production total. This may be related to the units either shipped to Mexico or knocked down overseas. More research is needed.

First Day of Production: September 1, 1954 (completion date was tagged as September 9, 1954)
Last Day of Production: September 19, 1955
Introduction Date: October 22, 1954
Final Production: 16,155 (official figure may be 16,202, including cars built in Mexico—see below)
Export: Of the 16,155 cars produced at the Dearborn Assembly Plant, 619 were exported as assembled units, and forty-eight were shipped knocked down for assembly at a Ford facility overseas. An additional forty-seven cars were shipped to Ford's assembly plant in Mexico City, where they were given serial numbers that included "MEX" in place of the Dearborn Assembly Plant's "F" code. Of these forty-seven, six have Ford-O-Matic, twenty-nine have overdrive, and twelve are three-speed versions. One car was imported fully built, probably to provide an example for assembly at the La Villa plant in Mexico City. (Source: *Early Bird*, September-October 1993, p. 25.)
Additional Information: No breakdown of engine/transmission combinations has been found by the author

1956
Production by Month

Oct. '55	Nov.	Dec.	Jan. '56	Feb.	Mar.	Apr.	May	June	July	Aug.
104	1,489	1,458	1,434	1,297	1,755	1,852	1,764	1,751	1,709	1,018

First Day of Production: October 17, 1955 (date first '56 completed)
Last Day of Production: August 24, 1956
Introduction Date: November 9, 1955
Final Production: 15,631 (official figure may be 15,722, including cars assembled in Mexico—see below)
Export: Of the 15,631 cars produced at the Dearborn Assembly Plant, 694 were exported as assembled units, and ninety were shipped knocked down for assembly at a Ford facility overseas. An additional ninety-one cars were shipped to Ford's assembly plant in Mexico City, where they were given serial numbers that included "MEX" in place of the Dearborn Assembly Plant's "F" code. Of these, nine were built with 292/3-speed, thirty-three with 312/Ford-O-Matic, and forty-nine with 312/overdrive. (Source: *Early Bird*, September-October 1993, p. 25.)
Additional Information: No breakdown of engine/transmission combinations has been found by the author. Nine out of every ten hardtops sold were with the portholes installed. No cars were delivered from the factory with the 260hp dual-carburetor package; this was a dealer-installed accessory.

1957
Production by Month

Sept. '56	Oct.	Nov.	Dec.	Jan. '57	Feb.	Mar.	Apr.	May	June	July	Aug.	Sept.	Oct.	Nov.	Dec.
365	1,802	1,872	1,898	2,077	1,565	1,714	1,553	1,500	1,456	1,295	1,159	1,022	671	954	477

Note: November-December figures are extrapolated, as no figures were given for those months.

First Day of Production: September 17, 1956
Last Day of Production: December 13, 1957
Introduction Date: October 3, 1956
Final Production: 21,380 (official figure may be 21,439, including cars assembled in Mexico—see below)
Production by Engine/Transmission:

C-series 292/two-barrel 212bhp, with 3-speed[1]	3,247 (estimated)
D-series 312/4-barrel 245bhp, with overdrive[2]	625 (estimated)
D-series 312/4-barrel 245bhp, with Ford-O-Matic[3]	15,848 (estimated)
E-series 312/twin 4-barrel, 270 or 285bhp (racing kit), with 3-speed[4]	197
E-series 312/twin 4-barrel, 270 or 285bhp (racing kit), with overdrive[2]	275
E-series 312/twin 4-barrel, 270 or 285bhp (racing kit), with Ford-O-Matic[2]	977
D-series 312/4-barrel supercharged (phase I) 300bhp, with 3-speed, overdrive	14
F-series 312/4-barrel supercharged (phase II) 300bhp, all transmissions	197
Total	21,380

Production Notes:

1. C-series production was estimated at 3,500 in the November-December 1986 *Early Bird;* figures may be high in light of others given when compared to total production. The figure 3,247 is based on the assumption that all other figures given in this list are correct when compared to total production.

2. Estimate for D- and E-series cars with overdrive is approximately 900 (*Early Bird,* September-October 1981, p. 41); Langworth places E-series/overdrive count at 275, from which 625 for the D-series motor is derived, based on the previous information.

3. The figure for D-series/Ford-O-Matic is derived from subtracting the estimated 625 units from the total production of 16,423 D-models with both overdrive and Ford-O-Matic.

4. The figure from the *Early Bird,* November-December 1980, p. 10; Langworth, p. 136.

Sources: *Early Bird,* November-December 1986, p. 17, 18; November-December 1980, p. 10; September-October 1981, p. 41; and Richard Langworth *Personal Luxury: The Thunderbird Story,* p. 136

Export: Of the 21,380 T-birds built, 580 were exported, and an additional seventy-two were knocked down. Mexican production figures for knocked-down cars sent to La Villa plant (engines unknown) include twenty-five with Ford-O-Matic and thirty-four with overdrive. Final production for 1957 is adjusted to 21,439 units to include Mexican cars. (Source: *Early Bird,* September-October 1993, p. 25.)

Additional Information: McCulloch rated output of the supercharged motors at 360bhp, but a more accurate range may be 325–340bhp. (source: *Early Bird,* November-December 1986, p. 17, 18)

1958

Production by Month

Dec. '57	Jan. '58	Feb.	Mar.	Apr.	May	June	July	Aug.	Sept.
152	1,479	2,319	3,866	5,600	5,461	5,211	5,212	6,555	2,037

Note: Production by month was derived from data obtained from Ford Motor Co. production records and from data compiled by the VTCI's collection of recorded owners' surveys. Actual production per month has not been verified.

First Day of Production: December 20, 1957
Last Day of Production: September 16, 1958
Introduction Date: February 13, 1958
Final Production: 37,893 (35,758 hardtop and 2,134 convertible)
Additional Information: Convertible production commenced on May 5, 1958. Production of 332ci 4-barrel export/low-compression models are included in 352ci 4-barrel totals; at least four hardtops and one convertible have been registered with the VTCI, all with the Ford-O-Matic transmission. This combination was not advertised as being available in the United States. Breakdown of cars equipped with either the 3-speed or overdrive transmission has not been documented, but it is believed by the author, based on data compiled from the VTCI's collection of owners' surveys and data from the 1959 and 1960 model years that approximately 1 percent (3,790) may have been outfitted with the 3-speed and another 1 percent with the overdrive.

1959

Production by Month

Oct. '58	Nov.	Dec.	Jan. '59	Feb.	Mar.	Apr.	May	June	July	Aug.
3,800	5,700	6,900	4,600	6,500	6,800	6,400	6,700	7,800	7,800	4,356

Note: Production by month is estimated from data compiled by the VTCI's collection of recorded owners' surveys. Actual production figures were not available.

First Day of Production: October 3, 1958
Last Day of Production: August 22, 1959
Introduction Date: October 17, 1958
Final Production: 67,456

Hardtop	57,195
with 352ci	54,041
with 430ci	3,154
Convertible	10,261
with 352ci	9,093
with 430ci	1,168

Additional Information: Production of 352ci 4-barrel export/low-compression models are included in 352ci 4-barrel totals. An estimated 1 percent of total production (6,750) was equipped with the 352ci motor and 3-speed transmission, and an additional 1 percent with the 352ci motor and overdrive transmission. The 430ci motor was only available with an automatic transmission. (Source: *Automotive Industries,* March 15, 1961.)

1960

Production by Month

Sept. '59	Oct.	Nov.	Dec.	Jan. '60	Feb.	Mar.	Apr.	May	June	July	Aug.	Sept.
3,800	3,800	6,250	7,800	6,600	6,300	8,800	8,800	9,200	10,350	5,500	9,900	3,543

Note: Production by month is estimated from data compiled by the VTCI's collection of recorded owners' surveys. Actual production figures were not available.

First Day of Production: September 8, 1959
Last Day of Production: September 13, 1960
Introduction Date: October 8, 1959
Final Production: 92,843

Hardtop	78,447
with 352ci	74,547
with 430ci	3,900
Sunroof	2,536
with 352ci	2,159
with 430ci	377
Convertible	11,860
with 352ci	10,606
with 430ci	1,245

Additional Information: This was the highest production year for the Vintage Thunderbird. Production of 352ci 4-barrel export/low-compression models are included in 352ci 4-barrel totals. An estimated 1 percent (9,290) of total production was equipped with the 352ci motor and 3-speed transmission and an additional 1 percent with the 352ci/overdrive. The 430ci motor was only available with an automatic transmission. (Source: *Automotive Industries*, March 15, 1961.)

1961 Production Data

Production by Month

Oct. '60	Nov.	Dec.	Jan. '61	Feb.	Mar.	Apr.	May	June	July	Aug.
2,500	6,700	7,665	7,945	7,350	5,574	9,891	9,070	7,742	4,449	2,721

Note: Production by month between October and December 1960 is estimated from data compiled by the VTCI's collection of recorded owners' surveys. Actual production figures were not available. Figures for Jan.-Aug. 1961 from *Automobile Industries*, March15, 1962.

First Day of Production: October 3, 1960
Last Day of Production: August 10, 1961
Introduction Date: November 10, 1960
Final Production: 73,051

Hardtop	62,535
Convertible	10,516

Additional Information: Production of 390ci 4-barrel export/low-compression models are included in 390ci 4-barrel totals. A total of fifty convertibles designated for use in the inaugural parade for President John F. Kennedy were built on December 30, 1960. Verification is accomplished by a notation in the remarks section of the ROT/Build sheet. Indianapolis pace/festival cars: Two cars were built to serve as official pace cars for the 1961 Indianapolis 500 race. Modified by Bill Stroppe, the number one car was presented to the race winner, A. J. Foyt (disposition unknown as of this writing). Another thirty-three cars were prepared to serve as festival cars for use by VIPs and in prerace activities; these received different graphics from the two pace cars.

1962

Production by Month

Aug. '61	Sept.	Oct.	Nov.	Dec.	Jan. '62	Feb.	Mar.	Apr.	May	June	July	Aug.
2,447	7,118	5,407	9,902	8,591	7,981	6,589	6,561	6,470	6,835	4,269	3,648	2,193

Source: *Automotive Industries*, March 15, 1963

First Day of Production: August 21, 1961
Last Day of Production: August 8, 1962
Introduction Date: October 12, 1961
Final Production: 78,011

Hardtop	68,122
with 390ci 4-barrel	68,091
with 390ci triple 2-barrel[1]	25
Landau[2] (included with Hardtop totals)	
with 390ci 4-barrel	note 2
with 390ci triple 2-barrel[1]	6
Convertible	8,457
with 390ci 4-barrel	8,443
with 390ci triple 2-barrel[3]	14
Sports Roadster	1,427
with 390ci 4-barrel	1,299
with 390ci triple 2-barrel	120
with 390ci 4-barrel (export)	8

Final Production Notes:

1. M-series figures for hardtop and Landau production are derived from the 1962–63 M-Series Registry compiled by William A. Wonder, and from owners' surveys submitted to the VTCI. These numbers represent actual cars for which documentation has been obtained as of the time of publication. Actual production numbers were not kept separately by Ford. Total M-series production may account for more than what has presently been estimated. Production of the M-series option began in January 1962. Hardtop production with 390 4-barrel is derived from accounted "M"s.

2. Landau production figures were not compiled by Ford during 1962 model year. An estimated 15 percent (about 10,220) of hardtop production may be Landaus. Landau production may have begun on October 23, 1961. Very early examples (through the end of October) may have been given the same coding has hardtops (63A/83). From November 1961-on, Landaus were coded 63B/87.

3. Previously published data had assumed that nine convertibles were equipped with the M-series motor. Records on file with the VTCI and the Wonder registry indicate that additional cars exist as of the date of publication.

Additional Information: Production of Sports Roadsters began on September 13, 1961, with serial number 2Y85Z-105844. Change to "76B/89" coding took effect mid-December 1961, based on data from the VTCI's Owners Survey collection and on information obtained from surviving factory gate releases. Production of 390ci 4-barrel export/low-compression models are included in 390ci 4-barrel totals unless specifically noted.

1963

Production by Month

Aug. '62	Sept.	Oct.	Nov.	Dec.	Jan. '63	Feb.	Mar.	Apr.	May	June	July
987	6,578	8,041	8,162	7,222	7,172	6,282	4,884	5,263	3,975	4,082	665

Source: *Automotive Industries*, March 15, 1963

First Day of Production: August 20, 1962

Last Day of Production: July 17, 1963

Introduction Date: September 28, 1962

Final Production: 63,313

Hardtop	42,806
with 390ci 4-barrel	42,785
with 390ci triple 2-barrel[1]	21
Landau	12,139
with 390ci 4-barrel	12,124
with 390ci triple 2-barrel[1]	15
Limited Edition Landau (Monaco Trim Package, all with 390ci 4-barrel)	2,000
Convertible	5,913
with 390ci 4-barrel	5,892
with 390ci triple 2-barrel[2]	21
Sports Roadster	455
with 390ci 4-barrel	411
with 390ci triple 2-barrel	37
with 390ci 4-barrel (export)	7

Final Production Notes:

1. M-series figures for hardtop and Landau production are derived from the 1962–63 M-Series Registry compiled by William A. Wonder. These numbers represent actual cars for which documentation has been obtained and were current as of the publication date. Actual production numbers were not kept separately by Ford. Total M-series production may account for more than what has presently been estimated. Production of the M-series option ceased by mid-January 1963.

2. Previous production figures for the M-series convertible has assumed eighteen were built. Records compiled by the VTCI and the Wonder registry have accounted for two more as of the date of publication.

Additional Information: 1963 was the last year for the Sports Roadster and M-series 390ci triple two-barrel packages. Production of the Limited Edition Landau began on January 3, 1963, and continued through end of production. Production of 390ci 4-barrel export/low-compression models are included in 390ci 4-barrel totals unless specifically noted.

1964

Production by Month

Aug. '63	Sept.	Oct.	Nov.	Dec.	Jan. '64	Feb.	Mar.	Apr.	May	June	July
1,253	4,487	9,155	9,535	9,928	11,482	11,134	9,427	9,573	6,524	5,808	4,159

Source: *Automotive Industries*, March 15, 1963

First Day of Production: August 12, 1963

Last Day of Production: July 24, 1964

Introduction Date: September 27, 1963

Final Production: 92,465

Hardtop	60,552
Landau	22,715
Convertible	9,198

Additional Information: No separate Sports Roadster model was offered during 1964. Cars fitted with both the Sports Tonneau Cover and Kelsey-Hayes Wire Wheels are considered as convertibles for production figures. An estimated forty-five cars were ordered from the factory with the combination. Production of 390ci 4-barrel export/low-compression models are included in 390ci 4-barrel totals.

1965

Production by Month

Aug. '64	Sept.	Oct.	Nov.	Dec.	Jan. '65	Feb.	Mar.	Apr.	May	June	July
4,344	7,614	7,007	4,714	8,453	8,137	6,780	9,335	7,002	5,492	5,041	1,053

Source: *Automotive Industries*, March 15, 1966

First Day of Production: August 3, 1964

Last Day of Production: July 9, 1965

Introduction Date: September 26, 1964

Final Production: 74,972[2]

Hardtop	42,652
Landau	20,974
Special Landau[1]	4,500
Convertible	6,846

Final Production Notes:

1. Approximately 10 percent (about 450) are believed to have been painted Wimbledon White; exact number is not known.

2. VTCI registered serial numbers indicate at least another 224 cars were built. See Note 2–1966 Production.

Additional Information: Production of 390ci 4-barrel export/low-compression models are included in 390ci 4-barrel totals.

1966

Production by Month

Aug. '65	Sept.	Oct.	Nov.	Dec.	Jan. '66	Feb.	Mar.	Apr.	May	June
4,248	6,151	7,528	7,559	7,384	6,934	6,382	6,903	6,228	7,183	2,676

First Day of Production: August 2, 1965

Last Day of Production: June 10, 1966

Introduction Date: September 25, 1965

Final Production: 69,176[1, 2]

Hardtop	13,389
Town Hardtop	15,633
Town Landau	35,105
Convertible	5,049

Final Production Notes:

1. Production figures for the 428ci 4-barrel motor option were not compiled by Ford for the AMA. The author estimates that 15–17 percent, and possibly up to 30 percent, of all 1966 Thunderbirds may have been fitted with the larger motor, based on data obtained from the VTCI's collection of owners' surveys.

2. Total production figures given by Ford Motor Company indicated that 69,176 Thunderbirds were constructed for the model year. However, serial numbers registered with the VTCI indicate that at least an additional 214 were numbered beyond the total production number. This indicates that either a group of cars produced during the year were damaged and/or destroyed between assignment of serial numbers and final invoicing (upon which production records were based) or that incorrect records were maintained.

Additional Information: This was the last year for convertible production and the last year for unitized body construction. This is also considered the last year of the Vintage Thunderbirds. Production of 390ci 4-barrel and 428ci 4-barrel export/low-compression models are included in 390ci 4-barrel totals.

EXTERIOR AND INTERIOR COLORS

1955 COLORS AND INTERIORS

Exterior Color/Sales Name	Data Plate Code	Remarks
Raven Black	A	-
Torch Red	R	-
Thunderbird Blue	T	1954 Ford Skyhaze Green
Snowshoe White	E	Added after January 1955
Goldenrod Yellow	V	Added March 1955
Special Deep Green	?	

Interior Colors	Data Plate Code	Remarks
Black/White	A/XA	-
Red/White	B/XB	-
Turquoise/White	C/XC	-
Yellow/Black	D/XD	Added March 1955

Note: All interiors were vinyl.

Convertible Top Colors
Black canvas with sewn-in back window

1956 COLORS AND INTERIORS

Exterior Color/Sales Name	Data Plate Code	Remarks
Raven Black	A	-
Colonial White	E	-
Buckskin Tan	J	-
Fiesta Red	K	-
Peacock Blue	L	-
Thunderbird Gray	P	Replaced midyear
Thunderbird Green	Z	-
Goldenglow Yellow	M	-
Sunset Coral	Y	-

Interior Colors	Data Plate Code	Remarks
Black/White	XA	-
Red/White	XB	-
Peacock/White	XC	-
Tan/White	XD	-
Green/White	XF	-
Brown/White	XG	-

Convertible Top Colors
Black canvas with tan lining
White vinyl with tan lining

1957 COLORS AND INTERIORS

Exterior Color/Sales Name	Data Plate Code	Remarks
Raven Black	A	-
Dresden Blue (Dark)	C	-
Colonial White	E	-
Starmist Blue (Light)	F	-
Cumberland Green (Dark)	G	Dropped midyear
Sun Gold	G	Midyear replacement for Y
Gunmetal Gray	H	Midyear replacement for N
Willow Green (Light)	J	-
Azure Blue (Light)	L	Midyear replacement for F
Gunmetal Gray	N	Code changed to H late year
Seaspray Green (Light)	N	Midyear replacement for J
Thunderbird Bronze	Q	-
Torch Red	R	Midyear replacement for V
Flame Red	V	-
Dusk Rose (Pink)	X	-
Inca Gold	Y	Dropped midyear
Coral Sand	Z	-

Interior Colors	Data Plate Code	Remarks
Black/White	XA	-
Red	XH	-
Bronze	XJ	-
White	XK	-
Dark Blue/Light Blue	XL	-
Dark Green/Light Green	XM	-

Convertible Top Colors
Black canvas with tan lining
White vinyl with tan lining
Blue canvas with tan lining
Tan canvas with tan lining

1958 COLORS AND INTERIORS

Exterior Color/Sales Name	Data Plate Code	Remarks
Raven Black	A	-
Winterset White	B	TB & Lincoln-repl. by E 8/58
Desert Beige	C	TB & Lincoln
Palomino Tan	D	-
Colonial White	E	Replaced B 8/58
Grenadier Red Metallic	I	Offered midyear
Everglade Green Metallic (Dark)	K	TB & Lincoln-Offered?
Gulfstream Blue (Blue-Green)	M	-
Platinum Metallic (Lt. Gray Metallic)	O	TB & Lincoln
Primer	P	Used with non-Ford colors
Casino Cream (Light Yellow)	V	TB, Lincoln & Mercury
Cameo Rose (Pink)	W	TB & Lincoln
Cascade Green (Light)	X	TB & Lincoln
Peach	X	TB & L-midyear addition
Monarch Blue Metallic (Medium)	Y	TB & Lincoln
Regatta Blue (Light)	Z	TB & Lincoln

Note: Two-Tones—2 letter code, 1st letter=body, 2nd letter=roof.

Interior Colors	Data Plate Code	Remarks
Bolster/Insert		

Vinyl and Nylon Highland Tweed Fabric

Dark Blue/Light Blue	XA	-
Dark Green/Light Green	XB	-
Black/Black	XC	-
Dark Turquoise/Light Turquoise	XK	-

All Vinyl

Dark Blue/White	XE	-
Dark Green/White	XF	-
Red/White	XG	-
Black/White	XH	-
Tan/White	XL	-
Turquoise/White	XM	-

Convertible Top Colors

Black Rayon/Gray Lining
Light Green/Green Lining
Light Blue/Blue Lining
White/Gray Lining
White/Blue Lining
White/Green Lining
White/Buff Lining

1959 COLORS AND INTERIORS

Exterior Color/Sales Name	Data Plate Code	Remarks
Raven Black	A	-
Baltic Blue	C	TB & Lincoln
Indian Turquoise	D	-
Colonial White	E	-
Hickory Tan (Buff)	F	TB & Lincoln
Glacier Green	G	TB & Lincoln
Tahitian Bronze Metallic	H	-
Steel Blue Metallic	J	TB & Lincoln
Sandstone Metallic (gold)	K	TB & Lincoln
Diamond Blue (light)	L	TB & Lincoln
Doeskin Beige	M	TB & Lincoln
Starlight Blue (dark)	N	TB & Lincoln
Primer	P	used with non-Ford colors
Sea Reef Green Metallic	Q	TB & Lincoln
Brandywine Red	R	TB only
Special	S	non-Ford color/special order
Flamingo (pink)	T	TB & Lincoln
Cordovan Metallic	U	TB only
Casino Cream (light yellow)	V	TB & Lincoln & Mercury
Tamarack Green Metallic	W	TB only
Platinum Metallic	Z	TB & Lincoln

Note: Two-Tones—2 letter code, 1st letter=body, 2nd letter=roof.

Interior Colors	Data Plate Code	Remarks
Bolster/Insert		
Beige/Light (Pearl) Beige	54	-
Red/Red	55	-
Black/Black	56	-
Medium Turquoise Metallic/		
Medium Turquoise Metallic	57	-

All Leather

Medium Blue Metallic/		
Medium Blue Metallic	82	-
Lt. (Pearl) Beige/Light (Pearl) Beige	84	-
Red/Red	85	-
Black/Black	86	-
Medium Turquoise Metallic/		
Medium Turquoise Metallic	87	-

Convertible Top Colors

Black Rayon/Black Lining	Light Blue Vinyl/Blue Lining
Turquoise Vinyl/Turquoise Lining	White Vinyl/Black Lining
White Vinyl/TurquoiseLining	White Vinyl/Blue Lining
White Vinyl/Buff Lining	

1960 COLORS AND INTERIORS

Exterior Color/Sales Name	Data Plate Code	Remarks
Raven Black	A	-
Kingston Blue Metallic (Dark)	B	TB, Lincoln & Mercury
Aquamarine (Turquoise)	C	-
Acapulco Blue Metallic (Medium)	E	TB & Lincoln
Skymist Blue (Light)	F	-
Beachwood Brown Metallic	H	-
Pale Turquoise (Light)	I	Lincoln-TB Special Order?
Monte Carlo Red	J	-
Sultana Turquoise Metallic	K	-
Corinthian White	M	-
Diamond Blue (Platinum)	N	TB & Lincoln
Primer	P	Used with non-Ford colors
Moroccan Ivory (Yellow)	R	TB, Lincoln & Mercury
Briarcliffe Green Metallic (Dark)	S	TB & Lincoln
Meadowvale Green Metallic (Medium)	T	-
Rose Glow Metallic	U	TB, Lincoln & Mercury
Palm Springs Rose	V	TB, Lincoln & Mercury
Adriatic Green (Light)	W	-
Royal Burgundy Metallic (Maroon)	X	TB & Lincoln
Gunpowder Gray Metallic (Dark)	Y	TB & Lincoln
Platinum Metallic (Light Gray)	Z	-

Note: Two-Tones-2 letter code, 1st letter=body, 2nd letter=roof.

Interior Colors	Data Plate Code	Remarks
Bolster/Insert		

Vinyl and Nylon Check Fabric with Silver Strands

Dark Blue/Light Blue	72	-
Dark Green/Light Green	73	-
Dark Beige/Light Beige	74	-
Black/Light Gray	76	-
Dark Turquoise/Light Turquoise	77	-

All Vinyl

Dark Blue/Light Blue	52	-
Dark Green/Light Green Metallic	53	-
Dark Beige/Light Beige	54	-
Red/White	55	-
Black/White	56	-
Dark Turquoise/Light Turquoise	57	-

All Leather

Tan/Tan	84	-
Red/Red	85	-
Black/Black	86	-
Turquoise/Turquoise	87	-

NOTE: All hardtops used a white headliner, except for Beige interiored cars, which used a tan headliner.

Convertible Top Colors

Black Vinyl/Black Lining
Blue Vinyl/Black Lining
White Vinyl/Black Lining

1961 COLORS AND INTERIORS

Exterior Color/Sales Name	Data Plate Code	Remarks
Raven Black	A	-
Aquamarine (Turquoise)	C	-
Starlight Blue Metallic (Light)	D	-
Laurel Green Metallic (Medium)	E	TB & Lincoln
Desert Gold (Yellow Gold)	F	-
Tawney Beige	G	Mercury-TB Special Order Only
Chesapeake Blue Metallic (Dark)	H	-
Green Velvet Metallic (Dark)	I	Lincoln-TB Special Order
Monte Carlo Red	J	-
Sahara Rose	L	TB & Lincoln
Corinthian White	M	-
Diamond Blue (Platinum)	N	TB & Lincoln
Nautilus Gray Metallic (Dark)	P	TB & Lincoln
Silver Gray Metallic	Q	-
Cambridge Blue Metallic (Medium)	R	-
Mint Green (Light)	S	-
Honey Beige	T	TB & Lincoln
Palm Springs Rose	V	TB, Lincoln & Mercury
Garden Turquoise Metallic	W	-
Heritage Burgundy Metallic (Maroon)	X	TB & Lincoln
Mahogany Metallic (Dark Brown)	Y	TB & Lincoln
Fieldstone Tan Metallic	Z	TB & Lincoln

Note: Two-Tones—2 letter code, 1st letter=body, 2nd letter=roof.

Interior Colors Bolster/Insert	Data Plate Code	Remarks
Vinyl and Nylon Bedford Cloth		
Light Blue/Dark Blue	72	-
Light Green/Medium Green	73	-
Light Beige/Medium Beige	74	-
Black/Medium Gray	76	-
Medium Turquoise/ Medium Turquoise	77	-
All Vinyl		
Medium Blue Metallic/ Medium Blue Metallic	52	-
Light Green Metallic/ Medium Green Metallic	53	-
Light (Pearl) Beige/Light (Pearl) Beige	54	-
Red/Red	55	-
Black/Black	56	-
Medium Turquoise Metallic/ Medium Turquoise Metallic	57	-
All Leather		
Medium Blue Metallic/ Medium Blue Metallic	82	-
Light (Pearl) Beige/Light (Pearl) Beige	84	-
Red/Red	85	-
Black/Black	86	-
Medium Turquoise Metallic/ Medium Turquoise Metallic	87	-

NOTE: All hardtops used a white headliner, except for Beige interiored cars, which used a tan headliner.

Convertible Top Colors
Black Vinyl/Black Lining
Blue Vinyl/Black Lining
White Vinyl/Black Lining

1962 COLORS AND INTERIORS

Exterior Color/Sales Name	Data Plate Code	Remarks
Raven Black	A	S-R;
Oxford Gray Metallic (Dark)	C	Lincoln-TB Special Order?
Patrician Green Metallic (Medium Turquoise)	D	TB & Lincoln
Acapulco Blue Metallic (Medium)	E	TB & Lincoln
Sky Mist Blue	F	TB & Lincoln
Silver Mink Metallic (Silver)	G	S-R; TB, Mercury & Comet
Caspian Blue Metallic (Dark)	H	TB & Lincoln
Castillian Gold Metallic (Medium)	I	S-R: Introduced Fall '61
Rangoon Red	J	S-R; -
Chalfonte Blue (Light Turquoise)	K	TB, Lincoln & Mercury
Sahara Rose	L	TB, Lincoln & Mercury
Corinthian White	M	S-R; -
Diamond Blue (Platinum)	N	S-R; TB & Lincoln
Green Mist Metallic (Medium)	O	TB & Lincoln; Late year add
Silver Moss Metallic	P	-
Tucson Yellow (Light)	R	-
Cascade Green Metallic (Dark)	S	TB & Lincoln
Sandshell Beige	T	S-R
Deep Sea Blue Metallic (Dark Turquoise)	U	TB, Lincoln & Mercury
Chestnut Metallic (Reddish Brown)	V	S-R (Late); TB, Lincoln & Ford
Royal Burgundy Metallic (Maroon)	X	TB & Lincoln
Fieldstone Tan Metallic	Z	-

Note: Two-Tones—2 letter code, 1st letter=body, 2nd letter=roof.
S-R=Sports Roadster color.

Interior Colors Bolster/Insert	Data Plate Code	Remarks
Vinyl and Nylon Bedford Cloth		
Light Silver Blue Metallic/ Medium Silver	70	-
Light Blue/Dark Blue	72	-
Light (Pearl) Beige/Medium Beige	74	-
Black/Medium Gray	76	-
Medium Turquoise/ Medium Turquoise	77	-
All Vinyl		
Medium Silver Blue Metallic/ Medium Silver Blue Metallic	50	-
Medium Blue Metallic/ Medium Blue Metallic	52	-
Light Green Metallic/ Medium Green Metallic	53	-
Light (Pearl) Beige/Light (Pearl) Beige	54	-
Red/Red	55	-
Black/Black	56	-
Medium Turquoise Metallic/ Medium Turquoise Metallic	57	-
Medium Chestnut Metallic/ Medium Chestnut Metallic	59	-

All Leather

Light Silver Blue Metallic/		
Light Silver Blue Metallic	80	
Medium Blue Metallic/		
Medium Blue Metallic	82	-
Light (Pearl) Beige/Light (Pearl) Beige	84	-
Red/Red	85	-
Black/Black	86	-
Medium Turquoise Metallic/		
Medium Turquoise Metallic	87	-
Chestnut Metallic/Chestnut Metallic	89	-

NOTE: All hardtops used a white headliner, except for Beige interiored cars, which used a tan headliner.

Convertible Vinyl Top Colors
Black Vinyl/Black Lining
Blue Vinyl/Black Lining
White Vinyl/Black Lining

Landau Top Covers
Black Cobra-Grain Vinyl
White Cobra-Grain Vinyl

1963 COLORS AND INTERIORS

Exterior Color/Sales Name	Data Plate Code	Remarks
Raven Black	A	S-R; -
Patrician Green Metallic (Medium Turquoise)	D	TB & Lincoln
Acapulco Blue Metallic (Medium)	E	TB & Lincoln
Silver Mink Metallic (Silver)	G	S-R; TB, Mercury & Comet
Caspian Blue Metallic (Dark)	H	TB & Lincoln
Castillian/Champagne Gold Metallic (Medium)	I	S-R; TB & Lincoln
Rangoon Red	J	S-R; -
Chalfonte Blue (Light Turquoise)	K	TB only
Sahara Rose	L	TB, Lincoln & Mercury
Corinthian White	M	S-R; -
Diamond Blue (Platinum)	N	S-R; TB & Lincoln
Green Mist Metallic (Medium)	O	TB & Lincoln
Tucson Yellow (Light)	R	TB, Lincoln & Mercury
Cascade Green Metallic (Dark)	S	TB & Lincoln
Sandshell Beige	T	S-R
Deep Sea Blue Metallic (Dark Turquoise)	U	TB only
Chestnut Metallic (Reddish Brown)	V	S-R
Rose Beige Metallic (Light Pink)	W	-
Heritage Burgundy Metallic (Maroon)	X	-
Fieldstone Tan Metallic	Z	TB only

Note: Two-Tones—2 letter code, 1st letter=body, 2nd letter=roof.
S-R=Sports Roadster color.

Interior Colors Bolster/Insert	Data Plate Code	Remarks

Vinyl and Pin Stripe Broadcloth

Light Blue/Dark Blue	72	-
Light (Pearl) Beige/Medium Beige	74	-
Black/Black	76	-
Light Turquoise/Dark Turquoise	77	-

Crinkle Vinyl/Vachette Vinyl

Medium Silver Blue Metallic/		
Light Silver Blue D/L	50	-
Light Rose Beige D/L/		
Light Rose Beige D/L	51	-
Medium Blue D/L/Light Blue D/L	52	-
Light (Pearl) Beige/Light (Pearl) Beige	54	-
Red/Red	55	-
Black/Black	56	-
Medium Turquoise D/L/Light Turquoise D/L	57	-
Medium Chestnut D/L/Medium Chestnut D/L	59	-

All Leather

Light Silver Blue Metallic/		
Light Silver Blue Metallic	80	-
Medium Blue Metallic/		
Medium Blue Metallic	82	-
White/White	83	Ltd. Ed. Monaco
Light (Pearl) Beige/Light (Pearl) Beige	84	-
Red/Red	85	-
Black/Black	86	-

NOTE: All hardtop/Landau headliners were white, except for Beige interiors, which used a tan headliner.

Convertible Top Colors
Black Vinyl/Black Lining
Blue Vinyl/Black Lining
White Vinyl/Black Lining

Landau Vinyl Top Covers
Black Cobra-Grain Vinyl
White Cobra-Grain Vinyl
Dark Brown Cobra-Grain Vinyl
Dark Blue Cobra-Grain Vinyl
Rose Beige Cobra-Grain Vinyl (Dark Maroon; Ltd. Ed. Monaco only)

1964 COLORS AND INTERIORS

Exterior Color/Sales Name	Data Plate Code	Remarks
Raven Black	A	Tonneau
Pagoda Green (Peacock)	B	-
Princeton Gray Metallic (Dark)	C	Lincoln-TB Special Order
Silver Mink Metallic (Lt. Gray)	E	Tonneau; TB & Lincoln
Arcadian Blue	F	TB & Lincoln
Prairie Tan	G	Tonneau; Dropped midyear
Caspian Blue Metallic (Dark)	H	TB & Lincoln
Florentine Green (Aztec Gold)	I	-
Rangoon Red	J	Tonneau
Samoan Coral (Bittersweet)	L	Tonneau
Wimbledon White	M	Tonneau
Diamond Blue (Platinum)	N	TB & Lincoln
Silver Green Metallic (Light)	O	TB & Lincoln
Palomino Metallic	P	Midyear addition
Brittany Blue Metallic (Medium)	Q	TB & Lincoln
Phonecian Yellow (Light)	R	Dropped midyear
Cascade Green Metallic (Dark)	S	TB & Lincoln
Navaho Beige (Light)	T	-
Patrician Green Metallic (Medium Turquoise)	U	TB & Lincoln
Sunlight Yellow (Light)	V	Midyear addition
Rose Beige Metallic (Light Pink)	W	TB & Lincoln
Vintage Burgundy Metallic (Maroon)	X	-
Chantilly Beige Metallic (Medium)	Z	-

Note: Two-Tones—2 letter code, 1st letter=body, 2nd letter=roof.

Interior Colors	Data Plate Code	Remarks
Bolster/Insert		

Crinkle Vinyl and Pompeii Pattern Cloth

Light Silver Blue/Light Silver Blue	71	-
Light Blue D/L/Medium Blue	72	-
Light Beige/Light Beige	74	-
Black/Black	76	-

Crinkle Vinyl

Light Rose Beige D/L	50	-
Light Silver Blue	51	-
Light Blue D/L	52	-
White	53	-
Light Beige	54	-
Red/Red	55	-
Black/Black	56	-
Light Turquoise D/L	57	-
Light Aztec Gold	58	-
Medium Palomino	59	-

Crinkle All Leather

Light Blue D/L	82	-
White Crinkle with Black Accents	83	Black carpet/trim
Red/Red	85	-
Black/Black	86	-

NOTE: Interior codes did not indicate use of a reclining passenger seat with adjustable headrest. Headliners for hardtops/Landaus were white, except for Beige-interior cars, which used a tan headliner.

Convertible Top Colors
Black Vinyl/Black Lining
Blue Vinyl/Black Lining
White Vinyl/Black Lining

Landau Vinyl Top Colors
Black Cobra-Grain Vinyl
White Cobra-Grain Vinyl
Dark Brown Cobra-Grain Vinyl
Dark Blue Cobra-Grain Vinyl

1965 COLORS AND INTERIORS

Exterior Color/Sales Name	Data Plate Code	Remarks
Raven Black	A	-
Midnight Turquoise Metallic (Dark)	B	TB only
Honey Gold Metallic (Medium Ivy Gold)	C	-
Silver Mink Metallic (Light Gray)	E	TB & Lincoln
Arcadian Blue (Light)	F	TB & Lincoln
Pastel Yellow (Light Ivy Gold)	G	TB & Lincoln
Caspian Blue Metallic (Dark)	H	-
Rangoon Red	J	-
Wimbledon White	M	Also Second Special Landau color
Diamond Blue (Platinum)	N	TB & Lincoln
Prairie Bronze Metallic (Palomino)	P	-
Brittany Blue Metallic (Medium)	Q	TB & Lincoln
Ivy Green Metallic (Dark)	R	-
Charcoal Gray Metallic (Dark)	S	TB & Lincoln
Navaho Beige (Light)	T	-
Patrician Green Metallic (Medium Turquoise)	U	TB & Lincoln
Emberglo Metallic (Reddish Copper)	V	Special Landau only
Rose Beige Metallic (Light Pink)	W	TB only
Vintage Burgundy Metallic (Maroon)	X	-
Chantilly Beige Metallic (Medium)	Z	-
Frost Turquoise	4	TB & Lincoln
Phonecian Yellow	7	Special order only

Note: Two-Tones—2 letter code, 1st letter=body, 2nd letter=roof.

Interior Colors	Data Plate Code	Remarks
Bolster/Insert		

Crinkle Vinyl and Pompeii Pattern Cloth

	w/o Headrest	w/Headrest
Light Blue D/L/Medium Blue	12	42
Black/Black	16	46
Medium Palomino/Medium Palomino	19	49

Crinkle Vinyl

	w/o Headrest	w/Headrest
White	20*	50*

*Though listed in Shop Manual, was not used—see letter-series codes.

Light Silver Blue	21	51
Light Blue D/L	22	52
Burgundy	23	53
Light Beige Metallic	24	54
Red	25	55
Black	26	56
Light Turquoise Metallic	27	57
Light Ivy Gold Metallic	28	58
Medium Palomino	29	59

Crinkle All Leather

White	30*	60*

*Though listed in Shop Manual, was not used—see letter-series codes.

Light Blue (Low Metallic)	32	62
Burgundy	33	63
Red	35	65
Black	36	66

Pearl Crinkle All Vinyl with Color-Keyed Accents

Seats/Accents (Carpet, Console, etc.)	w/o Headrest	w/Headrest
White/Blue	G2	P2
White/Burgundy	G3	P3
White/Beige	G4	P4
White/Red	G5	P5
White/Black and White	G6	P6
White/Aqua (torquoise)	G7	P7
White/Ivy Gold	G8	P8
White Palomino	G9	P9
Parchment/Emberglo	7D*	XD*

*Special Landau only

Pearl Crinkle All Leather with Color-Keyed Accents

Seats/Accents (Carpet, Console, etc.)	w/o Headrest	w/Headrest
White/Blue	H2	Q2
White/Burgundy	H3	Q3
White/Beige	H4	Q4
White/Red	H5	Q5
White/Black and White	H6	Q6
White/Aqua (torquoise)	H7	Q7
White/Ivy Gold	H8	Q8
White Palomino	H9	Q9

NOTE: Headliners for hardtops/Landaus were color-coordinated with seat colors

Convertible Top Colors
Black Vinyl/Black Lining
Blue Vinyl/Black Lining
White Vinyl/Black Lining
Tan Vinyl/Black Lining

Landau Vinyl Top Colors
Black Cobra-Grain Vinyl
White Cobra-Grain Vinyl
Dark Brown Cobra-Grain Vinyl
Dark Blue Cobra-Grain Vinyl

1966 COLORS AND INTERIORS

Exterior Color/Sales Name	Data Plate Code	Remarks
Raven Black	A	-
Midnight Turquoise Metallic (Dark)	B	TB only
Silver Mink Metallic (Light Gray)	E	TB & Lincoln
Arcadian Blue (Light)	F	TB & Lincoln
Pastel Yellow (Light Ivy Gold)	G	TB & Lincoln
Caspian Blue Metallic (Dark)	H	-
Nightmist Blue (Dark)	K	-
Honeydew Yellow	L	TB & Lincoln
Wimbledon White	M	-
Diamond Blue (Platinum)	N	TB & Lincoln
Silver Rose Metallic	O	TB & Lincoln
Antique Bronze Metallic	P	-
Brittany Blue Metallic (Medium)	Q	TB & Lincoln
Ivy Green Metallic (Dark)	R	-
Candyapple Red	T	-
Tahoe Turquoise (Medium)	U	-
Emberglo Metallic (Reddish Copper)	V	-
Vintage Burgundy Metallic (Maroon)	X	-
Sauterne Gold Metallic	Z	-
Mariner Turquoise (Dark)	2	TB, Lincoln, & Mercury
Phonecian Yellow	7	-

Note: Two-Tones—2 letter code, 1st letter=body, 2nd letter=roof.

Interior Colors	Data Plate Code	Remarks
Bolster/Inserts	w/o Headrest	w/Headrest

Crinkle Vinyl and Cloth

Light Blue D/L/Medium Blue	12	42
Black/Black	16	46
Aqua/Aqua	17	47
Parchment/Parchment	1D	4D

Crinkle Vinyl

Light Silver Blue	21	51
Dark Blue D/L	22	52
Burgundy	23	53
Emberglo	24	54
Red	25	55
Black	26	56
Aqua (Light Turquoise)	27	57
Light Ivy Gold Metallic	28	58

Crinkle All Leather

Seats	w/Headrest
Dark Blue	62
Red	65
Black	66

Pearl Crinkle All Vinyl with Color-Keyed Accents

Seats/Accents (Carpet, Console, etc.)	w/Headrest	
Parchment/Blue	B2	K2
Parchment/Burgundy	B3	K3
Parchment/Emberglo	B4	K4
Parchment/Black	B6	K6
Parchment/Turquoise	B7	K7
Parchment/Gold	B8	K8
Parchment/Palomino	B9	K9
White/Silver Mink	G1	P1
White/Blue	G2	P2
White/Burgundy	G3	P3
White/Emberglo	G4	P4
White/Black and White White Console	G6	P6
White/Aqua (torquoise)	G7	P7
White/Ivy Gold	G8	P8
White Palomino	G9	P9

Pearl Crinkle All Leather with Color-Keyed Accents

Seats/Accents (Carpet, Console, etc.)	w/Headrest	
White/Blue	L2	
White/Burgundy	L3	
White/Emberglo	L4	
White/Black and White	L6	White Console
White/Aqua (torquoise)	L7	
White/Ivy Gold	L8	
White Palomino	L9	

NOTE: Headliners for hardtops/Landaus were color-coordinated with seat colors

Convertible Top Colors
Black Vinyl/Black Lining
Blue Vinyl/Black Lining
White Vinyl/Black Lining

Landau Vinyl Top Colors
Black Levant-Grain Vinyl
White Levant-Grain Vinyl
Sage Gold Levant-Grain Vinyl
Parchment Levant-Grain Vinyl

THUNDERBIRD CLUBS

The Classic Thunderbird Club International (CTCI) is the premiere organization for 1955–57 Thunderbird owners and enthusiasts. Established in 1961, it produces *Early Bird* magazine, provides access to technical specialists and offers a whole range of items from shop manuals to restoration guidebooks to its members. National conventions are held during even years, with regional conventions during odd years.

For more information regarding CTCI, write to:
Classic Thunderbird Club International
P.O. Box 4148
Santa Fe Springs, CA 90670-1148.

The Vintage Thunderbird Club International (VTCI) maintains a tradition of proactive support for the four-seat Thunderbird. Along with its magazine, *Thunderbird Scoop*, it promotes and hosts regional and international conventions throughout the world, offers items such as reproductions of sales literature and other club-related items, and provides access to technical experts to answer the many questions owners may have. It also maintains a reprint service to make available past technical articles from the club magazine.

For more information on VTCI, please write to:
Vintage Thunderbird Club International
P.O. Box 2250
Dearborn, MI 48123-2250

INDEX